PATH OF AFFLICTION

Nick Campanella

Copyright 2021 by Nick Campanella

ISBN: 978-1-970153-31-6

Parental advisory: Violence, explicit language, and strong sexual innuendos.

La Maison Publishing, Inc.

Maison

Vero Beach, Florida
The Hibiscus City
lamaisonpublishing@gmail.com

The sublime is only one step from the ridicules.

—Napoleon Bonaparte

INTRODUCTION

Scott Draper kick started his custom-made black chopper and a low uneven grumble shook the ground. Gripping the tall handlebars, he revved the engine louder than the bike to his left. Out of the corner of his eye, he saw his oversized cousin dismount an iron horse, one hand raising to chest level.

"I could tell you didn't like my plan," Thaddeus "Thumper" Boyd barked over the many idling hogs parked outside the country bar they controlled.

Draper shook his head. "It ain't gonna work," he said, his long brown hair dancing in the cool autumn wind. "Hank's too paranoid."

"It's the *only* option," Thumper shouted. Glancing down at the new red patch stitched to his vest, he smirked. The letters were upside down, but he knew it read President. He then lifted his chin, locking eyes with his subordinate family member who was dressed just like him—hoody, vest, jeans, boots. All black. "It *has* to work. And you ain't leaving till we're on the same page."

"This is *our* mess," Draper said, his dark eyes narrowing. "We should just do it ourselves. Walk in there and tell him we need our shit. Then, after he gives it to us, he swallows two bullets. Win, win."

Thumper rubbed his meaty bald head. "Brother," he said in low baritone. "I feel your passion. But think for a minute. Me, you, Ax. We're gonna be the prime suspects no matter what. I'd rather be on camera at the casino when the shit goes down. Why not let the vatos do our dirty work? Enrique already said he'd take care of it. All I gotta do is give him the address."

"As soon as one of those immigrants' steps foot on Hank's land, he's gonna start shooting."

"That won't be a problem," Thumper growled, losing patience with the conversation. "You know damn well what they're capable of."

Opening his bearded mouth, Draper tried to ask another question. "How—"

Thumper held up a menacing hand, the action cutting him off before his number two could finish the thought. "Enough. It's done."

1

Frankie Buccetti gripped the handles of the jackhammer and drove it into the basement floor. His tall, thin frame stood in a growing cloud of cement dust. Despite wearing a protective mask, he could taste the soot in his mouth. He'd only been on the job for twenty minutes, but he could already feel the sweat forming under his dusty hat. Squeezing the trigger with his right hand, his body vibrated with the deafening rhythm of the machine. While following an outline in chalk, his flexed arms guided the jack to carve out a ten-foot rectangular section in the earth.

After two agonizing hours of stone cutting, Frankie's hat and shirt were wet. *On to the next step,* he thought, letting go of the trigger. The room became quiet. With ringing still in his ears, he dragged the heavy tool to the corner of the room and gently laid it down. Turning back to the work area, he saw a mound of rubble that needed to be removed by hand. He sighed and grabbed his arm. While massaging his sore tricep, he estimated four more hours of toil. His jaw clenched. A silent groan crawled up his parched throat. *There has to be an easier way to earn a living,* he thought, his head shaking tightly.

At the sudden ringing of his cell phone, his hand snapped for his pocket. *Conny!* He hoped it was her. When he read the screen on his phone, he swallowed his hopes that tasted dry.

Nonetheless, he pulled the soiled dust mask off his face and whipped it against the wall.

"Hello," Frankie said with a touch of irritation in his voice.

On the other end of the phone was Frankie's roommate, Giovanni Mariani, but everyone called him by his last name, initials, or sometimes just "G." "What are you up to?" he asked, his voice soft and raspy.

"The usual," Frankie said in monotone. "Just digging another trench. You?" Mariani snorted. "It's the day after Thanksgiving," he said. "They don't give you the day off?"

"I just do what I'm told," Frankie said and looked down at the shovel on the floor. "I need to make that money. I got bills to pay."

"Right on," Mariani said. "What are you up to tomorrow?"

"Not much." Frankie stretched his arms. "I'm gonna sleep till at least noon."

"Fuck that!" Mariani barked. "You been all cooped up in the house for a month."

"Yeah, well, between work and—"

"And what?" Mariani asked. "Between work and what? Missing her? Bro, I been there, but it's time to get out of the house. Time to start living again."

"I like the comfort of home. It's peaceful."

"Why don't ya come hunting with us in the morning? It will be fun. Me, you, Carlos, and Marcel—home team."

Frankie shook his head. "I can't. It's been a long week. I need a day of rest."

"C'mon, man!" Mariani insisted. "It will be worth it. Every man should experience deer hunting at least once."

"I got a felony on my record. If I get caught with a gun, I'm going straight to prison."

"We ain't getting caught," Mariani promised. "I got a felony, too. That don't stop *me*."

"I'm not you."

"Shit. I'd say you could use my bow, but that takes a skill you don't have."

"I ain't using no bow and arrow. That's primitive."

"Dude," Mariani said. "You're thirty-six years old and you've never been hunting with your boys. Answer me this question: in *all* your years, have you *ever* heard of a felon getting caught with a gun while hunting?"

Frankie let out a breath. "No."

"Then what's holding you back?"

"That was just an excuse, bro," he said, gazing out a tiny window at the blue sky. "I'd like to go. I just don't have any motivation. Maybe next weekend?"

"It's supposed to get cold next week. You wouldn't like that very much. It *has* to be tomorrow."

Frankie sighed. *He ain't taking no for an answer,* he thought. *I guess I could sleep in on Sunday. A good time with the boys might be worth the effort.* "Fine," he said. "What time?"

"We gotta head out early. Like 4:30 a.m."

"Holy shit. You gotta be kidding me?"

"We need to be in the deer stands before the sun comes up."

"All right," he said reluctantly. "Let me finish up work. We'll talk about it when I get home. I still gotta dig like five feet down. The plumber's replacing the sewer pipe tomorrow. I can't leave till it's fully exposed."

"Sounds good, brother," Mariani said. "Call Hank and let him know we're hunting on his land in the morning. I'd rather not talk to him. He irritates me."

"I'll text him. I need to make an appointment for my truck anyways. It's been pulling to the right."

"Probably a ball joint. Simple fix. Get that shovel swinging. I'll talk to ya later."

*****

Frankie's consciousness was suspended all night until his eyes cracked open. The alarm clock was buzzing. His skin felt hot — as if his dream placed him in the middle of a burning house. Frantically whipping the covers off himself, he rolled out of bed to end the dream and the racket. Half asleep, his eyes were nothing more than slits. The unfocused blur of darkness adjusted after a few deep breathes.

Standing in place, he aggressively stretched his sore arms and back. "Uggghhh…fuck…" he grumbled. *I just wanna crash,* he thought, glancing at his bed. *I should have said no. It feels like I didn't even sleep.*

Twelve minutes later, he was showered, fully awake, and alert. Standing in front of the foggy mirror with a towel wrapped around his waist, he wiped a spot clear with his right hand. The brown-skinned athletic man in the mirror bent forward to study his grief-stricken eyes.

"She's gone, Frank," he told himself, lifting the faucet handle so he could brush his teeth. "She's a stupid *fucking* gash. Just let her go." In his reflection, he saw a curly haired bitter man who lacked motivation, hope, and passion. He knew that his broken heart killed his drive.

He looked down his nose at the toothbrush holder on the counter of the sink. In the silver cup, two toothbrushes shot out in opposite directions. One was his and the other belonged to her. He clenched his teeth and reached for it before pulling away. *Not yet,* he thought with a shake of his head. Instead of tossing the toothbrush in the trash, he just let it sit there next to his, to collect dust and remind him of what he lost until he could build up the strength to let go. His mind couldn't stop thinking about the last time he ran his fingers through Conny's long brown hair as he held her in his arms.

After his mouth was fresh and minty, he pushed Conny out of his mind and entered his bedroom. Scabbing around in his closet, he grabbed a dark gray polo and a black fleece jacket. The sudden banging on the bedroom door, determined his pace.

Frankie winced at the disembodied voice of Giovanni Mariani on the other side of the door, "Strunzo!" Mariani said. "It's 4:45! Carlos and Marcel are here. Let's go!"

"I'm coming," Frankie hollered back, tucking his shirt into his jeans.

"Hurry up."

"Yah, yah," Frankie said under his breath. On the dresser in front of him was his cell phone, wallet, and a stainless-steel folding knife. Like every day before work, he stuffed all three in a different pocket. With his extreme-weather black bibs hanging over a chair, he grabbed them, stepped inside the legs, and secured the straps over his shoulders. After he covered his thick, wavy hair with a black knit watch cap, he reached for the door handle, pausing briefly to glance at a gold hockey medal with a blue ribbon that hung on the wall. *I'm still a champion,* he thought as he turned the knob. *I just live like a peasant.*

Swinging open the door, he crossed the threshold and the tautness of his cheeks relaxed into a sly grin. His diverse team of rivals was facing him. "Gooood morning, boys," he said to Mariani, Carlos, and, Marcel who were horsing around in the dining room — one white, one black, and one Hispanic.

"Frankie!" Carlos Zapata said with a smile.

"Whuuud up, bro!" Marcel Taylor said and opened up his arms to embrace his friend whose skin was two tones lighter than his.

Frankie bounced from Marcel to Carlos whose hand he clasped. "We taking two rides?"

"Nah. We'll just hop in with you."

Mariani clapped his gloved hands together. "We're late. Let's bounce!" He was wearing a long black parka, desert camouflage hunting pants, and a matching skull cap. His face hard like stone.

"All right," Frankie said, and then they proceeded to carry their hunting gear through the house and out the back door. It was dark, but the moonlight led them to Frankie's black Chevy Tahoe in the driveway.

Frankie swung open the rear doors. The dome light drove out the darkness.

"Put the gun cases on the bottom," Frankie said and stepped aside.

After the weapons were in, Frankie shoved his duffel bag on top and the others did the same.

"Shotgun!" Mariani said and shoved Carlos' husky frame which barely budged.

*****

From the back seat of the cruising vehicle, Carlos spoke over the voice on the radio. "Deer hunting with the good old AK-47," he said with a grin on his massive jaw. "*My* idea of fun."

"Your AK can't compete with my bow," Mariani boasted, then turned to face him. "You know that, right?"

Carlos chuckled. "In war or hunting?"

"Hunting," Mariani said. "You fire one shot with your AK, and you'll scare all the deer for miles away. Me, I could kill one and keep hunting."

"Okay, ya got me there," Carlos talked to the back of Mariani's hat. "But what about the battlefield."

Mariani turned his head slightly, tugging on the two-inch black scruff on his chin. "They wouldn't let me use a bow in Afghanistan," he said. "I used the M4A1. But there *are* some situations where a bow would serve a purpose in battle. I keep one in my truck at all times."

Marcel chimed in. "Ya gonna do a drive by in da hood with your bow?"

"What's the difference between hunting people and animals?" Mariani asked, then answered his own joke. "Ya can't eat the people!" He laughed shortly.

Frankie turned up the radio and climbed the hill. While listening to the morning weather forecast, he glanced at the clock on the dashboard. *4:50,* he thought and gradually pressed farther down on the gas pedal.

After a few minutes of no one talking, Marcel playfully grabbed Frankie's jacket and shook it. "Whuuud up, playboy!" His loud and flamboyant words forced a smile out of everyone. "I heard you're *single*...and ready to *mingle*. I'll have to introduce you to my wife's friend. She's *bangin'*."

"I'm single, but until she tells me to my face —"

Mariani jumped in. "She's gone, bro," he said. "After five years, she left you over a text message. I'd never talk to that bitch again."

"You can either meet a new woman," Marcel said, "or embrace the suffering for a while."

Frankie gripped the steering wheel. "I don't *want* to talk about this right now," he said and clenched his jaw. "I'm tired as fuck. I barely even slept."

"How 'bout this?" Marcel said. "Before we go hunting, we

should stop at the bank." He paused to place a hand on Frankie's shoulder. "Frankie, you run up in there, slam your fist on the counter, and tell 'em to give up all the money! That shit will wake you up *real* quick."

Frankie cracked a smile and took his right hand off the wheel. "Which bank?" he laughed, and everyone joined in. As he continued driving, the others kept talking and laughing and joking around. Frankie blocked it all out. *I almost forgot what it felt like to laugh,* he thought, following the broken yellow line on the road. *Mariani was right, this is gonna be fun!*

Frankie sniffled twice and turned his head slightly. "Damn bro," he said. "That shit stinks."

"What?" Marcel said.

"Your weed," Frankie said. "I just caught a whiff. It smells like a skunk."

"That's the good shit," Mariani said. "Light it up, Strunz!"

Marcel said, "I'll light it up if you tell me what strunz means."

"No." Mariani shook his head. He slightly turned in his seat to taunt his friend. "You better look that shit up on the internet, Strunzo!"

Frankie hit the steering wheel. "Eh!" he shouted, "Strunz means piece of shit, idiot. Now let me hit that blunt to take the pain out. My back's just killin' me."

With exception of Marcel, they all laughed. "Strunz?" He crossed his arms. "What the fuck? You used to call me rookie." He laughed out loud, smiling from ear to ear, holding the cigar in his near black fingers. He put a flame to it, took a big puff, and then exhaled a few seconds later. "Now I'm demoted to *strunz*?" Marcel said to no one in particular. "A fuckin' idiot."

Mariani shook his head. "It's meant to be sarcastic," he explained. "Something you say to your friends or your son. My own *dad* still calls me a strunzo. So, don't take it personal."

"Frankie," Carlos interrupted. "How's the jack hammer job going?"

"Not too horrible," he said. "When you add in the overtime, I keep my head above water. The days go by fast, but digging ditches is hard on the back. I'd start looking for a new job, but…"

Carlos unzipped his bulky black and white snowmobile jacket and took it off, exposing the matching bibs and the straps that rested on his broad shoulders. "I'd stay there for a full year if you can," he said, dwarfing Marcel who was sitting next to him. "It will look better on a resume. You might want to come work in the car business with me someday."

"I thought my criminal record was—"

Carlos cut him off with a louder voice. "I've been looking into that," he said and refused to hit the cigar that was going around in a circle. "The Statute of Limitations has passed. You just need a resume—" He paused as Frankie received the cigar. "—and *clean* piss. Then I can probably get you a job."

Frankie smiled as he brought the blunt to his lips. "I appreciate it," he said and took a hit. "I'll get sober soon. Right now, it's the only thing that takes the pain away."

"Might as well wake and bake then, huh?" Carlos chuckled.

"Breakfast of champions," Mariani said.

"Isn't that what got you kicked out of the Marines?" Carlos asked.

"No," Mariani said. "I took a selfie with a dead terrorist. When I got evaluated, they found pot in my system. Got me court-martialed. Dishonorable discharge."

"Dayam man!" Marcel said. "I didn't know about all that."

"The only person I've ever told was Frankie. It's kinda

embarrassing."

"Do you still have the picture?" Marcel asked.

"No," Mariani said with a widening mouth. "It was super cute though."

Carlos smirked. "Did *you* kill the guy?"

"It's hard to say. I can't count how many I killed in that battle. I *hope* he was one of 'em."

"And you thought it would be a good idea to take a picture?" Carlos asked. He flicked his lighter, the flame lighting his cigarette.

"Dude had a hole in his neck. He looked photogenic." Mariani took a puff from the cigar and then changed the subject. "I'm glad you came with, Frankie." He turned to pass the blunt to Marcel. "He's always had an excuse not to go hunting with me. 'It's too cold' or 'I can't be around guns.' Frankie finally grew a set. That's a good thing."

"I just don't like taking chances," Frankie said and hopped in the slow lane so a speeding car could pass him. They were now on top of the hill, approaching the city limits of Duluth, Minnesota.

Carlos hit Frankie's arm. "You don't like taking chances?" he laughed shortly. "You're rolling dirty as fuck. You got guns in the back and you're stoned out of your mind."

"I don't *like* taking chances," Frankie said. "I'd rather be at home sleeping right now, but instead I'm taking chances with you fools."

"I didn't put the poison to your lips," Carlos said.

"Poison?" Frankie glanced in the review. "You wanna talk about poison? That twelve pack a night you drink is about a hundred times more poisonous than this blunt."

"When I get home after a ten-hour day, I'm swimming in beer, but at least I ain't driving."

Marcel bumped the seat in front of him. "Hey, GM," Marcel said. "How far is this hunting site of yours anyways?"

"Kinda up by that trailer house Frankie used to rent back in the day," Mariani said. "You remember that place? Shit brown trailer; fire pits everywhere."

"Yeah," Marcel said. "I remember that. That was *way* back in the day."

Carlos laughed. "I forgot about that dump," he said. "That was like fifteen years ago."

"My old landlord lives there now," Frankie said. "He still works on my truck. He's a good mechanic. Works on the cheap."

"The guy can fix anything," Mariani said. "And he lets me hunt on his land whenever I want. All I got to do is flip him a hundo once a year, and then give him a heads up when I'm coming."

"How many deer you get this year?" Marcel asked.

"I only got one," Mariani said. "During hunting season that is. I got two more since then with my compound bow."

Frankie turned his head. "Wait, what?" he said. "It's not hunting season?"

"No." Mariani laughed shortly. "Deer hunting season ended a couple weeks ago. You didn't know that?"

"No. I didn't," Frankie said curtly. His head whipped toward the passenger seat with a lowered brow. "What the fuck are we doing then?"

"Breaking the law, fool!" Mariani said and everyone laughed except for Frankie.

Frankie looked in the rearview mirror. "What the fuck?" he said. "You two knew about this?"

"Yeah man," Marcel said with a smile. "I thought you knew."

Frankie let out an audible breath. "What's the penalty if we get caught?"

"What difference does it make?" Carlos said. "If you get caught with a gun, you'll be fucked."

"Thanks for reminding me." Frankie shook his head tightly.

*****

Twenty minutes later, Frankie noticed a gas station lit up on the right side of the road. "Does anyone need to stop for anything?" he said. "It's the last chance you'll get."

"I'm good."

"I got everything I need."

"Keep driving," Mariani said. "We need to be *in* the deer stand before sunrise."

Frankie cruised past the store at sixty miles per hour. "We'll get there," he said and accelerated.

"Hey Frankie," Marcel said. "Guess who moved back to town?"

"Who's that?" Frankie asked.

"Twan Davis."

"Fuck Twan," Mariani said. "If I ever see that dude again, I'm gonna break his fucking face."

Frankie's head shifted slightly. "I thought he'd be dead or in prison by now."

"Nah," Marcel said. "Dat nigga just got out the joint. Served five years for armed robbery. Guess he met some cartel people on the inside. Now he be movin' bricks of white."

Mariani slammed his fist against the door panel. "I should have took him out when I had the chance. We would have done society a favor."

"What happened?" Marcel asked. "I mean, I know you

guys fucked him up, but...."

"That asshole stabbed a friend of ours," Mariani said. "In the hospital, we promised him that we'd pay Twan a visit. We had to let Twan and his boys know how we respond to shit. Me and Frankie followed him to his car one night. We beat him down with brass knuckles. I was just about to bash is teeth in, but Frankie grabbed my arm."

"Forget about it," Frankie said. "The past is history."

Marcel lit up a cigarette. "Dat nigga ain't forgettin' shit. If he sees either of you, he'll be spittin' bullets fo' sho'."

"C'mon, man," Frankie said. "That was a long time ago."

"Twan ain't shit," Mariani said. "He better *hope* he don't see me. I won't need bullets."

"I roll with ya'll," Marcel said. "I just wouldn't underestimate dis nigga. Word on da street is they be cuttin' niggas up in little pieces."

"Yeah, right," Mariani muttered. "I've never heard of anyone in Duluth getting cut up."

Marcel lowered his voice. "Maybe not in Duluth, but in Chicago, the Flebotomia Cartel is feared. Guess what Flebotomia means?"

"Bloodletting," Carlos said and took a long drag from his cigarette.

2

Frankie pumped the brakes, put his blinker on, and then turned left down a primitive road that was curvy with hills and bumps. A half-moon peeked out from the dark sky and the beautiful orange landscape eased the muscles on his face. "Looks like the weatherman might be wrong."

Carlos agreed: "I know — he said it would be cold and windy, with either rain or snow."

"This is the Northland," Mariani said. "I wouldn't be surprised if a blizzard struck."

"It ain't gonna snow," Frankie said and pressed down on the gas. "Not today."

Frankie drove for another ten miles, and then he saw the twinkle of the road sign he was waiting for. *No need for a blinker out here,* he thought, tapping his brakes a few times before he hooked a right.

"Dodge Road!" Frankie boasted. "Feels like home."

The truck vibrated down the poorly grated dirt road. It was his favorite part of the drive — the quiet hum of the tires, the isolation of the deep woods. *I miss this road,* he thought to himself, his mind wandering back in time to his first visit to this area. He remembered standing in front of a rundown trailer house, a scrawny man waiting to greet him. As Frankie drove closer, a thin smile grew on his face at the first sight of

Hank Lindberg's shoulder length mullet. Another step and his new landlord's hooded eyes met his. Frankie reached out his hand.

"Thanks for meeting with me today," Frankie remembered saying.

In response, the man scowled, his gaze lingering on Frankie's dark skin. He unclenched his fist and took one cautious step forward. Gripping Frankie's hand, he squeezed it tightly. *"This here,"* he said, applying more pressure, *"is the first colored hand I've ever shook…"*

*****

"The fuck!" At the vehemence in Mariani's voice, Frankie blinked, his mind jumping back into the present, just in time…

"Heads up!" Frankie barked, his hands gripping the steering wheel to avoid hitting a black SUV that was parked on the right shoulder of the narrow road. He immediately slammed on the brakes and yanked the steering wheel to the left. The truck skidded almost sideways.

"Holy shit!" Marcel shrieked as the truck jerked sharply, his body slamming against the locked seat belt.

After the sudden correction, a cloud of dirt lingered in the air behind them. As soon as the truck was stabilized and moving forward once again, Frankie raised his voice. "My bad, guys," he said. "I was totally zoning out."

"What the fuck, man?" Carlos said. "That was close."

"Sorry," Frankie said. "I drifted off there for a minute."

"I guess you did need your beauty sleep," Mariani quipped.

"His little wake and bake didn't help," Carlos piled on.

Frankie smacked the steering wheel. "Well, what the fuck is that truck doing parked way out here anyways?"

"They're probably asking the same thing about us," Carlos said. "Only *they* think we're drunk."

Frankie didn't respond. He just kept driving down the secluded road. For the next two miles there was nothing but gravel and trees. A white mailbox appeared on the left and Frankie slowed the truck to a crawl. "That's the trailer house I used to rent from Hank," he said. "He lives there now."

"Hank's all methed out," Mariani said. "He looks like a zombie."

"Awe, man," Frankie said and accelerated back to normal speed. "That shit is poison. He wasn't always like that. He used to work like fifteen hours a day."

"Exactly," Mariani said. "That's *how* he was able to work so much. He was always snorting glass. Don't be blind, bro. Hank's a junkie, and he always will be."

"Well, he helped me out a lot," Frankie said. "As long as he doesn't feed that shit to his kid, he'll always be my friend."

Mariani snickered. "I'm pretty sure Lenny be smoking that shit, too."

"Are you serious?" Frankie asked. "What the fuck?"

"Yeah. The apple doesn't fall too far from the tree. I mean, I haven't *seen* him smoke meth, but his teeth are all rotten, eyes all sunk in. Looks just like his dad."

"Man," Frankie said and gripped the steering wheel tightly. "I used to babysit that kid a few times a month. He was like two or three; I'd let him play in the front yard. He liked mac n cheese. Now he likes smoking meth."

"Don't be surprised," Carlos said. "Drugs are an epidemic. Destroys families."

Mariani pointed. "Right there!" he said. "The gap in the trees."

Frankie pumped the brakes and turned left at the entrance

for the hunting spot. The unnamed path was almost hidden by an overgrowth of vegetation and dense forest. Because of the unlevel surface, Frankie engaged the four-wheel drive and slowly crept over the rough terrain.

"Almost there, boys!" Mariani said enthusiastically.

"Dope!" Marcel said and clapped his hands once with excitement.

It was about fifteen minutes after six in the morning when the guys pulled up to the end of the path. Frankie made a three-point turn and parked the truck facing the road.

"We finally made it!" Carlos said with a raised voice, his arms stretching above his head.

"The deer stands are about a half a mile that way," Mariani said, gesturing toward the dark and murky woods off to their right.

As the four middle-aged hunters got out of the truck to load up for the hike, the sky got darker. A drop of rain landed on Frankie's neck and then his hand. He looked up and saw storm clouds that were brewing. *We're gonna get rained on,* Frankie thought. *Just my luck.*

Marcel pulled out two-gun cases from the back of the truck and placed them on the ground. "What are you rollin' wit', Frankie?" he asked. "The 30 odd 6 or the Winchester Model 70 hunting rifle? It's got a 4x12 ranging scope."

Mariani was also looking at the two guns. "I'd take the Winchester," he suggested, "but that's just me."

Frankie took Mariani's advice. "Thanks, bro," he said softly. "That's a nice gun. You sure you don't want to take it?"

"No. It's coo'," Marcel said and smiled, forcing a smile out of Frankie. "I hope you get a sixteen pointer with it. I'm just happy to be hunting with my friends." Marcel reached in the back of the truck and pulled out a shoulder holster with a black handgun in it. "Here. Take this, too. It's loaded."

Frankie smiled. "Holy shit!" he said and received it. "What's that for?"

"You wanna be ready in case a wolf or bear run up on you," Marcel said. "I got mines. And I bet GM got his."

*****

Mariani noticed that everyone was all geared up, rifles pressed against their chests. He smacked Frankie on the back. "Let's do this, boys," he said. "Follow Frankie."

Frankie started off toward the untamed path and the others followed behind him in a single file line. The group of eager deer hunters had begun their trek to the hunting stands. The ancient forest was cloaked with mist that lingered from the treetops to the damp ground. Most of the non-evergreen trees had bare branches and their leaves littered the forest floor, painting it orange and brown and yellow. All was quiet as the light rain transformed into sleet.

I was wrong about the weather, Frankie thought as his body stiffened-up. With one hand on the rifle, he used the other to tug his hat down over his ears.

After a quick fifteen-minute hike, they finally reached Mariani's deer stands.

"All right, boys," Mariani said softly. "We made it."

"That wasn't so bad," Frankie said.

Mariani pointed at the tree. "Me and Frankie are gonna take this stand," he said. "You and Marcel take that one." He then pointed to the second stand, forty yards to the right.

"Sounds good to me," Carlos said softly.

From the loose huddle, the guys all shook hands, quietly wished each other luck, and started toward their respective trees. With a gun and duffel bag strapped to his back, Mariani climbed up the ladder with ease.

Frankie, on the other hand made it halfway up the ladder and looked down. His bare hands gripped the cold steel tightly. After a deep breath of confidence, he pulled himself up the ladder. The moment he entered the large wooden deer stand that looked more like a kid's tree fort, Mariani started giving Frankie pointers.

"Okay, listen," Mariani said quietly. "It's important you stay calm and quiet at all times. It might take hours before we see one, so just be patient. When you do see a buck; take your time." He paused briefly. "Aim for the shoulder. Take several deep breaths. Become one with the rifle, and then squeeze the trigger." He paused again and looked at Frankie. He blinked twice then added. "This is your first time, so your adrenaline will start to pump hard. Only deep breaths will slow down your heart."

"Thanks," Frankie whispered. "My heart's already starting to pound." He took a deep breath then added. "Do ya think we'll see one today?"

Mariani gave a sly grin. "Of course, Strunz," he said, busting his friend's balls. "I baited 'em."

*****

In the other deer stand, Marcel had been scoping the area with his binoculars for some time. The ground was slowly turning white. "Footprints!" he whispered and followed them. "I see a couple doe."

"Let's have a look-see," Carlos said softly and stuck out his meaty paw.

Marcel handed the binoculars to Carlos. He then pointed in the general area of where he saw the doe casually eating the apples Mariani left for them.

Marcel reached for his bag. "I'm parched," he said and pulled a water bottle out.

"Grab me one," Carlos said and set the binoculars down.

"I only got four," Marcel said. "Sorry bro."

Carlos laughed shortly. "Get the fuck out of here."

"Just kiddin', bro." Marcel smiled and handed him a bottle.

"Thanks," Carlos said and cracked the top.

"Hey, you really gonna hook Frankie up with a job?" Marcel took a sip of water. "That hard labor's killin' his body."

Carlos tilted his gloved hand. "Not anytime soon," he said. "If he failed a drug test it would affect *me*." He poked his chest.

"I respect that," Marcel said. "I just wanna see him make some money, and not break his back doing it. Was thinkin' 'bout offering him a sales job at the mattress store. What do you think?"

"He'd never take it," Carlos replied with certitude. "Even if you handed it to him on a silver platter, he'd make an excuse. Even though he complains about digging ditches, I think he actually likes it. It keeps him in shape, and he gets to work alone."

"How could anyone like living check to check?"

"He probably thinks he's gonna win the lottery someday. I bet the first thing he'd do is build a bunker. Then he could close himself off from society."

Marcel chuckled. "That'll be the day," he said. "He'll get some motivation one of these days, and when he does, I'll hire him. He's a hard worker."

"Lack of motivation is what cost him Conny," Carlos said. "Her dad offered him a high paying job at the paper mill, and he turned it down. She wanted him to spend more time with her. Go on trips and shit. He said she wanted to get married or at least move in together. He dragged his feet."

"I feel bad for him," Marcel said. "I know he's been having a tough time lately. I think he needs a rebound and a new job. A fresh start. A new life."

"I don't know, man," Carlos said. "He still loves that girl. This one is gonna sting for a while. In time, he'll snap out of it."

*****

Frankie looked down at his phone that was vibrating in his hand. "Man," he complained softly. "My mom called me like ten times in the last hour."

"You think she's okay?" Mariani asked.

"She's okay," Frankie said. "She's just persistent. Doesn't like being ignored."

"Why don't you text her and tell her you're busy hunting?"

"Not a bad idea," he said and thumbed the screen on his phone. "I just...I kinda wanted to unplug for the day."

Mariani noticed that Frankie's hands were shaky. "You cold?"

"A little bit." Frankie nodded. "Yeah, my fingers are freezing. How 'bout you?"

"This ain't shit," Mariani muttered. "I take a cold shower twice a week just to prepare myself for shit like this."

Frankie smirked and shook his head. "Let me see those binoculars."

"Shiiiiit, negro!" Mariani said sarcastically with a flamboyant southern dialect, mocking Marcel. "Here ya go, playboy!"

Mariani handed Frankie the military-style binoculars. "Any time you start feeling cold," he said, putting a flame to a cigarette. "Just try to imagine the American heroes who fought bravely in World War Two." He paused, making eye contact before he continued. "They had primitive gear compared to ours, and they endured much colder weather."

"I wonder how they did it?" Frankie asked in a soft voice.

"They had no choice. Combat motivates people to survive."

Frankie continued to scope out the terrain. "These binocs are awesome. Everything's so clear."

Mariani nudged Frankie's arm. "Check it out," he whispered and pointed south.

Frankie shifted his sights. "I see it," he whispered, handing the binoculars back to his boy. "He's eating the apples you left for him."

Frankie picked up the rifle, his heart thumping as he aimed down field. It was freezing out, but yet he started to perspire. *He's mine,* he thought as he chewed on the inside of his lower lip.

"Not so fast," Mariani said quietly. "Don't shoot him. He's younger than I thought."

Frankie's eye was pressed against the scope of his rifle. He inhaled a deep breath. Exhaling out his nostrils, he created a white cloud of vapor that quickly disappeared and reappeared after each breath. His body began to tremble. "It's a four-pointer," he whispered. "I can't take him?"

Mariani shook his head. "You could take him with my bow if you want," he said with a low tone. "Otherwise, you gotta wait for the big boy." He paused and nodded his head up and down several times. "Trust me…he's coming."

"You gotta be kidding me." Frankie blew out an audible sigh. "He's in my sites…waiting for lead."

Frankie stood stiff with his jaw resting on the cold stock of the gun. His finger was on the trigger, waiting for Mariani to give him the word.

"Let the bambino grow up," Mariani whispered, "so we can get him next year. His dad must not be too far away."

Frankie kept breathing heavily. *This is what I've been missing out on,* he thought. *This feeling, right now. Mariani was right. I feel alive for the first time in my life.* "C'mon, man," he growled. "I *need* this."

The two old friends were debating the propriety of killing a four-point buck. As if to further fuel the debate, the men were suddenly hit by a bone-chilling arctic breath of pestilence that shook the trees and whipped frozen snow in their faces. It felt like a thousand tiny needles piercing any exposed flesh.

Even Giovanni Mariani looked uncomfortable in the deer stand when the freezing gust of wind smacked him in the face and neck. Instinctively, he pulled his hat down to cover his ears, and then he tried to hide his head in-between his shoulders.

At that moment, Frankie took a couple of deep breaths and tried to wield his heart to beat slower. He looked into the scope of the rifle. As the wind howled in his ears, he felt it slightly move his body. Keeping the target in the crosshairs was a struggle. He fought it.

When the wind died a moment later, his body then became steady. His eyes narrowed. *Mariani will forgive me,* he thought as his finger curled around the trigger.

"CRACK! CRACK!" Jerking, Frankie's heart lurched, and his head snapped to the distant woods. He knew that the thunder of gunshots did *not* come from him.

"CRACK! CRACK! CRACK!" Each eruption echoed throughout the forest and made the air groan.

"That's not Carlos!" Mariani said with his eyes wide open. "It's coming from—"

"RAT TA TAT TAT! ... RAT TA TAT TAT!" Multiple semi-automatic weapons erupted almost simultaneously without rest.

Frankie opened his mouth to suck in some air. His head shifted from Mariani to the report of the weapons that ricocheted off the tree trunks.

"CRACK! CRACK! CRACK! ... CRACK! CRACK! CRACK!"

Stunned but not shaken, the combat veteran grabbed a fist full of Frankie's jacket. "Let's get the fuck out of here be for we get hit!"

Frankie's eyelids lifted as a jolt of adrenaline shot through his body. He watched Mariani scurry down the ladder. His eyes glanced down at the duffel bag. *It's safe here,* he thought and strapped the rifle to his back. Reaching for the ladder, he grabbed it, swung his leg around, and then scampered downward.

3

Cutting through sustained icy wind, Frankie found himself in the middle of the pack of fleeing hunters. At the sound of another barrage of gunshots that reverberated off the walls of the otherwise silent forest, he ducked from the bullets he couldn't see. Following in Mariani's footprints, Frankie's heavy boots crunched against the snow with each determined step. Stumbling forward on a branch, he touched the ground and bounced back up. Fueled by panic and fear, the four-man group kept running in a single file line down the wooded path.

Frankie felt a sharp pain in his heart as he breathed in cold air, but he pushed himself to keep close behind Mariani. As the wind whistled in his ears, he turned his head slightly. *Is that a girl screaming?* he thought and pressed forward with low trembling shoulders. His eyelids flinching each time he heard the plaintive cry that was piercing the air.

*****

They'd no sooner reached the SUV when Marcel, scrambling into the back seat, blurted out: "We need to get the fuck out of here! Right now!"

"I know!" Mariani said, slouching in the front passenger seat. "Let's go, Frankie!"

Carlos smacked Frankie's jacket. "Turn the key."

At the command, Frankie instinctively reached for the ignition, but then his hand fell to his knee. "People are *dying* back there!" he said. "Didn't you hear those screams?" He paused and turned in his seat to look at each of his friends. "That was a *woman* or a kid. Probably Hank's kid."

"I heard it," Carlos said and pulled his phone out. "I'll call 911."

Mariani turned around fully. "Fuck that!" he barked. "We got guns on us. I'm a fuckin' felon. I'll get five years. Frankie, too."

"Well, let's get the fuck out of here then!" Marcel said, but it was clear he wasn't making a request. "What the fuck we waitin' fo'?"

Frankie hit the center counsel. "Hank needs help, damn it!"

"You gotta be kidding me!" Mariani said, his face twisting with disgust. "Fuck Meth Lab Hank. Let's get the fuck out of here."

Carlos nodded his head. "Come on, Frankie," he said. "What if the cops come? They might start shooting at us."

"There ain't no fucking cops coming," Frankie said. "The closest house is five miles away. Nobody heard them gunshots but us. When I lived out here, I used to shoot targets in my back yard every day. No one ever gave a shit."

"Bro," Marcel said and grabbed the shoulder of Frankie's jacket. "Let's go home! I'm not fucking around."

Frankie turned in his seat. "Fine," he said and then straightened himself. "Let's go then."

"Let's bounce!" Mariani tilted his hand.

Frankie turned the key and the truck growled. With his foot on the brake, he slammed the shifter into drive and the

SUV rolled forward. No one was speaking.

That poor kid, Frankie thought. *He's like sixteen years old. I got him a present for his second birthday. And now he's probably dead.*

Frankie's eyes grew gritty as the truck crept to the end of the path, his fingers tightening as he turned right on the vacant road. Speeding up to twenty-five miles per hour, his eyes searched for the white mailbox. When he found it, he slowed down to a complete stop.

There it is, Frankie thought, raising his eyebrows. "I see blood," he said and hit the gas pedal.

Marcel was still gazing out the window. "Them mutha' fuckas' got it!"

"Oh my God," Carlos said. "That was the most horrible thing I've ever seen."

"It's shit like that," Frankie said, shaking his head. "Makes me doubt there's a God."

After driving down the road for a minute, Frankie caught his breath in his throat and then—his arms cranked hard on the wheel as he whipped the truck around with the rear wheels spinning.

Mariani turned in his seat, his hands spread apart and shaking. "What the fuck are you doing?"

"I-I can't just do nothing," Frankie said and turned his head briefly. "I have to see…w-what if there was something we could do? I can't, I can't just leave them."

Marcel raised his voice louder than everyone else. "What if you get killed?" he said, and Carlos saw a vein bulging on the side of his neck. "Someone's posting up over there with a big ass fucking gun!"

"I'd never lead you guys down the wrong path," Frankie said. "I-I just know it's the right thing to do."

Carlos shoved Frankie's shoulder. "You're putting our lives in danger," he said. "I'm getting fucking pissed, dude! Turn this shit around—now!"

"Or what?" Frankie said with contempt. "Shame on you. Shame on all of you. There're only few times in life when you have to step up as a man and risk everything to save a life. I'd do it for any of you. I'd even do it for a stranger—so, how the hell could I just leave a friend to suffer? How could I look in the mirror after that?"

After a brief moment of silence, Mariani's head snapped toward Frankie. "There's no glory in death, Frankie," he said. "Prison doesn't sound too fun either. I get what you're saying, but use your head, bro. Be smart."

"Look guys." Frankie said. "I'm sorry. I…I have no choice. Just drop me off—I'll find a way home."

"Are you listening to yourself right now?" Carlos raised his voice. "Do you not care what we think?"

At the small opening in the woods, Frankie tapped the brakes and turned left. Rolling swiftly over bumps on the path, the truck bounced back into its original parking spot. "I've made my decision," he said and threw it in park. Opening the door, a crack, he shifted to face Mariani. "I'm gonna check it out—with…or without you."

With a lowered brow, Mariani gave Frankie a withering glare. He heaved out an audible sigh and raised his eyebrows. "I'm not letting Frankie go in alone," he said and shook his head. "I don't like it, but I got his back no matter what."

"You can't help those people," Marcel said. "Don't do it, Frankie."

"How 'bout you, Los?" Frankie asked with a low tone. "Are you in…or out?"

"I think it's bad idea," Carlos said. "It's too dangerous."

"All right," Frankie said. "You two wait here. We'll be right back." He pulled his hat over his ears and opened the door.

"Wait," Marcel said. "If I can't stop ya, I'm gonna join ya."

Carlos squinted at the review mirror. When he met eyes with Mariani, he felt the pressure, just like when they were kids, and Mariani passed him the whiskey bottle for the first time.

"We could use your eyes, Los," Mariani said, looking at the mirror. "We'll scope from fifty yards. If it looks dangerous, we'll turn back."

"This is a job for the police," Carlos insisted, a muscle in his jaw flexing steadily as his eyes passed from Mariani to Marcel before landing on Frankie. He released a tight breath. "But if something happened to you guys and I wasn't there to have your back...I'd never be able to live with myself."

"Good," Mariani said and clapped his hands together once. "Now, let's make a plan."

*****

After a mission plan was settled upon, everyone got out of the truck. A cold gust of wind scratched at Frankie's face and he lowered his head.

Mariani approached Frankie. "If us three all have rifles," Mariani said. "You might as well just take the pistol. I need someone to be able to move fast with free hands."

"That works for me," Frankie said and placed the rifle in the far back of the SUV.

Mariani looped the strap on the binoculars around Frankie's neck. "Take these," he said. "This is your idea. You lead the way."

"Let's go save some lives," Frankie said and started

walking. He followed the packed down footprints that they'd made earlier. With each crunch forward, he sucked in cold air.

The four men continued marching onward. Head on a swivel, Frankie saw nothing but trees and bushes and snow. The wind screamed, pushing them down the trail and past the hunting stands. The heavy bleat in their hearts sped up, but their pace had finally slowed down. Passing tree after tree, his thoughts asked him a trembling question with no answer, just a beacon in the shadows of his mind, pulsating in his mind's eye, guiding him down a path of self-destruction.

With each forward step, Frankie's thoughts were betraying him. *Would Hank or his kid risk everything to help me?* he thought. *Probably not, but that's what makes me better. I'll do whatever it takes to help a friend in need.* Deep down in Frankie's gut, he felt the sting of fear, doubt and anger. He knew what they were doing was risky, but there was no turning back now.

Maneuvering around trees, Frankie and the boys steadily crept closer to their first checkpoint. When Frankie squinted, he could see Hank's fire pit mound in the distance.

"Frankie," Mariani said from behind him.

He stopped and turned. "What's up?"

"I should take the lead from here. I did recon in Afghanistan."

Frankie nodded. "Go for it."

Mariani moved to the front of the pack and closed the distance to the objective. Crouching low, he made a gesture with his right arm—a clenched fist to indicate a halt in forward movement.

"Let's take cover behind the fire pit," Mariani said softly. "Keep your heads low."

They approached the mound of carbonized junk slowly. Frankie crept up to the edge and got down on one knee. Pulling out the binoculars, he pressed them to his face. Hank's driveway became close. "Holy shit," he said, inhaling a short breath. He lowered the binocs, turning to his friends. His face was ashen, hollowed, shrunken.

"What?" Marcel asked, "What is it?"

Frankie let out a breath in the form of a small cloud. "I saw a-a...fuck, there's a dead body in the driveway!"

"Let me see," Mariani said and reclaimed his binoculars. Scanning from left to right, he first saw the rusty brown trailer house, and then a few vehicles, and then he saw a man on the ground. *Dark skin in the middle of the boonies,* he thought. *Hmm...* Handing the binoculars to Carlos, he said, "Frankie's right. Look on the side of the black SUV."

Frankie stood with a vacant gaze; the vision of red snow was fresh in his mind. His breathing was heavy and fast. *First dead body I've ever seen,* he thought. *Whoa, that looks just like the truck I almost hit earlier.*

Carlos swore under his breath, passing the binoculars to Marcel, the latter swallowing heavily as he brought them to his eyes.

An unnatural stillness met Marcel's gaze, splattered with garnish stains of blood and violence—a muted sort of destruction made apparent by a black SUV, every square inch seemingly riddled with bullet holes.

"Dayam, dog!" Marcel said a little too loud. "It's a fuckin' bloodba—"

Mariani jerked his hand. "Shhhh."

Marcel nodded with his lips pressed together.

Frankie was trembling inside.

"I'm gonna take a closer look," Mariani said. "Carlos, I want you and Marcel to creep around to the left." He pointed to the edge of the forest. "Take cover in the bushes next to that big ass spruce tree. Just keep your eyes peeled and watch our back. Check the windows of the trailer for movement."

Carlos and Marcel swooped around back.

Mariani took a step closer to Frankie. "This is what you wanted," he said with a low growl. "You better be ready."

Frankie took in a deep breath and let it out. "I'm ready."

"Good," Mariani said. "Pull out the pistol and press the safety off."

Frankie unzipped his jacket halfway and reached for his holster. When his bare hand touched the cold steel, his heart ticked a beat faster.

"Prepare to defend yourself at all cost," Mariani said. "Follow my lead and prepare to see dead people up close. It's ugly."

"What should I do if Hank pulls a gun on us?" Frankie asked, the black pistol dangling at his side.

"If it's me or him, it's gonna be him."

"Don't ya think he'd recognize us?"

"We tried to stop you for a reason," Mariani said with raised eyebrows. "Hank will shoot before thinking. If you hesitate, you die; if you pull the trigger, it's murder."

Frankie swallowed saliva. "I have to find out where those screams came from. They might be alive still."

Mariani pulled out his walkie talkie. "Los. Do you read?"

"Copy."

"You got me covered?"

"Positive."

"Going silent," Mariani said and put the device in his jacket pocket.

With the pistol in his right hand, Frankie tilted it and glanced down.

"We'll creep down the tree line," Mariani said, "and take

cover behind the trailer."

"Then what?"

"Then we'll leapfrog from the van to the SUV...and then we'll search the trailer."

"Right now?"

"Yeah." Mariani motioned to Hank Lindberg's home. "Let's move."

Frankie nodded once. Emphatically. "All right."

*****

Hidden from behind foliage, Carlos had binoculars pressed against his eye sockets. His wide stance kept him still as he watched his friends maneuver from the trailer to the van. "This is the stupidest shit I've ever done," he said to Marcel. "I hope we make it out of this with no trouble."

"So far so good," Marcel said, looking down the scope of his rifle. "I don't see any movement."

"Someone could be held up in the trailer."

"Keep your eyes on them windows. I'll watch the front yard."

"This is all your fault," Carlos complained. "Earlier, when you changed your mind—I was the odd man out. I couldn't say no. Now look at these two. They're walking toward a dead *fucking* body."

"*This* is Frankie's fault," Marcel said. "But we're all in it now."

*****

Mariani peeked around the side of the van toward the shot-up SUV. *Passenger side door wide open,* he thought and pulled back. *Spidered windows.* He let out a deep breath. "I'll go first,"

Mariani whispered. "I wanna get closer to that SUV. I can't see in through the windshield. Gotta clear the cars before we check the house."

"What do you want me to do?"

"Cover me," Mariani said. "When I get there, look at me, and then follow my signal. No words."

Frankie sucked in a breath. "Okay."

Mariani crouched to the passenger side of the SUV. Swinging his gun toward the trailer, he scanned the area. *No movement,* he thought, pivoting to the dead man face down in the snow. Narrowing his eyes, he grimaced at the stout body in black clothes. With the barrel of his rifle, he poked him in the back. *He's a goner.*

Lifting his head and turning, Mariani waved Frankie toward him.

Frankie closed the gap and Mariani pointed to the driver side of the vehicle. With a curt nod, he slowly lifted his gun and braced it with his left hand. Crouching low and moving steadily forward, his grip got tighter. With trembling hands, he aimed toward the driver's side door. The window was shot out. He could feel his breaths quicken as he reached the door.

Peeking inside, Frankie froze.

"Holy shit," he whispered silently, his eyes widening.

There was someone in there. Breathing!

And then the full head of black hair rolled. Frankie gasped in horror as the man's dark menacing eyes locked with his. Frankie's stance stiffened. "Psssst!" he got Mariani's attention. Releasing his left hand from the gun, Frankie pointed at the brown-skinned Hispanic individual in the driver seat.

Mariani aimed his long gun at the shattered windshield. Sidestepping a dozen paces, he planted himself next to Frankie. Mariani set his jaw.

*****

From inside the truck, a harsh voice croaked, "Are you cops?"

"Don't move mother fucker!" Mariani ordered the afflicted man who had steam rising from his chest.

"Fuck you, white boy," he said and then coughed up blood on his chin. "If you killed me, you'd be doing me a favor."

Frankie breathed heavily as he studied the man whose skin was a shade darker than his. Like the SUV, the stranger was riddled with bullets. His black coat was wet and completely covered in blood. The black hair on his face and neck was less than a beard but more than stubble. Crawling on the middle of his neck, a small tattoo of a black spider caught Frankie's eye.

"You want me to kill you, tough guy?" Mariani taunted him. His throbbing finger was on the trigger and he contemplated squeezing it. He took a determined step forward.

Frankie noticed that Mariani was getting antsy, and probably considering the proposition.

"Hold up," Frankie said, instinctively taking one hand off the gun, warding off Mariani. "This guy just killed our friends." He paused and looked at Mariani. "We should let him suffer."

The man spit out blood. "Hank was a rat," he said. "He wasn't your friend. He didn't have any friends."

Frankie opened his mouth, but no words came out.

"Eh, bro," Mariani insisted. "He's got a gun on the passenger seat. I'm gonna disarm him right quick. If he moves one inch, blow his *fucking* head off." Mariani circled around the front of the truck.

Frankie took a wider stance. Looking down the barrel of the gun, he could feel his cold hands trembling. Suddenly, the lip of the man in front of him curled. *What the fuck is he smiling at?*

From inside the SUV, the stranger jerked his right hand inside his jacket.

In the time it took Frankie's eyes to snap wider, his finger squeezed the trigger. At the earsplitting explosion of the gun, Mariani hit the dirt. Frankie took two steps back, dropping his jaw and the gun at the same time. "Oh fuck," he said to himself. "What did I do?"

*****

Mariani came running around the back side of the truck. He saw Frankie on his knees, and then pivoted to the driver side door. The stranger was slumped against the steering wheel. Steam was rising and lines of blood were flowing from his head. Rushing to his friend, Mariani dropped down to his knees and placed a hand on his back and chest. "Are you hit?"

Frankie shook his head as he gasped for air.

"You did that?"

"H-he reached in his jacket," Frankie said and covered his mouth.

"Get up," Mariani said and lifted him to his feet. "Everything's gonna be all right, but we gotta fix this before we go home."

Frankie's eyes were blinking, and his breaths were shaky.

Standing face to face, Mariani forcefully grabbed Frankie's jacket with both hands. "Calm down, bro," he growled. "You just saved our lives. You did good, but right now, I need you at your best."

"Okay." Frankie unzipped his jacket and pressed his hand against his chest. "What are we gonna do?"

"First things first," Mariani said. "Find the spent shell

casing. Look for a hole in the snow."

Frankie looked downward and pointed off to the right. "It's gotta be in this area."

Mariani reached in his pocket and pulled out the walkie talkie. "Los. Do you read?"

"Copy."

"I need you up here right now. Tell Marcel to keep an eye on that trailer."

"On the way."

*****

Frankie pointed at a tiny hole in the snow. "I see it!" He got down and carefully plunged his hand into the snow and pulled out a short brass shell casing.

"Put it in your pocket," Mariani said. "Don't lose it."

Frankie's head shifted at the sight of Carlos approaching.

Mariani turned to face Carlos, who was huffing and puffing. "We got a problem."

"I *see* that," Carlos said, his gaze bouncing from the dead man to Frankie, and then landing on Mariani. "What the fuck happened?"

"The guy reached for his gun. Frankie put him down."

Carlos looked at Frankie who had his lips pressed together. "This is *exactly* what I was worried about," he said and let out a breath. "Now what?"

"He found the shell," Mariani said. "I'm gonna find the bullet. You two search the house."

"Search the house?" Carlos asked. "For what?"

"That bullet has Marcel Taylor's name on it," Mariani said. "We have to find it, and right now…we could be sitting ducks. Search the fucking house. Don't touch anything."

Carlos lowered his eyebrows. "Should we knock first?"

"Yeah," Mariani said. "Pound on the door a few times. Shout that you're here to help. Do it twice, then go in. Three minutes. In and out."

"What about Frankie?" Carlos asked angrily. "He doesn't look stable."

Frankie plunged his hand in the snow and came up with his pistol. "I'm fine. Let's get this done."

*****

Mariani watched Carlos' and Frankie's progress toward the dilapidated trailer house. Turning to face the man who Frankie killed, he sighed. *I need that bullet, asshole.*

With his gloved hand, Mariani grabbed the door handle and yanked open the door. Grabbing the man by his jacket collar, he ripped him from the front seat to the ground. Getting down on one knee, he examined the small entrance wound under the right eye. The hole was oozing dark blood that was streaming down the side of his face. Mariani grabbed him by the jacket and rolled him over. *No exit wound,* he thought. "Hmmm." He rolled him on his back again.

Mariani unzipped the dead man's jacket and frisked him. *No gun,* he thought. "You sure put my boy to the test," he said. "Frankie passed."

Reaching for the sheath that was strapped to his chest, Mariani gripped the one-piece combat knife. He slowly pulled it out and cradled it in his hands, slowly rolling the leather handle. "Stay still, you piece of fucking shit."

Mariani put the tip of the tanto blade in the hole and held it still with his left hand. Raising his right hand in the air, he dropped his palm down on the butt of the handle. The bone cracked and the noise made Giovanni Mariani cringe.

4

From inside a small bedroom in the trailer, Frankie and Carlos hovered over a pale woman who laid still on the bed. Her shoulder length blond hair was dark red at the tips.

Frankie cautiously leaned forward and grabbed her cold wrist. "No pulse."

"Looks like a painful death," Carlos said, cringing as his eyes landed on the two black holes in her midsection.

"I bet that was her screams we heard," Frankie said. "She must have crawled into bed to bleed out."

Carlos turned around. "Let's check the other rooms." He walked out.

Frankie let out a long sigh. "Rest in peace, Candace," he said. As his gaze left his old friend, he noticed that her drawers were all ripped out of the dresser, clothes scattered on the floor. *I wonder what they were looking for?* he thought. *The Hank I knew was broke.* He then followed Carlos out the door.

Carlos pointed. "Footprints!" he said and walked slowly through the kitchen. When he got to the door, he flicked the light on and slowly walked down the creaky steps.

As soon as Carlos reached the basement floor, he stopped. "Three bodies," he said, his heart sinking to a new low.

Carlos stepped to the side and Frankie descended next to him.

Frankie winced and took in a sharp breath. "That's Hank right there!" he said. "The one with the mullet."

Hank Lindberg was face down in a puddle of blood. He was wearing blue jeans, a red and black flannel shirt, and his matted flop of brown hair hung on his shoulders and back.

"Who are these guys?"

"Looks like one of Hank's cronies. The other guy must be one of the killers."

"Mexican standoff. Everyone dies." Carlos poked Hank with the barrel of his rifle. "No survivors. No kid," he said with a heavy touch of irritation. "You satisfied yet?"

"Yeah," Frankie said and paused, a stream of memories flashing in his mind. The winch on Hank's truck, pulling his SUV out of the ditch on a cold winter day. Fishing with Hank on his boat. No luck, but the three-hour tour and the conversation about the obstacles of life stuck in his mind. Now Hank lay at his feet. "I don't know if Hank was a good man, but...he *was* good to me. Rest in peace, Hank."

*****

As Frankie got back to the shot-up SUV, all he saw was red on white. The snow around the dead man was splattered. Mariani was leaning against the front fender with a coy smirk on his blood-stained face.

"Holy shit," Frankie said under his breath, turning to see Carlos' eyebrows drop.

Carlos took a step closer. "Oh my God," he shouted, one arm shooting into the air. "What did you do?"

"I got the bullet," Mariani said, stooping to clean it off in the snow. "We can go home now."

Frankie squinted. "You found it?"

"Check it out." Mariani opened his fist to reveal a slug that was flattened.

Carlos scrunched up his face. "We were gone for like *five* minutes," he said, glancing down at the bloody head and gaping wound. "And you dug a *hole* into his brain?"

"This bullet would have given us all life in prison," Mariani said and put the evidence inside his breast pocket. "What'd you guys find?"

"Hank and his w-wife are dead," Frankie said with a trembling voice. "Didn't find the kid, but we...we found three other bodies. One Mexican on the front porch, one in the basement, and a white dude."

"All right," Mariani said. "Let's go home, boys."

Carlos nodded his head. "Good idea," he said, both words drenched in contempt.

"Hold up," Frankie said. "We should search the Navigator. Hank's house was ransacked. They were looking for something."

Mariani picked up his walkie-talkie and spoke directly to Marcel: "Breaker, breaker, one, nine."

The sound of static was heard and then Marcel replied. "Copy."

"Head to the truck," Mariani said. "Get it started."

From the brush in the distance, Marcel took one more look through the lens of the binoculars. He saw his team and the surrounding area, snow still falling from the sky. "Bet," he said and then retreated into the woods.

*****

Frankie gazed at the man whose life he took. The hideous face was split open and dripping with blood. In this moment of silence, he cauterized that picture in his head. The crevice that Mariani carved, the dark eyes that seemed to be watching him, the tiny tattoo of a spider in the middle of his neck.

From behind the truck, Carlos popped the back hatch of the SUV. Three medium-sized black duffel bags were resting on the carpet. Climbing inside, he snatched the closest bag, unzipping it quickly. Carlos' fingers shivering a little, he peeled back the sides of the canvas.

"What the...?" Whispering in disbelief, Carlos' eyes widened, his throat bobbing thickly. "Fuck," he cried, his head jerking up roughly, those expressive eyes exploding when they found Frankie.

"What is it?" Frankie asked, leaning forward.

Carlos smiled, his mouth stretching larger when he glanced back down at the contents in the bag. Then, with a swift swing of his arm, he pushed it toward Frankie. "Take a look!"

Frankie opened the bag wide and saw a mountain of money. "Fuck yeah!" he shouted.

Mariani bowed his head over the bag, his eyes estimating the contents. "That's a lot of fucking green!"

"The third bag is filled with dope," Carlos said, tilting the bag to show the bricks. "Looks like coke — or — maybe heroin."

"Fuck the coke," Frankie sputtered. He lifted his head to look at Carlos, and then returned his eyes to the money. "This must be a million bucks! It's the answer to all our problems."

Mariani zipped up the bag. "Los," he said. "Me and Frankie got to stage the crime scene. Grab a bag of cash and get back to the truck. When you get there, unload all the guns and put them in their cases."

"No prob'," Carlos said and scooted out of the truck.

Frankie patted him on the shoulder. "We'll be right behind

you, brother."

Carlos took a deep breath and grabbed the short handle of the duffel bag. "Make it quick."

*****

Frankie gazed at the large silhouette of Carlos, lumbering through the snow. As their friend got further away, he got smaller and smaller, until he disappeared in the darkness of the murky forest.

Frankie's eyes then swiveled from Carlos to the corpse — and the sudden weight of their reward. The burden of ending a man's life.

Mariani kicked the dead man. "Fucking punk!" he said and turned to Frankie. "Unless you wanna set him on fire, there's not much else we could do. The cops will wonder what happened to his face, but we didn't leave any evidence. Let's grab the bags and bounce."

Mariani marched to the back of the truck. Grabbing both bags, he tossed one in the snow near Frankie's feet.

"Wait. Leave the dope here," Frankie said. "Just the money. Drugs are poison."

"What?" Mariani insisted enthusiastically. "The coke must be worth a half a million dollars or more! We could cut it with Aspirin and turn it in to a million."

"You wanna poison your own people?" Frankie asked, a tinge of anger in his voice.

"How 'bout this?" Mariani said, "We take the dope and stash it in the woods. That way the pigs don't get it." He paused to see the expression on his friend's face then added, "It's a business decision, bro. Let's take it."

Frankie slowly shook his head. "No," he said. "Please. Just

trust my judgment on this. The cops will rule out a search for other suspects if they find drugs. They'll assume it was a big drug deal gone wrong. Case closed. Right?"

"They can search for suspects all they want," Mariani said defiantly. "What does that have to do with us? How would they know we were here?"

Frankie placed his hand over his heart. "You're missing my point, bro," he said. "We *want* them to think that no one got away. Plus, this is the type of thing that could ruin our whole crew. Just imagine— money, coke, idle time. C'mon, man. Let's take this loot and get the fuck out of here."

Mariani picked up the tool he used for the surgery. He looked at it briefly, wiped it clean on his pants, and then put it back in its sheath. "Maybe you're right," he said and threw the dope bag inside the SUV. "Fuck it. Let's bounce."

The two friends abandoned the crime scene, but one left bloody streaks in the snow.

5

Advancing with tremendous haste through the forest, Frankie felt the bushes and low hanging tree branches scratch against his jacket. The weight of his wet boots against the heavy snow slowed his climb, but the shadow of Carlos' footprints guided him steadily onward. His mind began to crank.

Hank was a racist, Frankie thought. *Why would he do business with Mexicans? He seemed pretty poor to be a dope dealer.* With each urgent step forward, the flowing adrenaline kept him warm in the face of freezing wind. His desire to escape forced him to ignore the pain in his lower back. He could rest once he was home and free and safe.

As Mariani put one foot in front of another, his nostrils flared as he revisited the very recent past. The fuel for his forward thrust was the fact that he'd just saved the day. Finding the slug in the dead man's head eliminated the evidence that they were there. The thought of cracking the skull made him feel proud. Mariani's blood was still pumping as he obsessed about what he had done. *How many people can say they've done that?* he thought and picked up the pace.

*****

Meanwhile, Carlos and Marcel sat inside the idling SUV, both puffing on cigarettes, their heads cocked toward the woods.

Carlos flicked the butt out the window. "There they are!" he pointed to the woodland.

"Mariani's covered in blood!" Marcel said, pushing open the door.

"Don't worry. It's..." Carlos didn't finish his thought because Marcel was already running toward his friends.

*****

Marcel reached out to grab Mariani. "Bro'!" His hands holding the lightest tremor as his eyes raked over the soiled jacket. "You okay?"

"Yeah, I'm good," Mariani said, shrugging him off. "Dude was a bleeder." He then began to remove his jacket. "We gotta burn this shit right now!"

"It's too suspicious," Frankie said. "They'd find the ashes. They'd know we were here."

Mariani shrugged. "Ashes are better than evidence."

"What, are we gonna wait here and make sure it burns all the way?"

"I need a bag then!" Mariani hollered over the wind. "We'll have to take it with us."

Frankie ran to the truck.

Mariani stepped out of his boots and camouflage snow pants. "Los," he said. "Get me some water. I need to clean my face."

Grabbing two contractor bags from the back of his truck, Frankie double lined them. He turned and opened it wide. "Toss your clothes in here," he said. "I'll shove it under the hood of my truck."

"Good thinking," Mariani said and stuffed the rolled-up

jacket and pants in the bag. "We'll burn this shit later."

Carlos handed him a towel and then a bottle of water. "You better hope he don't have the HIV."

"Fuck off." Mariani hurriedly shoved his boots in the bag. His huddled figure was starkly pale in the glow of the snow. Pouring cold water on his bald head, he stiffened against the bitter winds as he scrubbed his face and neck with the towel.

Frankie pried off the snowsuit he was wearing and gave it to his naked friend.

*****

The men clamored into the idling vehicle. Frankie jerked down on the transition. The truck began to roll down the trail. Glancing at the rearview mirror, he barked. "Seatbelts!"

Carlos reached for his seat belt. "You're just a ball buster, aren't you?"

"No," Frankie said. "This is the type of shit that could put us all in prison for life. We can't take any chances. We don't wanna get pulled over."

"What's the plan, brother?" Mariani asked from the passenger seat as they reached the end of the rutted path.

"We probably shouldn't go down the main road," Frankie said, talking aloud, feeling out the weight of his thoughts as they passed through his lips. "If the cops come, that's the road they'll take for sure." He paused, shifting his gaze in the opposite direction. "If we take a left *here*, then another left, we'll end up in the Meadowlands."

Turning on the road, Frankie registered the thought process in his head, spinning and fumbling through options. *Got it!* "From there, we could hop on the highway to Rice Lake. You guys remember Ivan, right? He lives out there."

"Fuck that," Mariani said. "Can't we get a hotel or something? Ivan's fuckin' nuts."

"It's safe," Frankie said, accelerating up to speed. "It's low key. No cameras. No signatures."

Carlos shifted in his seat. "Mariani's right," he said. "We should get a hotel or just go home."

"We need to burn the evidence," Frankie reminded everyone. "We need to split up the money."

"We can always go to my cabin," Marcel said. "It's in Wisconsin though."

"That's too far," Frankie said. "We need to get off the road as soon as possible. I'm going to Ivan's. It's close."

"He better not get nosey," Mariani said. "Or we'll be burning his body next."

"I'll keep him in check," Frankie said. "He owes me a favor."

"Fuck it, guys," Marcel said. "The sooner we get rid of the evidence the better."

At the end of Dodge Road, Frankie took another left. Leaning forward in his seat, he peered out the snow-obscured windshield. Blinking rapidly, Frankie tried to look past the slanted onslaught of snowfall as his hands gripped the steering wheel tighter. "This storm is insane," he said. "I can barely see twenty feet in front of me."

"You want me to drive?" Mariani asked.

"I got it," Frankie said.

Frankie continued to drive on the primitive old highway that led north, and the wicked stormfront followed them. The speed limit was fifty miles per hour, but he was going less than thirty.

Mariani hit the door panel. "Can't this beast go any faster?"

"Any faster and we'd be in the ditch," Frankie said. "Once we get on the main highway, we'll be able to go faster." He squinted his eyes. *Looks like we're driving into a giant wall of snow,* he thought, pressing his boot on the pedal to appease his friend.

*****

Twenty miles further north, silence took ahold of the vehicle as they waited to get caught—each man unable to fully exhale until they were safe. Frankie's eyes were glued on the windshield. Mariani gazed off to the side at the evergreen trees that lined the road. Marcel was thinking about his kids.

Carlos plopped a hand on Mariani's shoulder. "Can I ask you a personal question?"

Mariani turned his head. "It depends," he said. "Why? What is it?"

"How'd you get that bullet out?"

"I put the tip of my Kabar in the hole," Mariani said, jerking his hand in a downward motion. "Then I smashed it with my hand. It split his skull open. I had to pry it open, then dig in there with my fingers for a few minutes."

"I know," Carlos said. "But seriously—how did you stomach it? I couldn't have done that."

Mariani shrugged. "That's what sets me aside from most men."

"You're fucking nuts, bro," Carlos said. "But you saved our asses."

"Things don't always go as planned, my brother," Mariani said with no shame. "The moment Frankie shot that dude, I knew we needed that slug. I ain't goin back to prison."

Carlos cracked open the window. "Frankie should have

never shot someone," he said. "We should have never been there."

"Woulda, shoulda, coulda, but didn't." Mariani sparked up a cigarette, rolled the window down, and then flicked the slug into the ditch.

Frankie turned the radio up a few notches to drown out the tension that was building. He drove just a little bit faster and tried to justify their recent actions in his mind. *But we were there, Carlos,* he thought in his head. *The guy reached for his gun. He woulda shot me. We better not get caught.*

*****

The long drive was taking a toll on Frankie's back. Wincing in pain, he dropped a hand from the wheel, aggressively twisting his torso. As his body turned, he felt something digging in his side. He reached inside his fleece jacket and felt leather and steel. His eyes grew wide, a curse word breaking silently out of his mouth. "Fuck."

Instead of pulling over, he kept driving with beads of sweat rolling down his side. Scanning the highway while wondering what to do, he saw a white sign with red letters in the distance. As he got closer, he pumped the brakes, swerving into the unplowed parking lot of a small dive restaurant. When Frankie parked the truck, he immediately peeled off his fleece jacket.

Mariani whipped his head toward Frankie. "What the hell are you doing?"

"I forgot to stash my sidearm," Frankie said and let out a deep sigh. After he removed the shoulder harness, he handed it to Marcel in the back seat. "Can you stash it in one of those duffel bags?"

"Fo' sho'," Marcel said and received it.

"Damn." Mariani pointed. "A fucking trooper just rolled down that road."

"He could have pulled us over," Frankie said. "I can't believe I was driving around like that."

Carlos clasped his shoulder. "And you bust my balls for no seatbelt?"

*****

From within the confines of the restaurant, the owner stood and looked out the window. This was the first vehicle to roll into his parking lot all day. An eager smile was pulling up the corners of his mouth as he awaited the customers. The old man noticed them, but they didn't notice him. For a minute or two, he just stood there behind the large window and observed. *The driver's got some dark skin,* he thought. *Must be lost. Haven't seen a colored out here in years. I hope he's hungry though.*

A minute later, the black Tahoe suddenly spun all four tires in reverse, and then it ripped forward out of the parking lot. The rev of the engine was heard inside the restaurant.

"Fucking animals," the owner scowled. "Go back to the city where you belong."

6

From the bedroom of his hotel suite, Thumper slid his cellphone in his vest pocket. Opening the door, the first thing he saw was his number two, Scott Draper, sitting on the love seat, drinking a beer. "That was Enrique." Thumper tilted his left hand that was fully desecrated with tattoos. "He said Cezar isn't answering his calls either."

"I told ya." Draper popped up out of his seat dressed in black. "I bet Hank shot them spics dead."

"Nah," Thumper said, briefly scratching his grizzly beard. "Enrique assured me everything's fine. The prick actually told me to never doubt him."

Draper lit up a cigarette. "What are we gonna do if your pal Enrique's wrong?"

"That would be a problem," Thumper said, pushing up the sleeves of his black sweatshirt, revealing more ink on his thick forearms. "But I don't think he's wrong. Cezar was with three trained killers."

"We should come up with a plan B. I mean…for all we know, Hank's in protective custody."

"We don't know shit. I bet Hank's dead and Cezar fell off the grid."

"Let me send someone to drive by Hank's house. Might be able to get some information at least."

"Cops might be there by now. Can't risk it."

Draper spread apart his arms. "We need information. We're in the dark right now."

"We need to wait this out." Thumper squinted. "If Cezar got took out by Hank, Enrique would come at Hank with everything he's got. Trust me. We need to follow the plan."

"Thumper, if Hank lives, this alibi won't mean shit. The pig said Hank's been an informant for two years. Probably got enough dirt on us to put us away for life."

Thumper took a step closer. "I appreciate your advice." His voice lowered. "But I've made my decision. There's nothing else we can do right now. We're gonna spend the day at the casino until I hear back from Enrique, then I'll tell you what we're gonna do next."

"You're the boss," Draper said with a touch of mockery, his thin frame turning slightly.

"That's right." Thumper grabbed a fistful of his cousin's vest and jerked him closer. "I decide."

7

The main highway was plowed. Frankie was cruising north at fifty miles per hour. While increasing the speed of the windshield wipers, he felt his phone vibrating in his pocket. *Mom*, he thought. *You just don't stop, do you?*

He pulled out his phone and pressed it to his ear. "Hello."

"Where have you been?" Frankie's mom, Diana snipped. "I've been trying to get a hold of you all day. What the fuck's wrong with—"

Frankie cut her off with his baritone. "Stop!" he ordered. "I'm driving. It's dangerous. I'm gonna call you back. I love you."

"I need—" Frankie hung up the phone and tossed it on the center console.

Dropping one hand from the wheel, Frankie grabbed a fist full of denim. "My mom's been calling me all morning," he said. "I had to let her know I was okay. She's panicking."

"My phone's been off all day," Mariani said. "When I go hunting, I fully unplug."

Frankie grabbed his phone and turned it off. "There," he said. "Unplugged."

"*Until* you get to Ivan's house, that is." Mariani laughed a short laugh. "Then, *he's* gonna try to plug you."

Everyone laughed until Marcel spoke up without notice. "I

only met dat dude once," he said, his brows furrowing. "Musta been like ten years ago."

"You made a good impression," Frankie said. "He still asks about you. Thinks you're like the coolest dude ever."

Marcel smiled. "Why is that?"

"He loves black people," Frankie said. "He was sheltered as a kid. That's probably why he likes me, but I'm only half black. *You* on the other hand…you're black as night."

"Growing up black, I've had many people hate me for the color of my skin. But I've never had someone love me for it. I might have to have a conversation with this dude. Sounds like he's down for the struggle."

"He's got jungle fever," Carlos laughed.

"After ten minutes of talking to him," Mariani said, "you'll probably never wanna see him again."

"He couldn't be that bad," Marcel said. "I thought he was a little weird, but at least he was respectful. How the hell did you ever meet that guy, anyways?"

Frankie glanced in the rearview mirror. "Ya know what?" he said, "Ivan the Terrible wasn't always crazy, and he wasn't always terrible. He *was* a good dude. Believe it or not, he was the valedictorian my senior year." Slightly turning his head to the right, he saw a green sign fly past them. *Highway 4*, he thought. *Five miles. Almost there.*

"Ivan's the most terrible person I've ever met," Mariani claimed. "The sick thoughts that go through his mind are evil. I can't stand to be around him. He's a fucking nutcase."

"What made him lose his mind?" Marcel asked.

"I'm not sure," Frankie said. "After his dad died, he fell off the map. No one heard from him for a couple of years. The next time I saw him, he was bat shit crazy. He said the state committed him to the sanitarium, and they tested him like a guinea pig."

"They shoulda never let him out," Mariani said coldly. "He's a danger to society."

"He's harmless," Frankie promised. "Sure, he's a paranoid schizophrenic with bipolar tendencies, but he doesn't go nowhere. He just sits in his house and smokes his life away."

Mariani snorted. "But every time he goes to town for smokes or meds, he's at least a risk on the road." He lit up a cigarette and then went on. "How does that crazy fuck even have a driver's license? Do you know how much medication he's on? He must take at least twenty pills a day just to function."

Frankie put two hands back on the wheel as a semi-truck barreled past them. His breath was hitching as he tried to tune out Mariani's attack on Ivan's character. Leaning just slightly forward, Frankie squinted at the vehicle fast approaching in the review. It was a truck of some sort, but what stood out was the white license plate.

Carlos laughed out loud. "I drove with him once," he said. "Almost fucking ki —"

"Shit. Fucking shit," Frankie said suddenly, his voice cutting off Carlos, the very tremor of his words alerting everyone else. "Don't look back; we got a fuckin' cop behind us."

"What?" Mariani said sharply, his eyes shifting to the passenger side mirror. "Fuck." He hit the door panel.

Frankie looked in the mirror again. "Still no cherries, but he's riding my ass."

"Were you speeding?" Carlos asked.

"We were probably going too slow," Mariani said.

At the flash of red and blue lights, Frankie sat upright in his seat. "All right," he demanded. "Everyone stay calm. We're getting pulled over. Keep your mouths shut, just like we planned." Frankie put his right blinker on, tapped the brakes, and then turned on the shoulder.

*****

Staring at the driver side mirror, Frankie watched a tall Minnesota State Trooper walk toward them. Feeling a sharp pain in his neck, his hand shot to the source. As he massaged it, he took several deep breathes. "Don't say anything," Frankie said with a lowered tone. "Unless he asks you a question, don't even nod your head."

As the lawman in the classic sheriff's hat got close to the truck, Frankie pressed the button on his door and the window rolled down. An invisible torrent of cold air entered the truck and overpowered the heat. "Nice day, eh." The corners of Frankie's mouth lifted upward.

"No, it's not," the sheriff said, removing the shiny sunglasses from his head. After he put them in his black parka, he arched his dark eyebrows and leaned forward. "Do you know why I pulled you over today?"

Frankie slowly shook his head. "I'm not sure," he said. "Was I speeding?"

"No," said the sheriff, his thick mustache twitching the slightest. "You got a brake light out." He paused and observed each of the passengers, his eyes finally landing back on Frankie. "And your license plate's covered with snow. I couldn't read it. It's illegal to not have visible plates."

"It snowed a lot today, sir," Frankie said and narrowed his eyes. "I'll make sure it's clear from now on."

Fingers clenched in laps, cheekbones hollowed out by a steady stream of breathing, eyes glittering with exaggerated attention, Mariani, Carlos, and Marcel sat frozen in their seats, waiting for the situation to be over.

"I'm gonna need your driver's license and proof of insurance."

Frankie looked at the sheriff. "It's in my wallet," he said and slowly reached for his back pocket.

The sheriff reached out his hand and grabbed it. "Thanks." He sniffed twice, and then shifted

his head to eye the men in the back seat. "You boys hang tight."

The moment the lawman turned, Frankie rolled up his window. "What do ya think?" he asked a question for anyone to answer.

"He seems stiff," Carlos insisted. "I bet he's ex-military."

"Did you see the way he looked at me?" Marcel said. "That dude's a *racist*. I'll bet you any money he tries to search."

Mariani took his hat off, setting it on his lap. "He's just running Frankie's name for warrants," he predicted. "He'll be letting us go shortly. Fuck 'em! That pig ain't shit."

Waiting for the sheriff's next move, the windows started to fog from the heavy breathing. Frankie turned the dial on his dash from heat to defrost. They were in the hands of the law now, and at his mercy. The drum beat sound of time thumped in their ears as they waited to meet their fate.

There's no probable cause. Frankie thought silently as he trembled. *I ain't letting him search. Cuz if he does…we're going to prison for life.*

*****

For a long ten minutes, Frankie breathlessly watched the mirror. *Feels like purgatory,* he thought. Turning to look at

Mariani, he saw him nervously tugging at the scruff on his chin. Whipping his head back to the mirror, Frankie's heart sunk as the sheriff's door opened. "Here he comes," he said under his breath. He sat upright and cleared his throat, thinking about what to say. When he rolled the window down, the sheriff gave Frankie his cards back.

"Frank. I'm gonna need you to step out of the vehicle."

"Am I being detained?" Frankie asked.

"Not yet," the sheriff said. "Just step out of the vehicle, please. Don't make me say it again."

Frankie nodded his head, took his seat belt off, and then slowly opened the door. Stepping out of the truck, he rolled the window up and shut the door firmly. Through the window, Mariani lifted a single finger to his lips. Turning to face the sheriff, Frankie took in a breath of ice-cold air.

The sheriff cautiously looked down the wind-swept road. With no cars in sight, he waved Frankie in-between the two vehicles.

Frankie clamped down on his tongue, tucked his head in-between his shoulders, and cut through the fierce wind.

Instead of speaking immediately, the sheriff's features stretched across his mouth while he waited for Frankie to lift his head.

"You boys are a long way from town," the sheriff said, locking eyes with Frankie. "What brings you boys out—to *my* highway?"

Frankie paused for a few seconds, his eyes shifting to the left. "We were heading to Virginia to buy a new work truck." He cleared his throat. "The roads are horrible. I was actually just about to turn back to town."

"Ten cars in the ditch already," Sheriff Anderson said, pointing across the highway. "The thing is...I saw you pull into Joe's Diner from Old Highway 6. That road hasn't been plowed yet." He paused and rubbed his chin. "If you're going to Virginia, why would you take that road?"

*****

Meanwhile, in the truck, the boys started debating amongst themselves.

"What's taking them so long?" Carlos asked, watching Frankie and the sheriff in the rearview mirror.

"If he searches us," Marcel said, "we're fucked. Butt fucked!"

Mariani turned in his seat. "Frankie's got it handled," he insisted. "That pig has no lawful reason to search us. This is just a traffic stop."

"Why'd he tell him to get out of the car?" Marcel asked.

"They do that sometimes," Mariani said. "They wanna see if you walk a straight line. He probably thinks he's drunk."

"Well," Carlos said. "What if he takes the law into his own hands? He could say Frankie's drunk or high, and then search the truck?"

"He ain't gonna search," Mariani said. "But if he *does* try to search…" He paused dramatically, settling his hat loosely on his head. "I ain't going back to prison. I reserve the right to put him down like a sick dog."

"You're kidding, right?" Carlos leaned forward and touched Mariani's arm. "We ain't killing no *fucking* cop."

Mariani rubbed his hands together. "I hope it doesn't come to that."

"Don't even think about it," Carlos said. "We can beat this. We can prove that we were the first responders, not the killers."

"That *sounds* good," Mariani said, "but the reality is—we got bloody clothes under the hood. Not to mention the murder weapon, the bullet shell, *and* two bags of money. Do you wanna go to prison?"

Carlos folded his arms across his chest. "I'd rather go to prison on trumped up charges, than for killing a cop. Don't you fucking dare."

"Don't tell me what to do, Los."

*****

Without a jacket, Frankie shivered in the cold. Looking up at the authority figure who towered over him, his body stiffened. "I got off the main highway because I had to take a piss."

The sheriff took a step closer. "Let's cut the shit," he said. "Who's got the pot?"

"We don't smoke pot, sir." He slowly shook his head.

"Bullshit," the sheriff said. "I smelt the skunk right away. Now you're acting all nervous and skittish. Do me a favor. Let me search your vehicle."

Frankie's eyes narrowed. "I can't do that, sir."

"Why not?"

"I…I think the Constitution is on my side."

"You got some balls, son," Sheriff Anderson said and looked from left to right, and then behind him. "Take a look around. You're a long way from home, boy. Lift up your arms; I'm gonna frisk you."

Frankie did as he was told. Eyes forward, he could feel strong hands patting down his body.

In Frankie's fifth pocket, the sheriff pulled out a stainless-steel folding knife. With the wind swirling around them, he flicked open the blade, tilted it, and then snapped it shut. "It's my word against yours in the court of law." He gave the knife back to him. "Now, you can either let me search it the easy way…or the hard way. What's it gonna be?"

Frankie's veins were throbbing in his ear. The sheriff was so close he could smell whiskey on his breath. "You gotta do what you gotta do, but I'm gonna do what I *have* to do. I have to say no. I'm perfectly sober, and I'll take any test you have to prove it."

The sheriff let out a breathy grunt. "I smelt pot and you look real nervous. That's probable cause. The only way I'm not searching that vehicle, is if you put something in my hand that makes me forget about the marijuana."

"What?" Frankie scrunched up his face.

"You deaf, boy?" the sheriff said slowly. "Quid pro quo."

"What's that mean?"

"Pay to play."

Frankie tilted his left hand. "Is this a trick?"

"No," the sheriff said. "I'd rather make a few bucks than search your truck. I don't want to bring you to jail for a little pot. Doesn't that sound logical? The paperwork's a headache."

Frankie nodded. "I don't have much money, sir. I think I got a hundred twenty bucks."

"That ain't gonna cut it," the sheriff said and gestured to the truck. "Maybe your friends will pitch in to save your ass?"

"How much?"

"I'm a reasonable man. A hundred each and you're free to go."

Frankie let out a breath. "You want me to go ask?"

"Go ahead. Tell 'em it's your lucky day. Make it quick."

*****

The sheriff stood in the snowy wind and waited for Frankie. When the door opened a minute later, Frankie hopped out and closed the door. As he walked in-between the two vehicles, the sheriff smiled thinly.

Frankie handed him a folded wad. "Four hundred."

The sheriff nodded his head and put the money in his jacket pocket. He stuck out his hand and Frankie shook it. "Nice doing business with you, Mr. Buccetti," he said. "One thing: don't ever tell no one about this. I'm gonna remember your name. If this ever gets back to me, I'm gonna take four hundred bucks and pay my cop buddies to make life difficult for you." He was still squeezing Frankie's hand. "You understand me?"

"My lips are sealed," Frankie said. "Am I free to go?"

The sheriff let go of Frankie's hand. "Consider this warning," he said. "Get that brake light fixed. Get off the dope. Next time will cost you double." He bent forward and wiped the snow from Frankie's licensed plate with his bare hand. "Don't forget—this is *my* highway."

8

At the sight of an approaching driveway, Frankie let out an audible breath. *We're safe,* he thought and turned down the only path carved in the wall of forest. Envisioning a rickety gray house, Frankie cracked a brief smile for the first time in hours. When the truck came to a stop in front of the garage, Frankie threw the shifter in park.

"Hey," Frankie said, twisting to look in the back seat. "You two chill for a minute. I'm gonna smooth things over with Ivan. He's more than paranoid. If he sees four of us walk up uninvited, he might blow a gasket." He looked at Mariani and smiled. "Ivan loves you. You should come with me,"

"Oh, God," Mariani said and shook his head with disgust. "He *loves* me? What the fuck?"

"Come on. He'll be happy to see you." Frankie opened the door and stepped out of the truck.

The two co-conspirators walked twenty yards to the front deck. Looking up at the two-story house with a big bay window, Frankie stopped and leaned toward Mariani.

"I'm not gonna tell him much," Frankie said. "But he's pretty smart. He knows I'd never come without calling…unless it was an emergency."

"The less he knows the better," Mariani agreed.

Frankie climbed three steps that were buried with snow

and Mariani followed behind him. From the patio, they faced a solid wood door with a small peephole at eye level. *I bet he's watchin'*, he thought.

Just as Frankie raised his knuckle to knock, the door creaked open. A cloud of white smoke hurled out the door and quickly rose into the air.

"Homie?" Ivan said in a soft, timid voice, his wire framed glasses resting on his sharp, pointy nose. Behind the thick lenses, two blue eyes were wide open, shifting back and forth.

"Ivan!" Frankie, he said cheerfully, smiling at his heavyset friend who was wearing a black fleece jacket and a faded pair of baggy jeans that he held up with one hand. "How's it going?"

"I'm good." Ivan waved them in with two burning cigarettes in his fingers. "Come inside. It's cold out there."

Frankie walked through the doorway. "So, what's new?"

"Take a look at the digital watches my mom got me for my birthday." Ivan smirked and lifted both of his wrists. "Nope. I haven't been too terrible lately." He pressed a button that made a beep noise.

Mariani gave a puzzled look. "What's the second watch for?"

"This one I use to tell time," Ivan said, tilting his right hand. "And this one I use to time how long my company stays. Sometimes I time how long I can hold my weed hits."

Frankie bent over and untied his boot laces, but Ivan prompted him. "Don't take your boots off," he said and took a drag from the cigarettes burning in his fingers. "I'm sorry. The carpet isn't very clean."

Then without another word, Ivan turned on his heel and started walking toward the living room.

Frankie and Mariani looked at each other then followed

behind Ivan's lumbering bulky form; they were greeted by dim lighting and the strain of residual smoke wafting through the air. Beyond the smoke there was a faint but mysterious odor that existed throughout the living quarters.

Mariani wrinkled his nose. "Jesus, Ivan," he swore. "What the fuck is that smell?"

Taking a seat in a hideous green recliner, Ivan adjusted his glasses. "I like it when you say my name," he muttered. "Nobody ever says my name." He brought the cigarettes to his mouth and sucked in smoke. Pulling his hand away, he pressed his lips together. After a minute, his pale face turned red, and then an explosion of smoke exited his mouth. A brief coughing fit ensued. "I'm not sure what the stench is." He tried to cover his mouth as he coughed. "It doesn't bother me too much."

Mariani stared down at the tan carpet. There was a suspicious-looking brown stain in front of Ivan's chair. Mariani cringed. *Probably fucking vomit,* he thought. *Fucking nasty.*

"Frankie," Ivan said with a smile. The few teeth left in his mouth were the color of yellow chalk, but much darker by the gums. "Why am I so lucky to have your company? ... Is everything okay?"

"Yeah," Frankie shrugged. "Everything's fine. But the roads are *real* bad. We almost went in the ditch." He paused and looked at Mariani. Lifting two fingers, he worded, *two minutes,* then he turned his attention back to Ivan. "Can I ask you for a small favor?"

Ivan's eyes narrowed. "What's that?"

Frank winced as he imposed his will on an old friend. "We just need a spot to crash for the night," he said. "And it's not just me and Mariani." He aimed his arm toward the window and added, "Carlos and Marcel are in the truck."

"You know I don't like having more than one or two people here." Ivan took another drag from the double barrel cigarette. The cherries sizzled because it was all filter and no tobacco. His eyes widened.

Frankie scrunched his face up. "Blow that shit out, man. You're suffocating yourself."

Holding the smoke in his lungs as long as he could, Ivan coughed out a toxic cloud. Pressing his hands on his belly, he continued coughing, smoke still seeping from his nose and mouth.

"Marcel said he wants to smoke a blunt with you."

Ivan coughed out the last of the smoke. "Marcel smokes?

"Hell, yeah he smokes. That dudes got the skunk shit."

"Skunk?"

"Bomb shit."

"I've only met Marcel once. I thought he was cool."

Frankie opened his left hand. "When your name came up, he said that he thought you were a pimp."

"He thinks I'm a pimp?" Ivan smiled.

"In a good way," Frankie said. "That's just how he talks. He must think you're a pretty awesome dude."

Ivan's whittled down teeth were showing. "I don't wanna miss out on smoking with him. I-I just feel uncomfortable around a group of people. I don't know how I'll react."

Frankie dropped his hand on Ivan's shoulder. "How 'bout this," he said and pulled back. "Let my friends play pool in the basement, and I'll just hang up here with you. We'll smoke the night away and talk about old times. Then…if you feel comfortable, I'll have Marcel smoke a blunt with just you."

Ivan snubbed out the two cigarette butts in an overfilled ashtray. "As long as I get to smoke with Marcel, you guys can stay one night."

"Thanks, brother," Frankie said and reached out his hand. "I greatly appreciate it. One night. That's it."

"My pleasure."

*****

Mariani stood in the middle of the kitchen, arms crossed over his chest, a look of disgust radiating off his person. Swatting the air by his head, he dodged the buzzing in his ear. As he stepped back, he saw a cluster of fruit flies that were floating in the area around the sink. Feeling something crunch under his boot, he looked down at countless rat droppings on the linoleum floor. With a shake of his head, Mariani turned. *Filth and squalor,* he thought. *Fucking disgusting.*

Mariani stomped back to the living room where he found Frankie on a faded brown couch. "You done talking yet?" he said. "I got attacked by fruit flies in the kitchen. It's a little more peaceful in here."

"I was just about to ask Ivan if you could use his shower," Frankie said.

"That would be fine," Ivan whispered in a soft, almost feminine voice. "But I warn you, my bathroom is quite a mess."

Mariani rolled his eyes. "How messy?"

"Frankie was nice enough to clean it for me last summer," Ivan said. "I don't clean much."

Frankie changed the subject. "Do you mind if I go get Carlos and Marcel?"

Ivan smiled from ear to ear. "I was just thinking," he said. "Marcel is the first person to ever say a nice thing about me. How 'bout I invite them in?"

"Yeah," Frankie chuckled. "That's a good idea. Go get

them guys and I'll show Mariani where the bathroom is."

Ivan sprung out of his seat, scurried to the door, and replaced his shoes with moon boots. As soon as his jacket was on, he flung open the door and closed it behind him.

Frankie looked at Mariani. "I'll be right back." He walked to the kitchen and grabbed a garbage bag from underneath the sink. When he got back to the living room, he gave it to Mariani. "Put your clothes in here," he said. "I'll go outside and toss it in the wood-burning furnace."

Mariani snatched the bag. "Where's the bathroom?"

Frankie climbed the steps and Mariani followed behind him. When they reached the second floor, Frankie saw three doors in the small hallway, but one was cracked open. Light was radiating from the door, so Frankie pushed it open.

Mariani took one step inside the dilapidated bathroom and cringed. He saw filth from wall to wall, and it smelled like a public urinal. His heart contracted and the blood rushed to his face and neck.

"I'm gonna need some sandals," Mariani said. "My bare feet ain't touching that fuckin' floor. Look at it." He pointed. "He's got a pile of stained underwear next to the sink. Fucking disgusting. Hurry up and get me a bar of soap and some clothes." He let out a sigh while shaking his head.

"Yeah," Frankie said, nodding. "I'll see what I can find in the spare room. I'll be right back."

*****

Outside in the truck, Carlos and Marcel were slouching in their seats.

"Frankie said that Ivan hasn't brushed his teeth since 1997," Carlos insisted.

Marcel cringed. "No shit?" he said. "You would think he'd be dead by now."

"I guess he doesn't drink water either," Carlos piled on. "Only generic Mountain Dew."

"No water?" Marcel shook his head in disbelief. "That's ridiculous."

When Carlos opened his mouth to respond, he was cut off by the sudden rap of a knuckle on the rear passenger window. Carlos jerked his body and turned. "Holy shit," he said under his breath. "Speaking of the devil." He rolled the window down halfway. "Hey Iv'," he said. "How's it going?"

"Not too miserable lately," Ivan said with a bow. "Why don't you boys come inside?" He laughed softly like a child.

They hopped out of the truck and into the heavy wind.

*****

In the dark hallway, Frankie was restlessly tapping his foot. He could hear faint grumblings and cuss words from inside the bathroom.

Whipping open the door, Mariani threw the full trash bag at Frankie. "Burn that shit," he said. "Burn your fucking boots, too. You *and* Los." He slammed the door shut.

He's fuckin' pissed, Frankie thought before he hurried down the steps. When he reached the first floor, he saw Marcel, Carlos, and Ivan standing in the foyer.

"Welcome to Ivan's humble home." Frankie set the bag down. "I'm gonna run to the truck. I'll be back in a few. When I get back, we should help Ivan and clean the house. It's the least we could do."

Carlos glared at Frankie and shook his head.

"Until I get back, maybe you guys could get started with

the kitchen?"

"No problem," Marcel said and showed Ivan a rolled cigar. Ivan smiled. "I haven't seen a blunt in a long time."

Frankie looked down at Carlos' big black boots, and then he lifted his head to face Ivan. "You wanna bring Marcel to the kitchen? I need to ask Carlos something."

*****

Frankie popped the hood of his truck and grabbed the bag of evidence. Slamming the hood shut, he grabbed both bags, his heavy steps leading him quickly to the wood-burning furnace that was nestled behind the garage at the edge of the forest. Standing in front of it, he set the black bags on the snow.

It's all Hanks fault, he thought. *He ratted on his friends.* A gust of freezing wind made him briefly close his eyes. Leaning forward, he reached for the handle. With a forceful turn of the wrist, he opened the cast iron door, exposing the blazing inferno inside. The bright flash of orange light and the blast wave of heat opened his heavy eyelids.

The mocking wind spoke to him. It said, *do it.* So, Frankie tossed both bags in and watched them catch on fire. The plastic melted instantly but the clothes lit up and burned slower. He then took his boots off and set them inside. Carlos' boots were the last of evidence, and he shoved them in the oven as well. His eyes then shifted to the cord of logs next to the furnace. Reaching for the top, he grabbed four logs and dropped them on the frozen ground. Two at a time, he carefully set them on top of the burning heap.

The hatch was still open. The flames were lulling him into a trance; the sight, a backdrop of memory from Hank's house. The dark hand of the stranger that reached inside his coat, the instinctive pull of the trigger, the loud pop of the gun, and the slump of the body.

Frankie slammed the hatch and lifted the handle. "Good riddance," he said. "Piece of fucking shit."

*****

In the kitchen, Carlos felt his eyes widen, his nostrils flaring as he looked across the room, his gaze flickering from Ivan to Marcel.

"Would you like me to put some seeds in your tummy?" The echo of Ivan's last statement circled around the room.

"What the fuck you just say, dog?" Marcel growled.

Ivan laughed, ducking his head. "I was just kidding."

Marcel took one menacing step forward. "Do I look like I'm   laughing?"

Carlos grimaced. He'd almost forgotten how creepy Ivan could be — and Marcel didn't know that side of him.

"Would you like me to put some seeds in your tummy?"

That's what Ivan had asked when Marcel had commented moments before that he was starving, that he hadn't eaten since breakfast…

"Look at me, Ivan," Marcel commanded, his face a ruddy color. "If you *ever* say something like that to me again…" Marcel's next words cut off by the sound of Frankie shutting the front door.

*****

Frankie walked in the kitchen and the room was silent. Ivan was staring at the floor. Carlos' hand was covering his face. And the full force Marcel's gaze was on Ivan. The only play of emotion sat in the tic of muscles on one side of his jaw. "What happened?"

Marcel approached Frankie. "Your boy just made a pretty sick joke."

"Ivan!" Frankie slowly shook his head. "Will you *please* apologize to the man?"

Ivan lowered his head. "Marcel," he whimpered. "I'm sorry I said that. I was just kidding."

"Good," Frankie said and looked at Marcel. "Is that good enough for you?"

"Yeah." He nodded. "It's all good. I just don't play, ya know?"

Frankie opened his hands. "Can you two shake hands, please?" he asked politely, and Ivan lifted his right arm. Marcel met him halfway and shook Ivan's limp, clammy hand.

"All right," Frankie said. "Let's go downstairs."

*****

As everyone went to the basement, Frankie signaled for Ivan to stay put. "Ivan," he said in a disappointed tone. "What did I tell you about your sick jokes? ... That shit was funny twenty years ago, but people like Marcel take that shit personally. If I wasn't here, he probably would have fucked you up." He paused to look him right in his eyes. He then softened his tone. "You understand, right?" Ivan nodded his head, then Frankie continued. "You can't say dirty things to these people, or anyone for that matter. That's just not how civilized people act. Now, can I trust you to behave yourself?" Raising his eyebrows, Frankie gave Ivan a pointed glance as he waited for him to respond in acknowledgement.

Before Ivan could reply, they both turned at the sound of feet patting on the floor.

It was Mariani in a black T-shirt and gray sweatpants. "Where'd everyone go?"

"They're in the basement," Frankie said. "I'll be down in a minute."

"Right on," Mariani said and turned.

As soon as Mariani was out of sight, Frankie put his hand on Ivan's shoulder. "It's all good, Iv'," he said. "Look, I greatly appreciate you letting us stay here tonight. I'll never forget it. You're my brother, Ivan. You know that, right?"

Looking over at Ivan, Frankie's lips jerked into a crooked grin. The lens on Ivan's glasses enlarged his eyes, giving him a beseeching expression as he leaned forward, his head nodding along with Frankie's words.

"I know," Ivan said, bowing in a timid fashion. "I'm sorry. I should have taken my meds today."

"Why don't you go upstairs and take your meds? I'll come check on you in a little bit."

*****

Walking down the basement steps, Frankie felt all eyes on him. The room got quiet. He lifted the duffel bags, set them on the pool table, and unzipped the bag closest to him. Turning it over, he watched the bricks of money fall to the table and form a pile. Shaking the bag with a final snap, Frankie laughed, lifting his eyes, glancing at each of his friends.

"Holy shit!" Mariani boasted, "Look at all that fucking loot. Yeah...and it's all ours!" He grabbed the second bag, unzipped it, and quickly emptied the money. Two mounds now between them.

Carlos was rubbing his hands together greedily. "What's my cut?"

"Split it four ways," Frankie said. "Minus overhead."

"What's the overhead?" Carlos asked.

Mariani leveled one mound of cash with his arm. "Let's count this shit before we debate finances."

Marcel grabbed a few stacks and held them in his hands, gazing down with a smile from ear to ear. "I'm with Mariani," he said. "We need to find out what we working wit'."

"I think we should at least set some rules before we count it," Frankie said and lit up a cigarette.

"Rules?" Carlos lifted an eyebrow.

"This isn't 'Nam," Frankie said. "We need rules. Principles."

Carlos opened his hands. "Like what?"

"Simple stuff," Frankie said. "Never...tell...*anyone* about what happened today."

"My lips are sealed," Carlos said and lit up a cigarette.

Marcel raised his left hand. "I ain't saying nothing."

"You know *I* ain't saying shit," Mariani said.

Frankie rubbed the stubble on his chin. "Trust is important," he said. "I trust you guys, but we're the only ones who can fuck this up." He paused to look at each of his friends. "Your money's always safe here. I have a few holes dug throughout Ivan's hundred acres."

Marcel was still smiling. "We takin' some loot with us, right?"

"We're definitely taking some loot," Frankie said. "We need some spending cash, but this is where rule number two comes into play. It's *imperative* that we don't show off and flaunt how rich we are. We should all agree to be smart and wise with the money we spend."

"Los," Mariani said. "This means no diamonds for Jewlz. And for you," he pointed at Marcel. "No mink coats for May, and no fancy rims for your truck either."

Frankie continued, his words robbing either Marcel or Carlos the ability to defend themselves "I'm not asking much here," he said. "Two or three things. Don't speak about this to anyone. Don't flaunt your wealth. And last but most importantly..." he paused, looking around the room at his brothers. "Never rat on your friends. If you get questioned or charged with a crime, you *will* ask to see your lawyer and exercise your Fifth Amendment right. Basically, we all have to take an oath of silence, right here, right now."

"Loyalty," Mariani said and stuck out his hand for Frankie to shake.

Frankie shook it firmly. "Loyalty." He followed with a hug.

Each member of the crew embraced one another, repeating the same word: *Loyalty.*

*****

As day turned into night, the basement was thick with smoke. Two dozen neat stacks of money occupied the pool table. Carlos was standing with a notebook in his hands. "One million, two hundred thousand and change!" He dropped the notebook and put his fists high in the air.

"Holy shit!" Frankie said, his cheeks rising. "Fuck yeah!"

"We're rich, bitch!" Marcel gave Mariani a high-five.

The room erupted with raucous laughter and cheers as they embraced forcefully.

*****

From upstairs in his bedroom, Ivan sat in a chair with two cigarettes between his lips. His head cocked toward the open door. The celebration echoing through the hallway. *Why are they so happy?* The demon inside his head prodded him. *If they were grateful, they would have invited you to the party.* His gaze shifted to the bottle of antipsychotic medicine in his hands. Turning it with his fingers, Ivan read the directions.

Take two pills when experiencing high anxiety or violent thoughts.

It didn't take long before Ivan's mind replayed the memory of Marcel's pointed finger and harsh words. "They don't care about you," he said under his breath in a voice that was a little bit different than his. "They're just using you."

Ivan's nose flared as he took in a deep breath. His heart began to hammer in his chest. In the court of his mind, he just convicted Marcel for threatening him and Frankie for letting it happen.

Frankie took advantage of you, Ivan's demon told him silently. *If you don't do something, they're gonna team up on you. Surprise them. Now!*

"Fuck my meds," he said and whipped the bottle against the wall. "I want to *free* my mind." His eyes jumped to a wood framed picture of his dad that hung on the wall. Other than Frankie, Ivan's dad was the only person in the world to ever accept him for who he was (a lost soul). Now, Frankie was excluding him in his own house, possibly conspiring against him.

Ivan got up and waddled to his dresser. Opening the drawer, he pushed aside the underwear and clasped his fingers around the chrome plated revolver that his old man left him in the will.

Cradling the gun in his hands, he found his chair and sat down. With the gun on his lap, he started petting it like a cat. His mouth cracked open and a soft breathing noise came out.

Rocking himself back and forth, his voice box began rumbling in his throat. He had what looked like a smile or a devilish grin on his sickly, pale face. Curling his chapped upper lip, he stared into his father's eyes. "Sorry, Dad," he said. "I'd rather not disappoint you, but they left me no choice."

Turning his attention to the shiny pistol in his lap, his lip twitched. "Bang, bang," he scowled. "My little chrome friend will make them respect me." He slowly stood up and stepped closer to his dad's picture.

"Heee…" Spewed from his rotten mouth. A vision of him with the gun to Marcel's face burned in his mind. He pivoted to the opened door and walked through it. Slowly tiptoeing down the stairs, he made more soft outbursts. "Heee…"

When he got to the basement door, Ivan heard Frankie's voice. The same monotone voice he'd known for twenty-five years. His eyes widened.

Frankie, he thought, his mind flashing back through the years. A skinny twelve-year-old Frank Buccetti laughing at his sick jokes. A twenty-year-old Frankie, plucking him out of the gutter when he was living on the street. The thought of killing him made Ivan's eyes become wet. He then started panting.

Putting the barrel of the gun in his mouth, tears flowed down his face. His throbbing finger pulled the trigger halfway back. Hand shaking, he pulled the gun out and ran up the steps.

*****

Back in the basement, Carlos looked at his phone to check the time. "It's seven o'clock," he said, "Does Ivan have any food here? I'm starving."

"Yeah," Frankie said. "I bet he's got some pizzas."

"Do you think he'd mind if we cook a couple?" Carlos asked.

Frankie briefly chuckled. "Go for it," he said. "Ivan's mom brings him food, but he doesn't cook. He lives off potato chips and nuts, then sometimes he'll order a pizza."

Carlos bolted upstairs. In the kitchen, he swung open the freezer and grabbed two pizzas. With the counter tops corroded with grime, he set them on top of the refrigerator. After he preheated the oven, he returned to the basement.

Using the calculator on his phone, Frankie punched in some numbers. "$1.2 Million," he said. "Let's take a hundred thousand off the top for lawyer and ransom money, just in case Carlos gets abducted." He chuckled and continued. "I think we should give Ivan $20,000 to keep his mouth shut and ensure we have a safe house. For us…how 'bout we each take $10,000 home for spending cash?" He gazed around the room at his wide-eyed friends.

"What about the rest?" Carlos asked.

"$250,000 each," Frankie said. "We should bury it here for safe keeping till we find a better spot." He paused and took a drag from his cigarette, then asked. "What do you guys think?"

"Sounds fair to me," Mariani said. "But I think Ivan would keep his mouth shut for a G."

"I concur," Carlos said. "Twenty G's to Ivan? No way." He lit up another cigarette.

Frankie tilted his head. "You're right," he said. "Twenty's too much. We just need a safe place to lay low. And I want him to feel comfortable. Let's give him five G's, and if he needs more, I'll take it out of my share."

Marcel smiled. "We got to keep that dude happy," he said. "You see his eyes earlier? He looked possessed."

"He's pathological," Mariani said. "You would have done

society a favor if you choked him out."

9

The next morning, driving home from a weekend bender at his friend's house, Hank's son Lenny turned up the drive to his parents' home. Squinting, he saw wolves circling a black SUV. "What the...what the fuck?" Lenny shouted, but the words came out in little more than a hoarse whisper of sound.

Lenny rolled to a stop. "What the fuck are they chewing on?" He slammed the shifter in park.

Twisting in his seat, Lenny's arm snapped to the gun rack behind him. The shotgun jumped in his hands. Heart racing, he abruptly kicked open the door and jumped out of the truck. The blood-drenched wolves scattered into the dark forest before he could lift his rifle. Hot with adrenaline, he pumped the shotgun, fired a warning shot, and then repeated two more times. His stance was wide, his legs were trembling.

Lenny lowered the gun. His eyes snapped to the massive concentration of blood and guts in front the black SUV. "That's a lot of blood," he said under his breath.

What the fuck is that? he thought of the possibilities. *A dear? A dog?* His head lifted from the bloody snow to the bullet riddled SUV. He spun around to face the mobile home. "Mom!"

Pivoting quickly, he saw blood tracks leading to the house. Lenny angrily sprinted toward the door of the only home he had ever known. His breath gasping erratically up and out of his throat, almost choking him further as he approached the steps. The door was wide open. After only two steps inside, he froze. *Oh no,* he thought. *Blood everywhere.*

"Mom!" Lenny cried out. "Where are you?"

The boy's head was on a swivel as he slowly walked further inside of the doublewide trailer. The floor was wet with blood that was smeared on the linoleum floor. Red paw prints everywhere. The couch was soiled, and the walls were also caked with blood and black fur.

She's okay, she's okay, he thought, almost unable to breathe.

Jerking his eyes away, his throat bobbing precariously, Lenny saw a pair of small feet with white socks sticking out from behind the kitchen counter—and was that? *Oh God.* Covering his mouth with one hand, Lenny inhaled, closing his eyes briefly.

Dropping the shotgun, he scrambled to his mother's side. An uncontrollable sob erupted from his shaking form, his hands almost instinctively reaching out for her.

"Mom!" he cried and gently placed his hand on her cold back. Flinching, his fingers met a deep cut, felt the ripped flesh caused by wild animals. "Ohh, Mom." He sobbed uncontrollably. "What did they do to you?"

Candace's clothing was torn and shredded. She lay in a puddle of blood, shoved in the corner of the kitchen—her pale, white corpse face down. Lenny was on his knees next to her, choking down grief. He turned her over and immediately jumped back. "Ahh!" Lenny landed a few feet away on his back side. "No…!" The flesh on her face had been chewed off.

Lenny rose to his feet. *What am I gonna do?* he thought. "Dad!" he hollered.

With fast movements, he ran to his parent's bedroom and

saw a bloody mess. The once white linens were soiled red. He slammed his fist against the wall then continued his search. The basement door was open, and the light was on. Footprints led the way. Now, slowly descending the steps, he saw a man with his flesh chewed down to the bone. A black pool of blood surrounded him. Face down, the man's mullet draped over his mutilated back.

"Dad!" he cried, but instead of getting close to him, he ran back up the steps.

Horrified, his eyes traveled back to his mother; her petite body mangled almost beyond recognition. Her mid-length blond hair was wet and looked black from oxidized blood.

Scared, cold, confused, Lenny was trembling. He took his jacket off and covered his mom's mutilated face and upper torso. As his body rose, he inhaled. Looking down at the lump under the jacket, he exhaled. "I'm sorry, Mom." He sobbed. "I should have been here. I would have saved you."

Reaching in his pocket, he pulled out his cell phone. *I need help*, he thought and held it in his shaking hand. With his thumb, he pressed three numbers. It rang twice.

On the other end of the phone, he heard a strong female voice. "911, what is your emergency?"

"Uhh…umm… I." Lenny stumbled on his words, then eventually found his voice. "I need help. My name is L-Lenny Lindberg. I'm at 4894 Dodge Road. I-I jus—"

The dispatcher interrupted him. "Do you need police or an ambulance?"

"Would you just shut up and listen for a minute?" he wiped off his bloody hands on his white shirt.

"Calm down, sir. Stay on the line."

"My, oh God." Lenny sniffled. "They're dead. My m-mom and dad are dead."

Lenny heard her quick indrawn breath before she spoke again. "Are *you* okay?"

"No," Lenny said. "I'm not okay. Someone killed my fucking parents!"

"Sir, I need you to calm down," the operator said. "Help is on the way."

Lenny took a deep breath. "I know," he said in a calmer voice. "I'm sorry, I just need help. I don't know what to do."

"Are either of your parents breathing?"

"What the fuck is wrong with you?" Lenny shouted. "Why are you asking me these stupid fucking questions? ... No! You stupid cunt. They're not fucking breathing. They're dead!"

"I'm sorry, sir," she said with a soft tone. "Sometimes people cling to life. Can I get you to check for a heartbeat?"

"They're frozen stiff! Just send help."

"Do you know who did this?"

"No," he said. "I came home and found them like this."

"Okay, help is on the way. Stay on the phone with me."

"I-I can't believe this is happening to me. It hurts so bad."

"I know. I'm sorry. Can I get you take a deep breath?"

Lenny's eyes fell on his shotgun. "I'm gonna kill whoever did this. I swear to God."

"Stay calm, Lenny. Don't do nothing stupid."

"Fuck you, you stupid cunt. I'll kill your parents and see how you like it." He smashed his phone on the floor. The raw emotion flowed down his face as he sobbed hysterically. His blurry eyes looked down on the kitchen counter where a small metal pipe sat with a book of matches next to it.

I need to take the pain away, he thought and picked up the pipe. Striking a match, the flame lit the half-smoked bowl of meth. As he sucked in poison, his eyes snapped open, and then he blew out a dark cloud of smoke. He hit it again and staggered. Feeling lightheaded, he plopped down on a chair and picked at his fingernails.

"How am I gonna live here?" he asked himself. "Every time I go in the kitchen, I'm gonna see my mom. Every time I go in the basement, I'm gonna see my dad."

*****

Speeding up the highway with his cherries on, Sheriff Anderson grabbed his radio. "Be prepared for a anything," he said to his deputy. "The dispatcher said the perp was belligerent and making threats. Proceed with caution."

"Copy," Deputy Carlson said. "I'm en route."

"I'm ten minutes out," Sheriff Anderson said. "What's your ETA?"

Deputy Carlson put his foot on the gas and turned his sirens on. "Ten minutes."

*****

Lenny's eyes were now dry and red. He rose from his seat and bent down to grab the shotgun. Glancing at his mom, he sunk his head and wailed. "I don't want to live no more," he whimpered, tears gushing down his face.

Lenny set the butt of the gun on the floor. Looking down the barrel, he shook his head. *No way*, he thought. *Not like that.*

Lifting the gun, he held it with both hands and walked toward the front door. The moment he closed the door behind him, he took in a gulp of fresh air. The blinding sunshine warmed his freckled face, making him squint. As a reflex, he partially blocked out the sun's glare with his left hand. Clothes stained with blood, he marched through the snow in a daze.

Just as he reached the front of the truck, Lenny's body

jerked at the sound of sirens. Crouching against the front bumper, he pumped the shotgun. *I'm coming home, mom.*

Skidding to a stop at the edge of the driveway, one officer jumped out of the squad truck. Lenny stepped out in the open, shotgun pointed to the ground, eyes locked on the law.

"DROP THE GUN! DON'T FUCKING MOVE!" Lenny heard him scream at the top of his lungs. A rifle was pointing at him.

A second squad pulled up and two more officers hopped out. They took cover behind their squad car, handguns drawn. Lenny saw them and heard them. He didn't move one inch.

*****

Out of the corner of his eye, Sheriff Anderson saw a flash of red. His eyes flickered. In the same breath, he snapped his gaze back to the scrawny kid in a blood-stained T-shirt who was holding a shotgun at his hip. The barrel was angled downward.

"I said, drop the gun, boy!" Sheriff Anderson yelled. "I will shoot!"

The other troopers continued aiming their weapons at the gunman who was still frozen in place. He was not responding.

What the fuck is wrong with this kid? the sheriff thought in his head before he shouted. "You have three seconds to put that gun down!"

One. Two. Three, the sheriff worded slowly. No response. No comply.

The sheriff adjusted the butt of his rifle, pressing it firmly on his shoulder. Aiming at center mass, the sheriff sucked in air. "Drop the gun!"

With his finger curling around the trigger, he squeezed it. The single report echoed, and the young man fell to the ground.

Why'd you make me do that, kid? the sheriff thought and shook his head tightly. Sprinting up to the teenager who was twisted on the ground, he kicked the gun out of his pale hands.

Deputy Carlson kneeled beside Lenny and checked his pulse. Nothing, just a limp wrist which he set down gently. Reaching for Lenny's back pocket, he grabbed his wallet. "Here," Carlson said and stood up with his arm extended. After his boss took the wallet, Carlson looked down at the gaping wound in the kid's chest. With each passing second, the circle of dark snow around his body grew larger.

"Lennard Lindberg," the sheriff said with the driver's license in his hand. "Seventeen years old. I know that kid. Didn't recognize him at first."

"Yup," Carlson said. "It's been a while, but I been out here a few times over the years. I felt bad for that kid. Couldn't have been a good life. Parents drinking and fighting all the time."

Trooper McCoy opened his arms. "Why do you think he wouldn't drop the gun?"

"Suicide by cop," Carlson said.

"Yup," the sheriff said. "Probably killed his parents, then was too much of a coward to kill himself. So, he made me do it."

Carlson gazed at the out-of-date trailer house. "He must be strung out on drugs."

"That's right," Sheriff Anderson said. "He learned it from his dad. Hank's a junkie. I've busted him with meth twice." Bending down, the sheriff grabbed Lenny's shotgun and took a few steps toward his squad truck. Lifting the barrel, he fired one shot that peppered the vehicle and shattered the glass.

"What are you doing?" McCoy cried.

"Insurance policy," Sheriff Anderson said. "I ain't taking

any chances. The kid fired first." He handed the gun to the young state trooper. "Right, McCoy?" Anderson locked eyes with him.

McCoy nodded his head sharply.

*****

Walking through the trailer, Sheriff Anderson trampled over tiny shreds of bloody clothing and flesh. His handgun was out. Deputy Carlson and Trooper McCoy shadowed behind him. Once he made it to the kitchen, his heart sank. *Oh no!* he thought in his head. The body of a small woman was lying on the floor with a red flannel jacket draped over her upper body.

The sheriff peeked under the jacket. "Ugh!" He quickly set it back down. "No fucking face. You *poor* soul."

Carlson lowered his eyebrows and cringed.

McCoy held one hand on his stomach.

Anderson sighed. "I thought the kid made the mess outside," he said. "But look at all those paw prints. Wolves must have ransacked the house."

"But why didn't they rip her to pieces like the body outside?" Carlson asked.

"They probably got scared away before they finished her," the sheriff said.

Deputy Carlson shrugged. "Makes sense."

"I have a bad feeling there's another victim," the sheriff said and turned with his head studying the floor. "Follow those footprints."

*****

Climbing down the basement stairs, Sheriff Anderson stopped on the bottom step. He swallowed. A black puddle of blood came right up to his feet. "There's Hank Lindberg," he said to his fellow troopers behind him. Planting his boots on the wet concrete, blood splashed. Using slow movements, he took two steps forward. Looking down he took a deep, steadying breath.

"No one deserves that," Carlson said. "Not even Hank Lindberg."

McCoy turned away at the sight, bent over, and then vomited behind the stairs.

"It's okay, McCoy," the sheriff said. "The first time I saw a mutilated body in 'Nam, I did the same damn thing."

"Ugh," McCoy grunted and wiped his mouth.

Standing in the middle of the basement, Sheriff Anderson looked around the room. Light was shining from the back door that was propped open, a heap lying across the threshold. "One more in the back," he said and approached it.

"That's at least five bodies," Deputy Carlson said. "That's a massacre."

"This one ain't white," the sheriff said and turned to face his men. "And he's got an AK-47 next to him."

"Maybe the kid didn't kill his parents after all," Carlson said.

The sheriff pivoted and walked toward the stairs. "Looks like Hank had more dangerous enemies than his son." Lifting his head, his eyes scanned the room and landed on the work bench. Shining under the lightbulb, he saw two lines of a powdery yellow substance on top of a small mirror. "They came so quick; he didn't have time snort his meth."

Squinting, the sheriff examined blood spatter on the tan wall behind the work bench. Following the plywood up to the ceiling, he saw plastic tubing and wires leading behind the wall. Instinctively, he reached out and knocked.

"You hear that?" Sheriff Anderson asked. "It's hollow."

Deputy Carlson took a step closer. "False wall?"

The sheriff pointed at the skill saw on the work bench. "Cut it open."

Carlson grabbed the reciprocating saw and plugged it into the outlet on the wall. The deputy sheriff squeezed the trigger to see if it was operational. After the saw blade chirped, he then slowly lowered it to the wall as the tool screamed. Tearing into the wood, he broke through and cut a vertical line. He made three more cuts, and then pushed the center of the square, forcing the large piece to fall to the floor behind the bench.

"There's definitely a room back there," Carlson said and glanced back at the sheriff excitedly. "Let's see your flashlight." He held out his hand.

Instead of passing it to him, the sheriff turned it on. "Move."

Carlson got out of his path. Sheriff Anderson pointed the flashlight into the dark void. Climbing on top and over the workbench, he quickly crawled through the narrow space. When his feet hit the ground on the other side of the wall, Anderson swung the flashlight high and low around the room.

"Holy shit," the sheriff whispered when his light caught on two backpacks against the back corner of the otherwise bare space. Stepping over to the evidence, he quickly opened each one, his eyes flashing at the objects secured within them. "Bingo," he shouted, "Found it!"

"What'd you find?" Trooper McCoy asked.

"Drugs!" Sheriff Anderson said loudly and set one of the bags on the workbench, but he kept the second on the floor by his feet. "Go ahead and take these narcotics to the truck, then start searching all the vehicles on the premises."

McCoy slightly raised the muscles on his cheeks. "Yes, sir." He then grabbed the black bag and ran up the steps.

When McCoy was gone, the sheriff started climbing out of the hole with the second bag in his hand.

"What...?" Carlson asked, but before he could form the question on his lips, the sheriff smiled.

"Never was fond of our retirement package. You?" Unzipping the bag, he showed Carlson the stacks of money nestled inside.

Carlson grinned, his head tilting up the stairs in the direction McCoy had just traveled. "We letting him in on this?"

"McCoy? Hell, no. He'd fuck up a date with a hooker."

The co-conspirators shook hands; speaking quietly, making sure their voices wouldn't carry.

"More for us." Carlson smiled.

"We found drugs, guns, and multiple dead bodies," Sheriff Anderson said. "Case closed. We'll go down in the history books as heroes. After this is all over, I'll retire, and then you'll become sheriff."

Carlson raised his eyebrows. "Sheriff Carlson. It's got a good ring."

"Play your cards right, and it's yours."

"How much money do you think that is?"

"Enough," the sheriff said in a nearly inaudible tone. "It's probably a few hundred thousand."

"Damn. From the looks of his house, I figured he was broke."

"He must have been cooking meth."

Carlson stuck his nose in the bag.

"If McCoy asks what's in the bag, just tell him we found more dope."

"Good idea." Carlson smiled. "He won't question you."

"I'm not worried about him. Me and you need to be on the same page. I'm sure the press will be here soon, fighting over the first interview." He took a moment to think, then nodded a few times and continued. "When the gunman fired at my truck, I had no choice but to end the threat. We then breached the trailer, found multiple dead bodies—and that's when we found the methamphetamine.

"Dave, you always wanted your two minutes of fame. Here's your chance, just watch what you say. Be careful." Anderson laid a hand on his partner's shoulder.

"Thanks for trusting me," Carlson said. "Not just now, but for the last ten years."

"You should go help McCoy search those vehicles," Anderson said. "Distract him. I'll come out a few minutes later and put the loot in my truck. We'll split it up tomorrow."

10

Frankie and his boys had spent the morning stashing their money in the woods. Now, they were driving home. Their nightmare was behind them. The deed was done, and now they could finally take in a breath, but they couldn't let it out.

"Nothing ever goes as planned," Frankie said as the truck came to a stop in his driveway. "We have to expect bumps in the road, but we can't afford any unforced errors."

"I know, I know," Carlos said. "Lay low. Watch what we spend. Don't tell no one...I think we got it by now."

Frankie turned in his seat. "There's only two ways we can fuck this up," he said. "If we draw attention to ourselves or if we tell people."

"Loose lips sink ships," Mariani said. "Don't tell *no* one."

Marcel shook Mariani and Carlos' hands, and then he shook Frankie's hand last. "I can only speak for myself," he said with a low, serious tone. "I ain't saying shit." He opened the rear passenger door.

Before Marcel got out, Frankie turned in his seat. "Thanks for having my back. We were brothers before, but now we have a bond that will last a lifetime."

Marcel wore a massive smile. "Thanks guys!" he said. "I'll catch ya' on the flip side." He then shut the door and walked around to the back of the truck.

Carlos shook hands with Frankie and Mariani. "My word is bond," he said and got out. "We'll talk tomorrow."

"Have a good night, bro," Frankie said.

"You, too," he said and shut the door. Grabbing his gear from the back of the truck, Carlos walked behind Marcel toward the front of the house where their cars were parked.

Frankie turned his head to the passenger seat. "I was thinking about cooking a victory lasagna for dinner," he said. "Are you in or out?"

"I'm in," Mariani said, shaking Frankie's hand in a nonformal way.

"I'll head to Crado's. He's got the best ingredients."

"He's got some good food there, but I don't think he likes me," Mariani said and opened the door. "Be careful around that dude. He makes strong eye contact. It always feels like he's trying to read me."

"Ben's a good guy. My mom said he's a distant cousin of hers. They go way back."

*****

Frankie's mind wandered as he cruised through a yellow light. One hand was on the wheel. *I'm set,* he thought. *Set for life. All I got to do is —*

His peace was interrupted by a vibration in his pocket. For three seconds he took his eyes off the road. The screen on his phone read Mom.

"Hello," Frankie said.

"Where the hell have you been?" his mom scolded him. Biting down on his lip, Frankie took a deep breath at the hurling accusation. *I knew it,* he thought. *She's trippin'.*

"I'm sorry," Frankie said. "I was out of town."

"I been trying to get a hold of you for two fucking days,"

Diana snipped. "I was snowed in. Not one fucking thing to eat in this house. I had to put the dog bowl up; Marley was trying to eat it."

"I'm sorry," Frankie lied. "I had no reception."

Diana let out a loud sigh. "If you had no reception, it wouldn't ring," she snarled and continued to ridicule her son. "You were probably drunk as a skunk. You'd rather hang out with your friends than help your sick old mother."

Frankie sighed and shook his head. "Calm down, Mom," he said. "I'm here to help. What do you need?"

"You know what, never mind," Diana chuckled. "I've had a headache ever since I got on the phone with you." She paused momentarily to cough. "No wonder why Conny left you; you probably neglected her the same way you neglect me."

Frankie let out a careful breath. "Mom. I'm not gettin' into this right now."

"If you don't get her back," she said with the dog barking in the background. "You'll regret it. You'll never find another woman to tolerate you. I'm surprised you lasted so long with her. All you care about is yourself and partying with your drunk friends."

"I was actually having a good day," Frankie barked. "Now I'm fucking pissed. I gotta go." He hung up on his mom before he said anything he would regret.

*****

Frankie swung open the door at Crado's Italian Market and walked inside. The owner, Ben Crado, was stocking shelves with jars of tomato sauce.

Smiling over his shoulder, Ben spotted Frankie. "Ah, how's my favorite customer doing?"

Frankie only grinned, knowing that this position of esteem

was certainly helped along by the fact that he was a distant member of Ben's family.

"Not too bad," Frankie said with a slight tilt of his head. Stepping closer, the two gentlemen shook hands. "How's business?"

"Good. Real good. We delivered a lot of pizzas last night."

Frankie's eyes shifted to the left then came back to meet Ben's piercing blue eyes. "I have a confession," he said. "I ate a frozen pizza last night. It tasted like cardboard."

"So," Ben said. "You came to redeem yourself?"

Frankie let out a very short laugh, looking up at the tall man with dark but graying hair. "I'm making lasagna tonight," he said. "Could you set me up with everything I need?"

"I'll set you up real good." Ben gestured toward the transparent refrigerator door. "Help yourself to a pop. I'll be back in a few minutes." He hurried to the back room.

Frankie grabbed a can of root beer from the refrigerator and cracked it open. After his first sip, he pulled out his phone. Scrolling down his call log, he slowed down when it got to the C's.

His thumb pressed Conny's name and he proceeded to type her a message.

Hi. I want to talk to you. It's important. Frankie held his finger over the send button. Instead of pressing down, he deleted the words and tried again. *Will you please give me two minutes of your time? I need to talk to you. I have a good idea.*

Before he could hit the send button, Ben walked up holding a brown paper bag. Frankie put his phone in his pocket. "That was quick."

"Time is money." He set the bag on the counter.

Frankie's mouth parted. "How much do I owe you?"

Ben lifted his chin. "This one's on me," he said. "You're the only family member who hasn't asked me for a favor. And I know you'd be there for me if I needed your help."

"Anything for you," Frankie said. He stuck out his hand and Ben firmly shook it.

While squeezing his hand, Ben saw a man with dark bags under his eyes that were barely open. His handshake was firm, but his body was more slumped than the athlete who had always stood tall. "Is everything okay with you?"

Frankie let go of his hand. "Yeah. I'm okay." His head lowered.

"You just seem a little down today."

Frankie sighed. *He can read me that easy?* he thought. "I'm just a lil' tired. That's all."

"Frankie." Ben took a step closer. "I know you better than you think. You look stressed."

"I'm fine," Frankie said, concocting an excuse in his mind. *I got about a thousand problems, Ben…but I can only tell you about one.* "Conny dumped me a few weeks ago. I'll get over it. Just need some time."

"I'm sorry to hear that," Ben said. "She was a graceful woman."

"I thought she was the one."

Ben let out a breath. "I been there. Doesn't feel good. My wife left me when I was your age. It hurt, but I just pretended like I didn't give a shit. Three months later, she came pounding on my door. If Conny loves you, *she'll* come back. If she doesn't, then it's for the best."

"I never thought of it that way. I was just gonna send her a message."

"Nah." Ben swatted his hand. "That never works. Trust me. Women think indirectly. If you want to win a good woman, you have to think like a woman. Backwards."

Frankie inclined his head. "Thanks," he said, the left side of his face creasing into a smile. "I'm gonna try that."

"Let's do lunch sometime soon," Ben said. "It might feel good to vent to someone who's walked down that path."

"Sounds like a plan," Frankie said. "I look forward to it."

*****

Shuffling into the living room, Frankie and Mariani each grabbed a seat on one end of the dark green sofa set in the middle of the small space. Other than a ratty recliner and a scuffed coffee table, the room was adorned with only the flat-screen television against the back wall.

Frankie pressed the power button on the remote control, but the TV didn't turn on. *It's six o'clock.* He thought. *Come on.* He drove his thumb into the rubber button then tapped it on the hardwood table several times. When he pressed it again, the TV flashed on. Setting the remote on the table, he glanced at his steaming hot plate of lasagna.

"I don't even know if I can eat right now," Frankie said.

Mariani had his plate on his lap. His mouth was full. "This is some good shit, man."

"I'm gonna have to eat it later," Frankie said. "I keep envisioning our mugshots on the news."

"No way. I wouldn't get worried unless the feds get involved."

"Why is that?"

Mariani set his plate on the table. "Phone records. You called Hank on Friday to let him know we'd be hunting on his land. They'd question you harder. They'd turn over every rock."

Frankie's head rolled slowly to face Mariani, his face reddening. At the sound of the opening jingle on the nightly news, he shifted back and pointed at the TV. "This is it!"

Mariani leaned forward in his seat.

Frankie turned the volume up.

*****

The television screen zeroed in on a female news anchor, her golden hair polished and shined as she stared back at the camera. "A terrible situation is unfolding right now at a home just north of Duluth," she said. "Beth Seagull is live on the scene. Beth, I can see police working in the background behind the yellow tape. What can you tell us?"

"Well, Cindy. We don't have a lot of details right now." Beth paused, her dark hair flowing in the wind. "We do know there's been a shooting here. And I can confirm that one male suspect died in an altercation with the sheriff who was first on the scene."

"I'm told the sheriff is standing by to answer a few questions."

Beth stood with the microphone gripped in her hand. "That's right, Cindy. The sheriff and his deputy." She turned and the camera panned out. "Sheriff Anderson, can you give us any new information tonight?" She tilted the microphone toward his chin.

"I don't have a lot of new information," Sheriff Anderson said, "but um...I can tell you that multiple agencies from neighboring cities will be working around the clock to get to the bottom of this. To me, it's apparent that this crime scene is suspicious in nature. When we responded to the 911 call, we were confronted by a young man in the driveway who was holding a..." He paused, swallowing hard before he continued. "...A shotgun. From behind our squad cars, we attempted to talk him down. The gunman was noncompliant.

His language was threatening in nature. Then he fired a shot. My squad truck saved my life." He paused dramatically and lowered his head. "I-I had no choice but to use deadly force."

Beth took a moment before she spoke. "Do you have a name for this individual?"

"We can't release that information at this time."

"Okay. So, w-what happened next?"

"After the standoff, we noticed a large concentration of blood next to a vehicle that was riddled with bullets. I made the decision to immediately search the house. I hoped to find survivors. Instead, my men and I found a mutilated body, then another, and then another."

She slowly brought the mic back to her mouth. "N-not counting the gunman, you found three deceased victims?"

"The investigation may determine that there's more, but um...I'd say my count is five, actually. The blood in the yard could also be human. We believe a pack of wolves destroyed some of the evidence."

"Wolves?" she asked, her head moving back in disbelief.

The sheriff nodded. "That's correct. We found paw prints tracked all over the house and yard."

"Sheriff, what's the motive here?"

"At first, I thought this was a domestic murder-suicide, but we've learned there's something bigger here than first led on. We found a substantial amount of narcotics in a vehicle and also in the residence. It seems to have been a quarrel over drugs...or maybe a robbery gone bad." He gestured for his deputy to continue.

"In the actual search of the residence," Deputy Carlson said gravely. "When we were looking for victims, my mind and body was coping with it, telling me that these were m-mannequins, and that this was just a cruel prank." He shook his head. "This was no prank. Drugs and violence go hand and hand. The only good thing in all this…is that we took a lot of drugs off the street."

Sheriff Anderson leaned toward the microphone. "Words can't explain what we've encountered here today," he said. "We don't know exactly what happened, but what we do know…is that we have the remains of at least five victims." He covered his mouth and cleared his throat. "We also know that both parties were heavily armed. We found a total of twelve weapons on the premises. Some of which were long guns."

"We learned a lot tonight," the reporter said. "A lot more than we knew a few minutes ago." She paused, stiffening her body as she shivered in the cold. "I just have two more questions for you, Sheriff Anderson…then I'll let you get back to your investigation. Is there a manhunt for any other suspects? Is the community in any danger?"

*****

Frankie and Mariani were both desperately leaning forward in their seats, collectively taking in air. Sweat was pooling alongside Frankie's hairline and his heart rate was elevated. Mariani lit up a cigarette and Frankie did the same.

*****

Sheriff Anderson looked into the camera. "We have an ongoing investigation," he said. "But because of the large amount of narcotics found, federal authorities will build on our work. Until then, we have to be open to the possibility that other individuals could have been involved, either directly or indirectly." He paused to clear his throat again. "If anyone out there has any information, please call your local authorities to help us solve this heinous crime."

"Thank you, Sheriff An—"

*****

Swearing softly, Frankie turned off the TV. Running his fingers through his hair, he turned toward Mariani. "Federal authorities? I don't like the sound of that."

"I don't like it either," Mariani said and snubbed out his cigarette. "The feds will use the levers of government to find leads."

Frankie got up and walked to the window, lifting the blinds with his finger. "Do you think," he turned around, spreading apart his hands. "Do you think there's anything we're forgetting? Anything that could link us to the crime?"

"I don't think so," Mariani said and shook his head. "We all had gloves. We got the bullet. We burnt all the evidence. The tire tracks would have been covered with snow."

Frankie covered his mouth with his hand. "Fuck," he cried. "Fuck. What about…shit. The hunting gear we left in the deer stands."

Mariani's eyes widened, the only outside signal of his internal turmoil. *Deer stands,* Mariani

thought. A memory flashed in his mind. He remembered Frankie looking at his phone, complaining about his mom calling ten times. "Not only did we leave our stuff there, *you* were getting phone calls."

"I didn't answer any calls."

Mariani lit up another cigarette. "It doesn't matter. Any missed call, text, or voicemail would ping of the nearest tower."

"How do you know that?"

"I was in the military," Mariani said and brought his fist

down on the table. "People talk. I heard

your phone tracks your every movement. It's all recorded. Everything."

"What? You mean—"

"I mean, there's only a matter of time before the feds come knocking at your door."

"There's no way they could track my movements."

Mariani blew a stream of smoke upward. "Brother, trust me. Your phone tracked you walking through Hank's yard and his house. How could you explain that in court?"

"I hope you're wrong, but we should probably think about getting a lawyer." Frankie slumped in his seat. "We didn't go there to kill people. We went there to help them. The truth will set us free."

"Don't be foolish. The truth will lock you up."

11

Standing in a dimly lit basement, Thumper pressed his cell phone against his ear. Listening to the Spanish accent on the other end of the line, he waited until there was an opening to speak.

"He's dirty," Thumper said. "I-I know all about him."

"What did you just say?" the Hispanic voice asked.

"He's the one who tipped me off about the rat."

There was silence for a moment. "Do you know where he lives?"

"Yeah." Thumper put his hand in his pocket. "Why?"

"That gringo pig bragged about confiscating my narcotics. He made a big fucking deal about those drugs—too big of a deal...and I kept waiting and waiting but he never mentioned..." The man swore quietly under his breath, his voice gathering strength when he spoke next. "I'm pretty sure that pig took my loot."

"Enrique," Thumper said. "That place was crawling with cops. How would he get away with it?"

"You must not have been paying attention to what the pig was saying," Enrique said. "He was the first one on the scene. He said the drugs were in an SUV. That means my men found the stash, they just got sloppy. It's either my money was in that SUV or your friend Hank hid it." He paused, letting out a breath. "Unless, of course…*you* have it."

"You think I took it?" Thumper pointed at himself.

"If you did, this is what it would look like."

"If I took it, I'd be gone."

"Thumper, I like you. But I-I can't protect you if you don't come up with the money. I'll help you, but you got to prove that you didn't take the money. You pick up the sheriff, I'll get him to talk."

Thumper shrugged. "Hank probably hid it in the woods. He must have known his cover was blown."

Enrique lowered his voice to a low growl. "I just lost my only four men in this white bread town." He paused briefly. "They died because *you* let a rat hold on to *my* money. That rat is dead. *You* got a clean alibi, but *I* still owe someone for that fucking money. I'm gonna have a little talk with this sheriff, and I want *you* to make that happen."

Thumper paused before he replied. "I sell dope. I don't kidnap cops."

"This is your fuck up. And I'm gonna fix it, but I ain't doing all the work. You have one week. Your options narrow after that. We can't let this slide."

Thumper lit up a cigarette and blew out a line of smoke. "If I get the pig, am I even?"

"No. You're even when he coughs up the money."

"What if he doesn't?"

"Don't doubt me. It's insulting."

*****

On Monday night, Frankie got home from work, flipped on the light, and set his lunch cooler on the kitchen counter. Stepping through the kitchen, he peeled off his jacket and tossed it on a chair in the dining room. After he took his boots off, he fell into the couch and put his feet up. *That was the longest day of my life,* Frankie thought. *I should have just quit. If I can't sleep again tonight, I'm gonna have to retire. I don't need to break my back anymore.*

At the sound of Mariani walking down the steps, Frankie sat upright because he was hogging the couch.

From the landing, Mariani stretched his arms and yawned. "What time is it?"

"It's about 5:30," Frankie said. "What, did you just get up?"

"Yeah, I be straight hibernating," Mariani said, eyes half shut. "I'd sleep all winter if I could. Hey, you got a cigarette? I smoked a whole pack last night."

"Here ya go, bro," Frankie said. "Smoke 'em up. Less poison for me."

Mariani grabbed the pack and sat down on the other end of the couch. "Thanks bro," he said, averting his gaze to the window. "I didn't fall asleep till like five this morning. I keep thinking about those phone records. It's driving me nuts."

"Me too," Frankie said. "My body was shaking all night. My heart wouldn't slow down. I had to go to work with no sleep."

"I'm freaking out," Mariani said, holding a flame to the cigarette that dangled from his lips. "This shit could take us all down." A stream of smoke came out his mouth.

"I know. All I can think about is the feds kicking in my door."

"I ain't goin' back to prison, bro," Mariani said. "I might have to flee town. You gonna come with?"

"We got the money to flee if we have to," Frankie said. "We could just disappear."

Mariani sighed. "We could go to Italy. I got family there."

"Hopefully, it doesn't come to that," Frankie said. "It would be hard to walk away from friends and family."

"It's already come to that, Frankie. It's not safe here. We have to leave. Tonight."

"I can't just up and leave." Frankie spread apart his arms. "That would make us look guilty. Trust me, if they press charges, I'm gone. Until then, I say we don't break patterns."

"I ain't takin' that chance. A year or two in prison ain't shit, but life without parole for your little humanitarian mission. Fuck that. I'm gone, tonight."

"Whoa, whoa, whoa. You're gonna leave tonight? Seriously?"

"I'm not going to Italy tonight, but I ain't staying here."

"How 'bout this? Let's get something to eat and talk about it. If you're gonna leave, there's a chance we won't see each other for a while. You're gonna have to have a few drinks with me. You're my brother. I can't just say goodbye like this."

Mariani tugged the scruff on his chin. "You're making this harder than it needs to be. I love you, bro, but you have to be ready to give up everything." He snapped his fingers. "Just like that."

"This is all my fault." Frankie covered his face with his hands. "I'm sorry."

"It's not your fault. It's my fault for not stopping you."

"Nah, it's Hank's fault."

"What a fucking mutt. All right, I'll go have a drink with ya, but only cuz I need to take the edge off."

"You say that, but I don't think you're ready to say goodbye either."

*****

Frankie took a sip of his dark-colored drink and swiveled the bar stool toward Mariani. "If you leave

town, how ya gonna know what's happening?" Frankie straightened the collar of the brown polo shirt

that peeked out from underneath his black fleece jacket.

"I have a few tricks up my sleeve," Mariani said.

"Where ya gonna go?" Frankie shoved him gently. "Syria?"

Mariani chuckled. "Definitely not Syria," he said. "That's where you'd go. You'd blend in with all the other refugees. No, but I ain't gonna tell no one where I'm going. Not you *or* anyone else."

"Why? You think I'm gonna rat you out?"

"Not at all. We're brothers." Mariani lifted his chin. "I'm not even gonna tell Ma Dukes. It's just a peace of mind. If I get caught…it's on me."

Frankie tilted his glass of whiskey, letting it flow down his throat. "Four drinks down. I'm gonna have to switch to beer after this drink."

"Whiskey…is *exactly* what the doctor called for," Mariani said and finished his drink, setting the empty glass on the table. "It takes my mind off this shit…so I can pretend Saturday was just a bad dream. Beer is for pussies. I'm getting another round of whiskey." Standing with his bald head shining under the light, he reached into the inside pocket of his black leather coat. Pulling out a wad of cash, he peeled off a twenty and set it on the bar. "Two whiskey on the rocks." He said to the bartender who was in earshot.

The bartender filled two glasses and set them in front of the two men.

"Damn, man." Frankie shook his head. "I'm getting twisted tonight."

Mariani grabbed his glass and lifted it to eye level. "To

freedom!"

"To freedom!" Frankie said and the two old friends tapped glasses.

*****

At Mariani's request, Frankie went to the jukebox. He had five bucks folded up in his hand and a list of songs in his mind. Competing with the songs were two problems that were swirling. Freedom and Conny. His freedom was teetering in the balance, and his lover was haunting his thoughts. *Don't think about her*, Frankie thought. *Just make the most of the night. Mariani might be gone tomorrow.*

Elbowing his way through the crowded bar, his vision was blurred from hard alcohol. Always on guard, he scanned the room for potential threats and people he knew. There was no friends or foes, only a diverse group of strangers. His eyes hopped from a group of rugged looking twentysomethings huddled around the pool table, to a man and a woman with black hair talking intensely in a booth. His gaze then landed on a short and thin woman with dark wavy hair.

Is that? Frankie thought, squinting his eyes. *Tara?* He stopped abruptly, whiskey spilling on his hand. "Dayum!" he said softly.

As the crowd shifted, the woman's face got blocked out. "Fuck," he said and took a few steps closer. "It is her."

As Frankie approached Tara and her two friends, his smile grew smug. "Tara!" he said, his cheeks lifting. "It's Frankie. You remember me?"

"Oh, I remember you," she said softly, eyelids flickering. "You were on the hockey team."

"And *you* were a cheerleader." Frankie took a step closer and softened his voice. "It's really good to see ya. Can I get you a drink?" He paused, nodding back toward the bar where Mariani was sitting. "Bring your friends. This round's on me."

Tara smiled. "Thanks! It happens to be my birthday."

*****

After several rounds of drinks, Frankie stood in a circle with Mariani, Tara, and her friends. Shot glasses were raised above their heads.

"Happy birthday, Tara!" Frankie blurted out, and the others repeated before tapping glasses.

Frankie set the glass to his lips and snapped his head back. Scrunching his face up, he looked at Tara

and maneuvered next to her. Leaning down, his lips just barely brushing her ear, Frankie whispered:

"I can't keep my eyes off of you."

"Why is that?" Tara blushed and averted her eyes coyly.

Frankie placed his hand on her forearm. "I think you're super cute."

"Where's Conny?"

"She dumped me."

"What? Really?" Her eyes widened.

"Yeah. It didn't work out."

Tara took a sip of her drink. "Sometimes things don't work out." She nibbled on the inside of her lip.

"There's a flip side to that coin."

"Frankie, why didn't you talk to me back in high school?"

"That's a good question," Frankie said. "I-I guess I didn't want to insult you."

"Have you ever thought that maybe your silence was insulting?"

*****

As the night closed in, the group of newfound friends engaged in drunken conversation, the alcohol infusing a sense of dazzling bliss.

Leaning against Mariani, laughing over a shared joke, Frankie suddenly felt the weight of Tara's hand on his shoulder.

"Hey," she said, giggling as their eyes met. "We really got to take Tiffany home. She's…well, she's

getting pretty sloppy."

Glancing at her friend, Frankie nodded hesitantly. "Yeah…I mean, what if I don't want you to go?"

"I don't want to leave either," she admitted softly. "Maybe…maybe you could just follow us."

Frankie took in a sharp breath of guilt. "Not tonight," he said, gently touching her elbow. "I-I was thinking, I don't think it would be fair to you right now. You deserve my full attention, and I got a lot on my mind."

"No, it's okay," she whispered.

Frankie pulled out his phone. "Let me get your number. Maybe we'll chat sometime."

She told him her number and he typed it in his phone. He opened his arms and she fell into his embrace.

When she walked away, his eyes followed her to the door.

Mariani broke his concentration with a shove. "*You* are a stugots," he slurred his words. "That girl is a dime piece. I hope you got her number."

"I did," Frankie said. "I-I like that girl. If Conny doesn't come back, Tara will belong to me."

"Bro, Conny's gone," Mariani said. "She ain't coming back. And even if she did, would you really take her back?"

A vision of Conny's wide smile flashed in Frankie's mind.

He stumbled slightly, using the bar as a crutch before responding. "In a heartbeat."

"I've been there, brother," Mariani said. "It's hard to let go, but you just have to move on. Maybe a night with a girl like that would help."

"I need a cigarette." Frankie set his drink on the table.

*****

Out on the back deck, Frankie shivered in the cold. While inhaling cigarette smoke, his head turned to Mariani who was gazing off into the distance of the great lake.

"All I see is black out there," Frankie said.

"All *you* see is black," Mariani said. "And all I see is open space."

"That's what I'm trying to tell you, bro. We're the flip side of the same coin."

Mariani took one last drag from his cigarette and flicked it off the deck. "That's right, but I'm heads."

Frankie put his butt in the tall ashtray and then swung open the glass door. Mariani stepped inside and Frankie followed him. The bar was dying down, but the party lived on with loud dance music and stumbling college kids.

Frankie leaned toward his friend. "I'm gonna hit the men's room."

"You know where to find me."

Frankie's vision was blurred, and his body was buzzing. People were in his way. He carved his own path, gently nudging his way through the crowd. With the pool table coming up on his right, he noticed a group of ruffians in baggy clothes surrounding it. *None of these peasants could take me,* he thought and glanced at the black-haired girl who was standing next to them. *How do them dudes get that girl?* His head straightened, and he kept walking to the back of the room where he entered a narrow hallway.

Pulling open the door to the latrine, he walked inside and immediately smelled a strong odor. *Piss*, he thought, his head snapping to the left. The sight of a urinal overflowing made him scrunch up his face. He walked past it and found the single stall in the back corner of the bathroom.

Once confined within the fake granite walls, Frankie set his drink on the chrome toilet paper dispenser. With his hiking boot, he lifted the wet toilet seat and then un-zipped his pants.

Frankie enjoyed the moment of peace where he could plot and plan for a future, he hoped had not been written yet.

The very moment that Frankie zipped up his pants, he was startled by the sound of the bathroom entrance door slamming open and the brittle, sharp voice of a woman cussing.

"You piece of fucking shit!" Frankie heard a woman scream. "I know you fucked that whore, mother fucker!"

Frankie was in doubt of what to do, so he did nothing. From inside the stall, he tensed up. He leaned closer to the stall door, his ears stretching to catch their words. Frankie couldn't see what was going on, but he imagined a sharp clawed cat, scratching at her mate.

"Shut the fuck up, you stupid bitch!" the disembodied voice of a man said.

The screeching voice got louder. "I read the text on your phone—you sick fuck... I found a new man anyways." She laughed hysterically. "He's way bigger than you."

Suddenly, the laughing stopped, the woman's voice hiccupping into a frozen cry at the reverberation of something being slammed up against one side of the stall. Looking down, Frankie saw a pair of black pumps pressed up tightly to the back of the wall.

Using slow caution, Frankie crept out the door to witness a pale-skinned man in a yellow shirt and black ball cap, pinning a skinny black-haired girl against the stall. His left hand was gripping her by the neck and his right arm was cocked back. The man's fist was clenched — as if he was a second away from smashing her pale little face.

"Let go, Dane!" she cried.

In one swift movement, Frankie put the man in a headlock, one arm pressing dangerously against his throat. The flat brim hat fell off Dane's head. The more the man panicked and squirmed, the tighter Frankie squeezed. Dane's air supply was taken from him in short order, and there was nothing that he could do. He couldn't breathe so he couldn't fight; all he could do was surrender or black out.

When Frankie noticed that his victim's will to fight was fading, he whispered in his ear. "Shhh." Tightening his hold, Frankie's voice sounded again. "Shhh."

Dane squirmed and thrashed his body.

Applying immense pressure on his neck, Frankie growled. "You done yet?"

Frankie eased the pressure for a second so Dane could have the option to give up.

"Fuck you!" Dane coughed out.

Frankie tightened the vice. "Tough guy, huh?" he said then kicked Dane's legs out from under him, bringing him to his knees. While Dane was gasping for air, Frankie dragged him three feet to the overflowing toilet. Grabbing him by the hair, Frankie rammed Dane's face on the lip of the urinal that was frothy and wet. The man in his early twenties tried to fight it, but Frankie was too strong to be contained.

As Dane shook his head, the urine was contaminating his nose and mouth. With a fist full of dark brown hair, Frankie dunked his head in the yellow liquid. Watching him thrash helplessly for a few seconds, Frankie lifted his head clear of the bowl. Forcing his head on the porcelain, he lifted his fist as if he was about to strike.

Looking down at his defeated foe, Frankie's eyes zeroed in on his neck. *What the fuck?* he thought. *I've seen that spider before.* A cold chill ran down his spine and he released his grip.

When Dane fell to the wet floor, Frankie pointed downward. "Stay the fuck down!"

Dane sat humiliated on the tiles, breathing heavily. "You're gonna regret dis' nigga'."

"What, you gonna get your spider gang after me?"

"You have no idea who I roll wit'," Dane said, his dark eyes filled with malice.

"Who do you roll with?"

"Niggaz that be spittin' bullets," Dane said. "You better watch your back. We gonna find you."

Out of the corner of his eye, Frankie saw an empty beer bottle on top of the urinal. Grabbing it with his right hand, he lifted it above his head. "I don't like threats." He took a step closer, smashing the bottle on Dane's face.

Dane curled up on the floor. His hands pressed against his eye, blood seeping through his fingers.

"Keep talking, mother fucker," Frankie barked.

The black-haired girl stepped between the two of them. "Thank you," she worded so softly that her boyfriend on the floor couldn't hear.

Frankie nodded, his eyes softening in the light of her beauty. "Good luck with your life," he said. "You look way too good to be with that chump." He shook his head in disgust and turned for the exit.

She paused and watched him walk out the door. Briefly

looking down at her boyfriend who was groaning, she then bolted after Frankie. "Wait," she cried, stepping quickly behind him.

He stopped and turned around.

"What's your name?" she asked.

"Frank."

"I'm Misty," she said and stuck out her hand.

Frankie shook it. "Nice to meet ya," he said. "Look, I gotta get out of here. Do you

need a ride home?"

"Yeah. I-I came here with him."

"Let's go," he said, and they marched across the bar.

With the back of Mariani's bald head shinning under the light, Frankie stopped. "This is my brother, right here." He pointed briefly. "He's twice the man that chump will ever be."

"G," Frankie said from behind him.

Giovanni Mariani swiveled around on his stool, drink in hand. He looked up to Frankie, shifted his head to Misty, and then his eyes landed back on his friend. "What's up?"

Frankie leaned close to his ear, placing his hand on his shoulder. "Bro, we gotta get the fuck out of here." He squeezed. "I'll explain in the truck."

"What?" Mariani's eyebrows lowered.

"I think I hurt someone in the bathroom," Frankie whispered. "Let's bounce."

Mariani shot up off his stool. "Am I gonna have to put someone in the ICU?" he asked with a hushed growl.

"Not today."

12

At eight a.m. the next day, the wheels of justice were turning. The investigation of the mass-shooting at Hank Lindberg's property had just became a federal case. The F.B.I. sent two agents from the Minneapolis branch to Duluth to lead the investigation. Upon arrival, Special Agent Brett Abbott and Agent Derek Clark received a full debriefing by the head of the Homicide Division.

"That's just about everything." Captain Thompson handed the gray-haired Agent Abbott a business card. "Call Lieutenant Hubert and set up a time to meet. He handles confidential informants for the drug and gang taskforce. He'll have sensitive information about Hank Lindberg and his associates."

Agent Abbott tilted the card in his withered and bony hand. "This will be the first call I'll make," he said. "When an informant gets murdered in cold blood, all fingers point to the source."

Agent Clark glanced at the card but remained silent.

Dressed in a black uniform with a bright blue patch on the shoulder, Captain Thompson shook Abbott's hand firmly. "This area has never seen violence like that before," he said, shifting to shake Clark's brown-skinned hand. "We owe it to the people to get to the bottom of this…and make sure it never happens again."

"Our capabilities are unique," Agent Clark said and let go of the captain's hand.

"The technology at our disposal will help us get to the bottom of this," Abbott said. "You have my word."

*****

While swinging a shovel at work, Frankie felt his phone vibrating in his pocket. Pulling it out, he looked at the screen. "Who the fuck is this?" he said softly, not recognizing number. Watching it ring in his hand, he sighed while swiping the screen with his thumb. "Hello."

"It's me," Mariani said. "I got a burner phone. You should get one, too."

"I'll get one after work," Frankie said.

"I'm gonna stay in town for a few days. Gotta tie up some loose ends."

Frankie stabbed the shovel in the mound of dirt. "You probably need your loot, huh?"

"Yeah," Mariani said. "And I need to grab some clothes from your house. I thought I'd try to time it for when you're there. Maybe we can run up to Ivan's together. Talk about a few things."

"All right. When is best for you?"

"Friday. What time will you be done with work?"

"Probably about five o'clock. It all depends on the project."

"K. Just text me when you get the burner phone, so I got your number. Then I'll hit ya back on Friday."

"Sounds good," Frankie cleared his throat. "Hey. How'd the night cap go with Misty?"

Mariani chuckled. "Misty is a whore," he said. "I hope I never see her again."

"She's fucking hot, man. Must have been a fun ride?"

"Nah, her phone was ringing the whole time. It was a turn off. She looks good, but I don't like her. I think she's trashy."

"That was probably her dude calling. Dane. You shoulda saw me break that bottle over his head. You would have been proud."

"You're getting more and more like me every day. Pretty soon you're gonna have a bald head and a bow and arrow in your truck."

Frankie laughed shortly. "Oh shit. I almost forgot to tell ya...that Dane dude had a spider tattoo on his neck. It looked just like that dude's at Hank's house."

"So, what?

"You don't think he's part of the same gang?"

"Nah. Don't worry about that asshole. I'd be more worried about the feds. You should start shopping around for a lawyer, since you're not coming with me."

"I got a good lawyer in mind," Frankie said. "Keith Sundean. You ever heard of him?"

"Yeah, but you should shop around. The feds ain't no joke."

"Nah, can't get a better lawyer in this town than him."

*****

Agent Clark was hovering over a small metal desk. His eyes sifted through photos, thumbing through the pictures of the bullet-riddled Lincoln Navigator, the guns, and of course, the mutilated bodies.

"Seven bodies but we only have two names," Clark said. "I can't say I've ever had wolves tamper with a crime scene before."

"Be patient," Agent Abbott said from behind his desk. "All

the pieces will come together. We can't prosecute the dead. I bet Lieutenant Hubert will shed some light on things tomorrow."

Taking a seat to collect his thoughts, Agent Clark buried his chiseled brown face in his hands. After a few moments, he popped out of his seat and darted to the whiteboard on the wall. He picked up a red marker and wrote down the word — *Hank* — in the center.

"Hank Lindberg owns the mobile home," Agent Clark said and circled the name. "He was a long-term confidential informant with a criminal history of drugs and domestic violence. Deputy Carlson found a pound of methamphetamine in Hank's basement. Then Trooper McCoy found four kilos of pure cocaine in the SUV parked in the driveway." Agent Clark was half Abbott's age, but he had a military background and a master's degree in criminal science.

"The report says the SUV came back stolen," Agent Abbott said from behind the computer screen. "The fingerprints found in the truck come back blank, except for one that belongs to the original owner. All the guns found around the SUV had the serial numbers scratched off. Might take a day or two to get the DNA and dental records back."

Agent Clark drew a question mark underneath Hank's name. "I'm willing to bet my life that whoever was in that truck, came there to silence Hank. Somehow, they must have found out he was an informant."

"But who are they? And how did *they* find out?"

Clark crossed the room back to the desk. "Without a list of all Hank's associates," he said, "we're at a stand-still."

Abbott closed his laptop. "Until then, we've got to work with the hard evidence found on the scene. The drugs, the guns, the cell phones found. We need to comb through Hank

Lindberg's phone records, too."

"Hank's a small-time meth cooker," Agent Clark said. "I can't imagine him buying, selling, or possessing that much drugs. I just can't picture it. Hank's mugshot makes him look like a fiend. He ain't no kingpin."

"You have a point," Abbott shrugged. "All of Hank's drug convictions involved small amounts of meth, not kilos of coke. But he *did* have that big bag of meth in the basement. That shows that he *was* an active dealer."

"I still think it was a deliberate attempt to dispose of an informant," Clark said, opening his hands. "And Hank was the mark."

"Then why would there be coke in the back of that SUV?" Agent Abbot argued. "I've never seen a case where the hitman had a substantial amount of drugs on their person."

Agent Clark sighed in agreement. Running his hands through his dark, wavy hair, he nodded slowly. "Yeah, I guess me neither. But when you find four AK-47s on the scene..." he paused to shake his head. "It just...it's gotta be a hit."

"Maybe it's both," Agent Abbott said. "Maybe they took out the informant and robbed him blind. Maybe they thought Hank was dead until he shot at them from the window before they left."

"Do you think someone might have got away?" Clark asked, the muscles on his face tightening.

Abbott got up and slipped his thin frame into a black wool trench coat. "Even *if* someone got away," he said, "we need to find out who sent them. Before that, we got to get something to eat. I haven't eaten nothing all day. It's almost two o'clock."

"Hank's profile said that he was affiliated with a biker gang," Agent Clark said and put his black parka on. "I look forward to hearing what the lieutenant has to say."

Special Agent Abbott opened the door and his subordinate walked through it. "I want you to meet with Hubert. I'm gonna interview Sheriff Anderson. See what he has to say."

*****

Enrique Chaffetz dragged a suitcase out of the back seat of his Toyota SUV. Shutting the door, he turned and stepped in the direction of a rundown duplex on the hillside of Duluth. It was dark outside— quiet. The only noise was the wheels on the suitcase rolling behind him and the wind whistling in his ears. When he got to the front porch, he tightened his grip and heaved the black suitcase up each step. The door opened from the inside and a gray-haired, black man waved him in.

"It's fucking cold out there, Antwan," Enrique said, setting the suitcase on the linoleum floor.

The pear-shaped old man in a black jogging suit shut the door and locked it. "Only fo' more months of dis shit," Antwan said with a raspy southern accent.

"I ain't sticking around for that," Enrique said. "I'm just passing by."

"Good thing you passed by here." Antwan ran his eyes over the tall suitcase that stood at Enrique's side. Shifting his head slightly, he took in the attire of the thirty-some-year-old Hispanic man in front of him. *Looks like he's going to a funeral,* Antwan thought about the dark gray slacks, the brown leather shoes, and the black wool coat that hung to his knees.

Enrique lowered his tone. "I brought more than usual," he said softly, his hand running through his slicked back hair. "Can ya handle the extra work?"

"For sho'," Antwan said and gestured toward the living room. "My son's hungry. He's gonna make dat' scrilla."

"Good," Enrique said and followed Antwan in the living

room. His head tilted to meet the eyes of Antwan's son who stood a head and shoulders above him.

"Whud up, Big Rick," Antwan's son greeted Enrique with a slow and deep voice.

Enrique nodded. "What up, lil' Twan? You don't look excited to see me."

"What happened to Cezar?" Twan asked and crossed his massive arms.

"He got himself killed by a gringo. I'll be making the drops this month."

Twan pointed to the suitcase. "That fo' me?"

"Si." Enrique turned to Antwan who was handing him a leather satchel.

"That's all of it," Antwan said.

Enrique put the strap over his shoulder. "It feels about right. Five hundred thousand?"

"G'yeah." Antwan reached for the suitcase and laid it down. From his knees, he unzipped it and flung open the top.

"Dayam!" Twan said, bending over to get a closer look. "How much is dat?"

"Double," Enrique said, nodding his head. "I need the money faster this time. Saturday."

"No prob," Twan said, his mouth widening. "Shit. Dis gonna be a white Christmas fo' sho'. Snow for everyone!"

Enrique shook his hand. "You and your dad always come correct…and current." Enrique turned to the old man. "But more importantly, I don't hear of any problems. No busts, no rats. It's like you guys don't exist."

"We got a fool proof system," Antwan said. "Only family gets to push *my* shit. My family has a strong bond. Twan *did* make one exception though. And it's paid off so far."

Twan pointed to the wall. "My top earner." He lifted his

chin. "He's in the apartment next door. A major talent. Best I ever seen. You wanna meet him? Da kid will never get another chance to meet a real don."

Enrique smiled at the flattery. "You vouch for him?"

"Yeah," Twan said. "He's a white boy, but we tight. He's got the whole eastside on lockdown. Dem white bitches be fiending."

"Go get this gringo baller."

Twan pulled out his phone, touched the screen, and then put it to his ear. It rang twice. "Come over."

A minute later, a short Caucasian man in his early twenties opened the door and stepped through it. Stopping at the foyer, he nodded downward once with his flat brim hat somewhat covering his face.

"Come on, nigga'," Twan said, waving his white friend forward.

The man strutted forward in dark clothes that looked two sizes too big for him. A white bandage was covering his left eye. He extended a tilted hand. "Dane."

Enrique shook it firmly. "I hear good things."

"Thank you," Dane said with a trembling voice.

"What happened to your eye?" Enrique asked.

Twan spoke for him. "He got blind sided with a bottle at the bar."

"Did you have back up?" Enrique asked.

Dane swallowed. "I-I was in the bathroom," he said softly. "Didn't see it coming. H-he just smashed me with a bottle. Some mixed dude I've never seen before."

Enrique pivoted to Twan. "Your captain should have back up at all times. People should fear your crew." He turned back to Dane. "Money talks. Go pay for the surveillance tape at the bar. Find out who did this to you." He paused and met Dane's good eye. "Break his legs, or better yet…pluck out his *fucking* eyeball with a spoon."

Dane nodded.

Enrique's head shifted to Twan. "Did you teach him about Omerta?"

"Yeah," Twan said slowly. "He's fully committed to the cause. His lips are sealed. Only white boy I'll ever trust."

"Good. Then you won't mind if I explain the consequences for snitching?"

"Nah."

Enrique took one step in Dane's space. "I just made an example of another white boy in a different crew. Did you hear about the family that got killed on the news the other day?"

Dane swallowed hard, blinking rapidly.

Enrique leaned closer. "You rat, you die. Your whole family dies. Don't do that to your family."

14

On Wednesday morning, in a diner just north of Duluth, Special Agent Brett Abbott was sitting across from Sheriff Richard Anderson. Abbott took a sip of coffee and then set it on the table. "I've borne that burden before..." he said. "The burden of being forced to fire on a kid."

"So, you know what I'm feeling?" Sheriff Anderson said.

"Yeah," Agent Abbott said and let out a breath. "When someone fires on you, instinct and training kicks in. You know you did the right thing, but there's a sting in your heart that never goes away."

"Exactly." Sheriff Anderson took a sip of coffee. "I've had this badge for thirty years; it's only the third time I had to fire my weapon. But I-I just can't stop thinking about it." The sheriff lowered his head. "The whole crime scene reminded me of 'Nam. Bodies torn to pieces. Blood everywhere."

Abbott lifted his chin. "How old are you, Sheriff?"

"Sixty-six."

"I'm sixty-five. What company did you serve in the Marines?"

Anderson leaned forward. "Bravo company. Third battalion. How'd you know?"

"I noticed your Marine Corps ring," Abbott said and showed him the gold band on his pinky finger. "Semper Fi."

The sheriff smiled. "Semper Fi. Your stock just went up in my book."

The special agent's cheek muscles twitched. "I read your report three times, Sheriff. You found a lot of drugs, guns, and dead bodies. What do you think happened?"

"I think it was a drug deal gone bad." The sheriff lied through his coffee-stained teeth. "I bet the black SUV came to sell Hank some dope. And something went wrong. Who knows?"

"I've considered that theory, but what about the four AK-47s found on the scene?"

"I don't know. They must have been heavy hitters."

"Hmmm. Maybe."

The sheriff brought his cup to his lips and took a sip. "This area of the country has never seen anything like this. I hope you can get to the bottom of it."

"That's why I'm here. The F.B.I. won't rest until everyone involved gets brought to justice. I'm due to retire this year. Might be my last rodeo, Sheriff." He slid a business card across the table. "I want you to dig a little bit. Any new information would be greatly appreciated."

Before the sheriff could say *no problem*, a pot-bellied man with gray hair walked up with a tray in his hands. "Eggs Benedict for the good Sheriff." The owner of Joe's Diner set the plate in front of him, then turned to Agent Abbott. "And a Denver omelet for you, young man."

"Thank you," Abbott said and smiled up at a rotund man with a freshly-shaved face.

The waiter opened up his left hand. "Do you need anything else?"

"Joe," the sheriff said. "Surprise my new friend here with a piece of that famous apple pie."

"No thanks," Agent Abbott said. "I'll be full after the omelet."

"Come on," Joe said and gave a wide smile. "It's on the house. So, you can tell your friends."

Agent Abbot shrugged. "You talked me in to it," he said. "Thank you."

"No problem," Joe said and headed for the kitchen.

Sheriff Anderson took a bite of his egg and set the fork down. "Have you identified any of the remains yet?"

"No. The DNA will come back in a few days."

"I bet the pictures you saw were pretty gnarly."

"Almost as bad as it gets."

"I still can't believe it. Those damn wolves made quite a mess."

Agent Abbott nodded. "They sure did," he said. "Sheriff, how did you identify Mr. Lindberg anyways? He was unidentifiable."

The sheriff's eyes shifted to the left then came back. "The kid said his dad was in the basement. He said he had long brown hair."

Agent Abbott's head tilted slightly. "You never met him before?"

"Nope." The sheriff looked down, shaking his head slightly. "Not that I can remember."

"And you don't know anyone he associated with?"

"No."

Joe carried out the pie and ice-cream. "I hope you catch the jerks."

Agent Abbott looked at him, mouth gaped.

"Sorry," Joe said. "I overheard you guys talking earlier. Don't get me wrong, Hank was no prince, but he was a weekly customer for years. I kinda liked him."

"What did you like about him?" Agent Abbott asked.

"He worked hard. He was always filthy, fingernails caked with motor oil. He said he was a mechanic."

"Do you know anything about his personal life? Any reason someone would want him dead?"

"He seemed scrawny, dark sunk in eyes. I think he was a doper. Not a reason to kill a family though."

"Thanks, Joe." He gave him a card. "I'm Special Agent Brett Abbott of the F.B.I. If you hear any information about Hank or his associates, don't hesitate to call me. Day or night."

The two men shook hands. "Joe Nordstrom," he said. "Will do."

"One more thing, Joe. Did you notice anything unusual on Saturday or Sunday? That crime was only twenty miles south."

"Other than the blizzard," Joe said. "I can't think of anything. It was a slow day. Only a few customers."

"Are you sure?" Abbott tilted his hand. "Even the smallest things that sometimes don't seem related, could be helpful."

"Nope, nothing." He touched the bridge of his nose. "Except, well, there was a, um, a black SUV that pulled in the parking lot that morning. But whoever was in it didn't even come inside. After a few minutes, they just drove away." He paused to meet the federal agent's eyes. "I thought that was odd."

"Do you have surveillance cameras?"

"Yes, sir."

The sheriff squinted. "Black SUV, huh?" he asked. "Did you see the driver?"

"Yeah," Joe said. "Some colored guy with a black watch cap."

"Must've been lost." Sheriff Anderson said, quickly bringing his coffee cup to his lips.

Agent Abbott's eyes narrowed. *Did he really just say that?*

*****

Agent Seth Clark sat behind a desk in his temporary office, Lieutenant Doug Hubert across from him. A thick white binder rested between the two men. Reaching across the table, Clark pulled it toward him.

"The all-important Hank Lindberg file," Agent Clark said with a reserved smile. "Thank you. This should answer some questions."

Hubert cleared his throat. "I organized all my memos for you," he said in a rushed voice. "The computer file that you had was just the basic details about his criminal record and cooperation. This is the hand-written notes from every meeting I had with him. I put his phone records in there, too." He paused with a short laugh. "This whole time, I thought he was just lying about those people. But now, I'm pretty sure he was telling the truth."

Clark opened the binder and raised his eyebrows. "Bingo!" he said. "Thaddaeus Boyd, president of the motorcycle club. If it *was* a hit, I bet *he* made the order."

"He goes by Thumper," Hubert said, shifting his thin frame in his seat. "I guess no one calls him by his first name. But yeah. He's at the top of the food chain. Before Hank coughed up the info, these guys managed to stay off the radar for a generation. They operate deep in the woods and make the city people come to them." He threw up his hands and leaned back in his seat. "They cook meth and distribute it, they sell stolen guns, and they pimp out young girls." He shook his head and let out a breath. "Fucking lowlifes."

"This phone number belongs to Thumper?"

"It's a burner phone," Hubert said. "But we know it's

Thumper. We recorded three phone conversations between him and Hank on that line."

"That will be helpful," Clark said while skimming the first page. "Mr. Lindberg was giving you information for two years?"

"Yeah. A little more," Lieutenant Hubert said, nodding his head that was bald on the top, gray on the sides.

"What made him flip?"

"Routine traffic stop. Some sheriff up north busted him with a small amount of meth. Hank gave us just enough info to keep himself out of jail. Names, a few recorded phone calls with Mr. Boyd. A few controlled buys. Nothing substantial. But he had his foot in the door. He seemed committed. Spiteful. Promising big deals in the future."

"What else did he know?" the federal agent leaned forward.

Hubert shifted his body in the chair. "He also gave addresses, hang outs, phone numbers—which led to other phone numbers."

"Was Hank a biker? Was he in the gang?"

"No. He doesn't ride a bike, but he said he was a prospect in the club. He started as the club's mechanic some twenty years ago. That's how got into the inner circle." He paused momentarily to make eye contact. "He told me that sometimes they'd pay him in meth."

"How would they know he was a CI?"

"Not sure. Either they had a hunch—or maybe—a mole in the force. Because we never arrested anyone from Hank's info. We've just been building a weak case."

"Interesting." Agent Clark's cheek muscles flexed. "Tell me, how big is this biker gang?"

"It's hard to say," Hubert said. "They don't even have a

name. That list you read are the names of the thirteen members Hank gave us, but there's at least ten more prospects or wannabes like Hank."

"That's a pretty small gang," Agent Clark said. "But after seeing what they did to Hank and his family, it looks like they play for keeps."

Officer Hubert shrugged. "That's why we need to take them down. This cannot become normal around here."

Agent Clark set the binder on the table. "Did Mr. Lindberg ever express fear of this Thumper character?"

"Yeah, the last time I spoke with him," Detective Hubert said. "It was the Monday before Thanksgiving. We talked for about thirty minutes. He was begging to get relocated in the witness protection program." Hubert let out a breathy, short laugh.

"He knew he was a dead man," Clark said.

Hubert pointed at the binder. "Look at page three."

Agent Clark turned the page and saw a raw mug shot of Thumper with his thick, meaty neck, his dark menacing eyes, and his massive bald head. Clark's eyebrows hitched up. "That's one mean looking guy."

"His reputation matches his looks, but he's only had one arrest. He assaulted someone at the local bar."

"Hmm." Clark rubbed his temples. "But if this gang has no history of murder—why would they bring out the AK-47s to kill a small-time junkie? A guy who—at most—was a rat? I just don't get it." He opened his arms and looked across the desk. "Was Hank the greatest threat that they ever had? Was he worth wiping out an entire family?"

"I think Hank knew more than he was telling," Hubert said. "I think he was playing both sides. Maybe he made money for them while blowing smoke up my ass. We never had high expectations from Hank. Honestly, we have bigger fish to fry. The inner city is filled with drug gangs from Chicago and Detroit. They're flooding the streets with heroin laced with fentanyl."

"Black and brown people?" Clark said with a touch of contempt.

"Come on. You know it's not about color, it about saving lives. Getting the drugs off the street."

Clark opened his hands and shook his head. "Forget I said that. I just always see law enforcement soft on white gangs. I don't discriminate. White, black, brown. If they're bad guys, I'll do whatever it takes to stop them."

"I'm sure you've dealt with biker gangs before. They're dangerous, but not a priority. We were just happy to have an informant in their crew. We wanted to watch them over time."

"What about the drugs found in the black SUV?" Agent Clark asked.

"I'm not sure." Hubert leaned back and folded his arms. "The bikers are known for meth, not coke or heroin. The whole thing is pretty crazy if you ask me. I was debriefed on the killings. I don't understand why hitmen would have kilos in the back of their truck. Then, on top of that—*four* of the killers end up dead? I mean…what? Were they incompetent? Or was Hank surgical with the rifle? Doesn't that sound incredible to you?"

Clark slowly swayed his head from left to right. "I've seen several failed hits." He set the palm of his hand on the desk. "But you're right, I've never found dead hitmen with a bunch of coke in their vehicle. Maybe it wasn't a hit. Maybe Hank was trafficking narcotics under your nose."

*****

Special Agent Abbott set a leather binder on the honorable Judge Stolcis' desk. "I need a search warrant, your honor."

"Let's take a look and see what you got," Judge Stolcis said, leaning forward to grab it.

"We have reason to believe Mr. Boyd is responsible for the murder of Hank Lindberg, his wife, and a third individual who has not been identified."

The gray-haired female judge copiously read the application and then turned the page to take in Hank Lindberg's phone records. "Mr. Boyd called the confidential informant the night before the murder, then ten minutes later, he called the suspected hitman. Then he called the hitman again *after* the murder."

"Yes, Your Honor. Mr. Boyd is the boss of the motorcycle gang that Mr. Lindberg was a witness to. We're confident that he's responsible for this heinous crime. We need to search his residence and vehicles to find more evidence."

"So, you don't need an arrest warrant?"

"No, no. Just a warrant to search and seize anything related to the Hank Lindberg murder."

Judge Stolcis pursed her lips. "Warrant granted."

*****

Inside of a friend's garage, Thumper was screwing a stolen license plate on the back of a Lincoln Crown Victoria. Standing on the gravel behind him was Enrique Chaffetz in a long wool coat and a pair of black slacks.

Dropping the screwdriver in the dirt, Thumper stood up and turned around. "I know," he said with a low tone. "Give me a break. My house just got raided yesterday. I-I had to lay low."

"They've got nothing on you," Enrique said. "Otherwise, there'd be a warrant out for your arrest."

"The card on the door said I'm wanted for questioning by a federal agent. I'm fucked."

Enrique opened his hands. "This is the third time I had to tell you not to doubt me. Don't let it happen again."

"What do you want from me? You want me to go get him right now?"

"No. I don't want another fuck up. Make a plan and do it right."

"I have a plan."

Enrique shook his head. "That's what you said on Sunday. If Martos don't get the money in a few days, we're both dead." Enrique shifted his head slightly. "Well, *I* might just get a beating. You...you look like you could have stolen the money. Do you see what I'm saying? When a million comes up missing, someone has to go down no matter what the excuse. It's politics. Don't take it personal."

Thumper's eyes narrowed. "I-I understand," he said with a single nod.

"Good," Enrique said. "Tell me your plan."

Thumper patted the back of the car twice. "I'm gonna shove him in the trunk headfirst."

"I'm serious." Enrique took a step forward. "This guy was a fucking Marine. He's old, but he'll push your shit in if you're not smart."

15

An unconscious Sheriff Anderson was crammed in the cold trunk of a car. At the hum of the engine, his eyes opened to darkness. He found himself bound and gagged, heart sinking by the moment. He could feel a pounding in his head, a tenderness over the back of his scalp, the sweet taste of blood in his mouth. The sheriff groaned. His world shifted in and out for a moment as he adjusted to the darkness and now, fully wake, the memories reasserted themselves.

The sheriff remembered opening the door to his garage at the crack of dawn. After he flipped the light switch, the first thing that he saw was a husky intruder wearing a black ski mask, standing against his squad truck. A shotgun in his hands.

"Hey, now!" the sheriff said, raising his hands to his chest.

While staring into the deep blue eyes of the perpetrator in front of him, Sheriff Anderson felt the force of a blunt object smash him in the back of the head. He remembered the blow bringing him to his knees and then to the ground. The vision of his hand reaching for his sidearm was vivid.

"Ah, ah, ah…" The masked man in all black pumped the shotgun. "Don't fucking move, pig!"

Sitting upright on the cold cement floor, Sheriff Anderson put his hands up. "Okay," he remembered saying frantically.

"Don't shoot!"

"Grab his pistol!" the man in black barked at his skinny accomplice. "Then stand him up and frisk him."

"W-what do you want from me?" the sheriff asked, his lips quivering under his mustache. Shifting just slightly, he only hoped to offer them a distraction; the man who'd frisked him had confiscated his sidearm and his ankle pistol, but he'd missed the small knife on the side of his right hip.

"Shut the fuck up," the heavier of the men said to the sheriff then shifted his gaze to his wingman in black. "Go get the Crown Vic."

The masked man nodded then ran out the door.

The kidnapper leaned up against the sheriff's maroon squad truck. "Listen up, pig," he said. "We're gonna take a little drive. If you do exactly what I tell you to do, you might just live to see another day."

The big man slowly walked to the wall and pushed the button to operate the automatic garage door opener. The black car backed halfway inside. He poked the sheriff with the barrel of the shotgun. "Get up," he said. "You're goin' in the trunk."

A chilly fear took possession of the sheriff's body and he began to tremble. Reality reached a fever's pitch as he got closer to the vehicle with the trunk popped open.

"Get in." The man with the shotgun poked him again.

The sheriff stalled until he felt a third poke in his back. He then crawled in the back of the tarp-lined trunk.

The taller of the men reached in his jacket pocket and pulled out a dirty sock.

"What the fuck did I do?" the sheriff cried. "Let me g—"

Forcing the sock in the sheriff's mouth, the thin kidnapper growled. "How's that taste, pig?"

The sheriff groaned.

The big man stretched out the duct tape and then proceeded to wrap it around his head. After that, he taped his hands and feet together as well.

Knowing the statistics of resisting in the face of a gun, the sheriff didn't put up much of a fight. His body was stiff, and his eyes were shifty with fear.

"You're under arrest," the thinner one said and spit on his face.

The sheriff twisted and groaned as the fluid rolled in his eye.

The man with the shotgun turned his weapon around and smashed the butt of the gun on his jaw. He then slammed the trunk closed with authority—and just like that—the sheriff's world became dark.

It must have been at least an hour that he'd been unconscious, all scrunched in that trunk. Now he was listening to the muffled sounds of his captors in the front of the car. *That has to be Thumper and Scott Draper*, the sheriff thought, hoping to glean some information. *They think I'm gonna rat them out. I wish I would have.*

Through the masking sound of the tarp, all he'd gleaned was the low rumble of voices and the occasional bark of laughter.

*****

In the bathroom of his hotel suite, Enrique bent his knees, shoving an olive green back-pack under the sink. Feeling a vibration in his pocket, he shot up. When he pulled out his cell phone, a quick glance at the screen told him it was Thumper. A twinge of excitement flowed through him and he swiped the screen with his thumb.

"Si, como no?" Enrique asked and shut the door to the

vanity.

"Yeah," Thumper said in code. "I got that pork chop in the frying pan."

"Good," Enrique said and entered the kitchen. "Tenderize it for me." He cracked a smile as he looked down on a black suitcase that was standing upright. "I'll be there by noon. You know what not to do, right?"

"Yea," Thumper said. "I'll be careful."

"Bien." Enrique opened the oven, slid the suitcase inside, and then closed the door. Pressing the phone to his ear, he heard a muffled sound followed by Thumper's soft laugh. And then the phone cut out.

*****

With his hands taped behind his back, Sheriff Anderson sat in a chair. His gaze rested on a masked Scott Draper who was twisting a small knife a few feet in front of him. *If they were gonna kill me, why would they be wearing masks?* he thought, the duct tape preventing him from speaking his mind. *I know who you are, Scott.*

Sheriff Richard Anderson had survived a prison camp in Vietnam, and he'd walked away knowing a few things about captors. At the whistling sound of a torch igniting, his bruised head whipped to the kitchen of the small log cabin.

"Sheriff," Thumper said, crossing the room with a torch in his hands, stopping just two feet from his victim. "This is gonna suck for you. Might get real hot." Bending forward, he tilted the six-inch blue flame in front of the sheriff's face.

The sheriff's body stiffened, and his head snapped back. His muffled voice barked through the duct tape.

"What's that?" Thumper asked. "I didn't hear ya."

Draper stepped forward. Reaching for the sheriff's head,

he grabbed the corner of the duct tape and then ripped it from the sheriff's mouth, tearing whiskers from his thick mustache.

Sheriff Anderson shrieked in pain, his face scrunching up. "What do you want from me?"

Thumper gave a short laugh. "Listen up, pig. I'm only gonna to tell you this once. You have one fucking rule: speak when spoken to. That's it." Standing directly in front of him, he moved the whistling flame closer to his eyes. "Do you understand me?"

The sheriff nodded his head quickly: "Yeah, I understand."

"Good." Thumper turned the torch off. "You speak out of turn and the torch comes back on." He walked behind the sheriff and opened the back door.

The sheriff felt a rush of cold air scratch against the back of his neck. As his chair creaked and tilted backward, his eyes widened.

*****

Outside on balcony, the sheriff looked past his captors to the choppy White Face Lake. In the far distance, all he saw was gray in the sky with no rays of light.

Thumper broke the sheriff's gaze with the flicker of a lighter.

"You ready to answer some questions?" Thumper blew smoke in the wind. With the cigarette dangling from his lips, he threw a few warm-up punches like a boxer about to step into the ring.

The sheriff bit down on his tongue as a tremble of fear seized upon him. *Stay strong,* he thought, breathing through his nose. *I've been through much worse.*

Thumper nodded his head. "All right," he said, his voice grimmer than before. "Let's be frank. We know." Leaning closer, Thumper sneered. "We know you're a dirty cop, but I want details. How many times have you abused your power?"

"I'm elected by the people to protect and serve," the sheriff said, and then he cleared his throat. "I enforce the law, not break it."

"Wrong answer." Thumper spit in his face. "One lie is a thousand lies." He turned to Draper and nodded downward once, smoke venting through his mask as he spoke.

Stepping forward with a knife in his gloved hand, Draper poked a hole in the sheriff's uniform, just under the armpit. Reaching forward, he grabbed a fistful of fabric and yanked back with force. With the torn shirt in his hand, he dropped it on the snowy deck.

The sheriff's naked upper body stiffened sharper and he began to shiver. His voice grumbled but no audible words came out.

"I'm gonna give you one more chance," Thumper said, studying the sheriff's eyes. "Tell me one thing you've done that was beneath the dignity of your badge." Before the sheriff could even open his mouth, Thumper leaned down close and, with a twist of his wrist, snubbed out his cigarette on the man's chest.

As the red-hot cherry burned his skin, the sheriff groaned and shook his body so hard that the chair he sat on teetered. "All right!" Sheriff Anderson growled.

Thumper dropped the cigarette and stood tall.

"Fuck! I...I pulled over a drunk girl last summer. Told her she could earn a get out of jail free card if she'd let me bend her over." Sheriff Anderson put his head down in shame. "She said no at first, but..."

"That wasn't what I expected." Thumper laughed. "I thought you were gonna tell me how you gave up Hank

Lindberg for two G's."

"I knew that's what this was about," Sheriff Anderson said. "What? Do you and Draper think I'm gonna talk or something?" He shook his head. "I never said a word. I couldn't. That would implicate *me*."

"We crushed Hank…and *you* just happened to be the first pig on the scene." Thumper's head tilted slightly. "What a fucking coincidence."

The sheriff's lip quivered. "Hank was gonna take you *all* down. This is how you repay me?"

Thumper chuckled. "Okay, sheriff. I'm thankful for the paid tip. But that didn't give *you* the green light to show up at the scene and rob us."

"I didn't rob you."

"Bullshit." Thumper threw a right jab and shook the sheriff's mouth. "Where's the fucking money?"

The sheriff sunk his head and spit blood. "Okay. I-I found a bag of money. You can have it. Just let me go."

"How much?"

"Like a hundred thousand."

"Where's the rest?"

"That's it!"

Thumper lit up the torch. "Where's the rest?"

"I swear, that's it! What are you talking about?"

Thumper stepped forward, stooping slightly. "You better fucking tell me where it's at."

"A hundred thousand in the shed behind my garage. I'll give you the code."

"We don't need no fucking code." Thumper placed the blue flame on the sheriff's mustache.

The hair on the sheriff's upper lip singed. Smoke was rising in his nostrils. He screamed and thrashed his body to one side.

Raising a gloved hand, Thumper laughed and patted out the flame on the sheriff's mustache. "Where's the money?"

"I'm not lying!"

"You know what? Fuck this. I'm goin' inside for a while. I'll let the spic go to work on him. He'll have no choice but to talk then."

The sheriff shivered. "I-I told you the truth."

"No, you didn't. I don't think you understand what's happening here. This is not a debate."

"Go to my shed," the sheriff said frantically. "Take the money."

Thumper winked at Draper.

Draper rocked the Sheriff's jaw with his fist. "A hundred thousand ain't cutting it."

"Give me the fucking loot!" Thumper raised his voice. "Don't make me kill your wife!"

The sheriff's face scrunched up. "Leave her alone!" He screamed. "You got the wrong guy!"

"He look thirsty to you?" Thumper asked his cousin.

Draper grinned, guffawing. "Sure does." He bolted for the door.

Placing one finger against his lips, Thumper bent forward, his face inches from the sheriff. "Shh," he whispered. "It'll all be over soon." He straightened. "Or maybe not. Up to you." He laughed.

The sheriff trembled as a string of blood dangled from his chin.

Draper came back with a tall glass of water in his hand. Hovering above Sheriff Anderson, the ice in the glass was tinkling with the movement. "You thirsty, Sheriff?"

The sheriff tilted his head only to see the masked man

overturn the glass. The moment the cold water touched his skin, the sheriff's shoulders raised. Body jerking, he lunged against his restraints, his teeth clenching together but not before a guttural curse emanated out of his mouth.

Thumper chuckled. "Let's go inside. I'm fucking freezing."

*****

In a dank basement, Frankie swung a shovel full of dirt on a PVC sewer pipe that rested on the bottom of a trench. *Filling a ditch is easier than digging one,* he thought and turned back to the mound. Swinging again, more dirt flew on the pipe. Turning his body to repeat the action, he stabbed the shovel in the shrinking pile.

Before he could pull the shovel out, his phone started ringing in his pocket.

Looking at the screen, his eyebrows lowered. *Mariani,* he thought and then answered it.

"Hello."

"Whud up?"

Recognizing Mariani's voice, Frankie pressed the phone tighter to his ear. "Not much, just filling a hole. What do you got goin?"

"I'm just loading up my Jeep. You still free after work?"

"Yeah."

Mariani cleared his throat. "If I get there by six, you wanna run up to Ivan's with me? I need to grab that loot. I finally came up with a plan."

Frankie let out a sigh. "All right. I'll be there."

"I'll fill ya in on the way."

*****

If Sheriff Anderson had any chance of survival, it would fall on him. *There's only one way I'm going to survive this,* he thought to himself, eyes staring up at his captors.

But his thoughts were morbid. No one knew where he was. His wrists were taped behind the chair. *Only cunning will set me free,* he thought. *It's now or never.*

"Chop, chop," Thumper clapped his hands twice. "Back to business." He pursed his lips and nodded a few times. "Sheriff, where's the loot? Tell me and we'll go inside. I might even give you a finder's fee." He paused, crept closer, then crouched low to the sheriff's level. "If I don't like your answer, I'm gonna go back inside and let you freeze."

Sheriff Anderson's eyebrows made a V. "Fuck you!" he said and spat in Thumper's face.

Thumper stood up and wiped the fluid from his eye. "Mother fucker!"

Draper took a step back to give Thumper some space.

Thumper reached for his waistline where his pistol was concealed. *If it wasn't for Enrique…* he thought to himself as he touched the steel of his gun. Stepping up to the sheriff, he lifted the man's chin with his left hand. Raising his fist high, he thrust down on the sheriff's nose.

The raw force of the punch snapped the sheriff's head back and tipped the chair over. From the icy deck, his eyes widened at the sight of blood pouring out of his nose, pooling around his mouth.

Thumper got on one knee and hit him again, this time in the eye. "That hurts a little bit, doesn't it?" He gave a short laugh. "Trust me, I've been hit like that before. It makes you feel all defenseless. Your eyes water up, and everything gets all blurry. Then you start to panic because you don't know what's next." He stood up and watched the old man bleed and groan.

"Your hands are taped behind your back. You can't fight and you can't run. Give me what I want, and you go free."

The sheriff was laying on his side. With his feet taped together, all he could do was slither up against the railing. Blood was running down his face and dripping on the snow. "You hit like a girl."

Thumper bent his knees with a wide stance. "Don't fuck with me, pig! The next punch is gonna knock your fucking lights out."

The sheriff looked up and saw a gloved fist hovering over his face. "Go fuck your inbred mother!" he barked and spit out blood near Thumper's feet.

Thumper chuckled. "You're tougher than I thought, old man." He kicked him in the gut. "But if I were you, I'd smarten up pretty fucking quick. A foreigner is on the way. He isn't civilized like me. He uses tools to get what he wants."

"Suck my dick, bitch."

Thumper turned to his co-conspirator. "You see this?" he said, "This idiot wants to die over money he'll never see again. What the fuck's wrong with this guy?"

Draper shrugged. "Fuck him," he said. "Let this pig freeze to death."

On that note, the two men turned on their heels and entered the cabin, Thumper slamming the door behind him emphatically.

Entering the cabin, the men rubbed their hands together as the warmth of the room enveloped them. Heated by an old-fashioned fireplace in the corner, the place radiated a stark contrast to the freezing temperatures outside. Thumper took off his jacket and sat down on the sofa next to the fire. The old couch creaked when the oversized man dropped his weight into it.

"How long you wanna leave him out there?" Draper asked.

"I don't know," Thumper improvised. "Enrique will be here in an hour or two. We'll let him work his magic."

"What if he freezes to death?"

"He'll be all right. We'll take turns checking on him. No serious bodily harm, just a broken nose, a bit of fear, and maybe some frostbite."

"You're not gonna give me a chance to make him talk?"

Thumper's head shifted. "We'll see. Any more damage and he won't be able to talk at all."

For the next hour, Thumper and his cousin relaxed under the swelling heat of the fire while outside, in the billowing darkness of winter, a sheriff shivered alone.

*****

Peeking out the small window on the door, Thumper noticed that the skin on the sheriff's back was beat red. Steam was rising from his mouth and he was moving slightly. "He's still breathing."

"It looks like he's gonna crawl down the steps," Draper said.

On the other side of the door, Sheriff Anderson was lying on his side. His arms still awkwardly taped behind the chair. He moved his boots from the deck to one of many wooden balusters holding up the railing. Pushing off with his feet, his face scraped on the ice and snow. "This is nothing," he mumbled and slithered an inch toward the stairs. "This is nothing." He slithered again and moved a foot. Turning his head, he studied the staircase. *I just gotta get on my feet and break this tape,* he thought and heard the creak of the door.

Thumper pushed open the door and looked down. "Where

the fuck you think you're going?"

Following behind him, Draper grabbed the sheriff's ankles and pulled him back on the deck.

"Okay, pig," Draper said, flicking open his pocketknife. "Now it's my turn. Give up the info or I'm gonna gut you like the pig that you are."

"This is nothing," Sheriff Anderson muttered as he eyed the skinny legs of the man with a knife.

Thumper pointed and laughed at his cousin. "You — are nothing!" he mimicked the sheriff's mumbled voice.

"Yeah," Draper replied, pointing the knife at the sheriff. "You think I'm nothing? How 'bout I show you something?" He stooped low, gripping the sheriff's neck, slowly guiding the knife toward his eye.

A sudden burst of adrenaline filled Sheriff Anderson's veins. Spinning on his back, he coiled his bound legs and sprung them into Draper's knee as hard as he could.

Draper's knee buckled. "Fuck!" he cried, the knife falling from his hand. Instinctively, he reached for his leg, just in time to absorb another incoming boot. This time, Draper went down.

Thumper stepped over his cousin and dropped his weight down on the sheriff. Crawling on top of him, Thumper straddled his chest. With his hands gripped around the sheriff's neck, he squeezed and shook him violently. "Mother fucker!" He punched his face. Pulling back his fist, he thumped his skull again. Bouncing to his feet, Thumper lifted his knee and started stomping on the sheriff's head.

Thumper halted to catch his breath. He was panting. His gaze locked on the limp sheriff and the blood strewn around his head. He kicked him in the ribs and the body didn't respond.

Draper was cursing, both hands on his knee.

"Are you okay?" Thumper asked.

"He fucked up my knee," Draper grumbled.

"Can you get up?" Thumper asked and offered him his arm.

"Yeah, I'll be okay," Draper said gravely and grabbed Thumper's wrist.

Thumper lifted him up and held him in place.

"You gotta let me kill this pig."

"I think he's already dead," Thumper shrugged. "I just dented his forehead with my boot."

Draper tried to put weight on his foot but immediately leaned on Thumper. Looking down, Draper saw the sheriff twisted on the deck. "That's a lot of blood."

"It is," Thumper replied. "The steel toe does that sometimes."

The two goons silently hovered over the unconscious victim. The only sound was the wind surging through the trees, and Thumper's heavy breaths. At the sudden sound of a car door shutting, their heads both snapped toward the front of the cabin.

Thumper met Draper's eyes. "Fuck. It's Enrique." He suppressed his voice. "He's early. That spic said he'd be here at noon." He shook his head and let out a deep sigh. "Just let me do all the talking. Don't say a word."

*****

Shuffling quickly to the door, Thumper cracked it open, his eyes lighting hesitantly on Enrique. "Made great time I see," he said and stepped to the side.

"Take those masks off," Enrique ordered while crossing the threshold with a black plastic box hanging at his side.

Thumper and Draper pulled their masks off and tossed them on the hardwood floor.

"Good," Enrique said. "You won't need masks anymore."

Thumper nodded.

"Where is he?" Enrique asked.

"He's chillin' on the back deck," Thumper replied, nervously pointing toward the back door.

Enrique looked into Thumper's bloodshot eyes. "Did you get him to talk?" he asked, setting the box on the floor.

"Yeah, he confessed." Thumper looked away. "He said he only has a hundred thousand though."

"A hundred thousand?"

"Yeah. He's a stubborn fuck."

Enrique reached in his black leather jacket and pulled out a handgun. "Here's some motivation," he said. "Now, bring me to the pig."

Thumper led Enrique to the back door. Stopping before he opened it, he tucked his chin. "Things went a little off script."

Enrique charged past him. Opening the door, he stepped outside on the snowy back deck. He looked down at the twisted man with blood all around his head. Enrique's head snapped back up. "What the fuck did you do?" He grabbed Thumper by the jacket with both hands. "You better hope he's not dead, gringo."

"The pig," Thumper said frantically. "H-he kicked my guy's knee. We had a little tussle. Gramps didn't wanna give up, so I had to take him down the hard way."

"You had one fucking task." Enrique flinched his arm. "How the fuck am I gonna get him to talk now?"

Thumper shrugged. "I'm sorry. He was a fucking maniac."

Enrique dropped to one knee, pressing two fingers on the sheriff's neck. "You're fucking lucky," he said and got up. "He has a pulse. Cut that tape and bring him inside."

Draper pulled his knife out and limped toward the beleaguered sheriff.

*****

Enrique looked down on the sheriff sprawled out on the antique sofa snoring. "Thumper gave you quite the thumping," he said, soaking up the blood on his face with a hot, damp rag.

Dropping the soiled rag on the floor, Enrique shook his head and walked to the kitchen where Thumper was standing with a whiskey bottle gripped in his hand. He snatched the bottle, swore under his breath, and returned to the sheriff. Letting out an aggravated sigh, Enrique stooped above the sheriff, pressed down on his chin, and tilted the bottle above his mouth.

When the flow of alcohol met the sheriff's mangled lips, his eyes jerked open. Letting out a startled, gargled cry, he spit up the bitter drink. Confusion mounted in his eyes as they swung wildly to Enrique, his body thrashing as he attempted to sit upright. His right eye cracked open and he let out a sharp cry. Rising suddenly upward, he brought his hands to his mouth and swore.

Setting one hand against the protesting sheriff's shoulder, Enrique pressed him back down on the sofa. "Silencio," he whispered, leaning closer, pressing a fresh rag on the sheriff's lips. Enrique tried to absorb the sound of the sheriff's frantic breathing. "Sheriff, I know you took more than a hundred thousand. Tell me where it's at and I'll let your family live." He pulled the rag away from his mouth and dropped it on the floor next to the square box.

Narrowing his gaze, Sheriff Anderson studied the well-dressed Hispanic man who was before him. "I-I swear, I only have a hundred thousand." He licked his lips and swallowed. "That's all I found." He sniffled.

"Your choice." Enrique opened the plastic box. Reaching for the handle, he pulled the yellow and black circular table saw out of the case and snapped in the battery pack. He looked at both of his men who were approaching. "Pin him down, right arm on the table. He's gonna squirm."

Swinging his fist, Thumper punched the sheriff's swollen face. Grabbing him by the back of the neck, he slammed the sheriff on the table. The bucking sheriff wouldn't stay still so Thumper plopped his two hundred and fifty pounds on his back.

Using both hands, Draper quickly grabbed the sheriff's taut arm and pinned it on the table.

Two feet in front of the sheriff's face, Enrique pulled the trigger and the saw screamed.

"No!" Sheriff Anderson cried.

"It's too late," Enrique said. "Hold him still."

"Wait! I can get your money!"

"I bet you can." Enrique squeezed the trigger and slid the buzzing saw across the table.

*****

With the whiskey bottle in his lap, Sheriff Anderson sat on the couch between Thumper and Scott Draper. His amputated hand was resting on the coffee table in front of them. Enrique stood facing the sheriff whose nub was bandaged with a white towel and duct taped tightly.

"I'm gonna take your foot next," Enrique promised.

The sheriff took a pull from the whisky bottle. "I don't have your money, but I know who does."

"Who?"

"Frank Buccetti."

"Who the fuck is that?"

"The nigger who stole your money."

"Was he working for you?"

The sheriff took another drink of whiskey and stretched the truth. "No. I pulled him over that day. I smelled pot. H-he gave me a hundred thousand to let him go."

"You just extended your life a few hours. But if this is a lie, I'm gonna cut off the rest of your limbs. And then I'm gonna make you watch me do the same thing to your wife and grandchildren. After that, you'll know what the word affliction means."

16

Pressing on the gas in his four-door sedan, Thumper hopped in the fast lane and passed a semi-truck. Thumper's gaze was on the highway, but his ears were eavesdropping to the conversation Enrique was having on the phone.

"His name is Frank Buccetti," Enrique said in a low tone. "Half muck, half gringo.

Thumper slightly heard a muffled voice reply, but not enough to comprehend the words.

"Que bien," Enrique said. "I'll call back in an hour." Putting the phone in the breast pocket of his jacket, Enrique's head shifted to Thumper. "Slow down. We're in no rush. Might be a while before we get a location on him."

"Do you think the sheriff's telling the truth?" Thumper asked.

"He doesn't want any more of the Skilsaw."

Thumper shook his head. "People will say anything to stop the torture."

"That's what they say, but there's a science to it. Trust me. Most people tell the truth after the saw. Every once and a while, I get a tough hombre, then I just bring in a family member. They crack every time."

Thumper glanced at Enrique. "Hey, you're the pro. I'm just a back woods hick."

"When Martos calls back with his address and phone number, I'm gonna call this little mestizo. I want to hear the voice of a dead man."

*****

Finally home from work, Frankie turned the key and pushed the back door open. Two steps in the dark kitchen, he flicked the light switch on the wall. "What the fuck," he said under his breath because there was no light, only darkness. Stepping out of his muddy work boots, he let out a heavy sigh. The digital clock on the oven read 5:57 and the sliver of light guided Frankie through the kitchen. Turning the corner to the dining room, he hit another light switch. No light.

With his head tilted up at the light fixture, he heard the clack sound of a shotgun pumping. Sucking in air, a sharp pain of fear entered his lungs. He pivoted to the threatening noise. The shadow of an average sized man was standing in his living room. Frankie lifted his hands to chest level. "What do you want?"

"You know what I want, Frank," the shadow said with a slight Hispanic accent. "I found five thousand in a shoe in your closet. Where's the rest?"

"Y-You got the wrong house. I-I don't know what you're talking about."

Enrique snorted out a noise that sounded like a short laugh. "Que bien."

Frankie heard movement behind him. Swinging his right leg around, his body spun and faced a large black mass closing in on him. Crack. He felt a blunt object hit his knee. He went down on the coffee table, crushing its wooden legs. The attacker dropped the bat and descended on him.

Grabbing the man's jacket with both his fists, Frankie tried to force the heavy man off his chest. Both men were groaning. Frankie could feel incoming blows to his head, but he didn't let go until punch number four.

*****

Mariani's Jeep Cherokee crept through Frankie's alley and stopped at the driveway. "Who's got the Crown Vic?" he asked himself and stepped on the gas pedal, four tires spinning on a thin layer of snow. Turning right at the end of the block, he drove to the next street then turned right again. Finding a spot in front of Frankie's house, Mariani parked and killed the engine. He got out and sprinted to the front door, the cold wind pressing against his black parka.

Turning the doorknob, Mariani dropped his shoulder into the door, crossing the threshold into darkness. He felt a cold draft. The light switch wasn't working but his eyes adjusted quickly. Furniture was strewn across the floor, the coffee table in pieces. "What the fuck!" he bolted to the kitchen. The back door was wide open, and he saw red taillights streaking in the darkness of the alley. "Frankie!" he worded. "Oh, fuck."

Darting to the front door, Mariani whipped it open and ran full speed to his SUV.

He turned the key, threw the shifter in drive, and spun the vehicle around. "Fuck!" he said and hit his steering wheel repetitively as he raced down the block. At the stop sign, Mariani looked left and saw one set of taillights. Whipping his head to the right, the inclined road had at least four pair of red taillights in the distance. "Shit!" he dropped his fist on the center counsel. "Which way?" His head shifted back and forth.

Taking a few deep breaths, Mariani hit the gas and cranked the wheel to the right. Pressing the gas pedal to the floor, he closed the distance of three blocks and then climbed the gigantic hill, passing car after car. "Is that it?" he asked himself and let off the gas to navigate the s-curve on the steep incline.

Mariani's Jeep was in the slow lane, two vehicles behind the car in question. "That better be him," he said, gripping the steering wheel as tight as he could. *I should just run them off the road,* he thought and opened the center console.

Reaching inside, he felt the cold steel of his handgun. His fingers wrapped around the handle and he brought it to his lap. His hand let go and returned to the wheel. Mariani pressed down on the blinker and merged in the left lane, accelerating to fifty miles an hour. The first car he passed was a tiny crossover and the second was a loud pick-up truck.

"I'm coming for you, Frankie," Mariani said loudly, tailing just twenty feet behind the four-door sedan. *But it might be better to wait till they're off guard.*

*****

On the right shoulder of the highway, a big green sign flew past Mariani's Jeep. "Twenty miles to Virginia," he said to himself. "Where the hell are they bringing him?"

Tailing from three hundred yards away, Mariani saw red brake lights in front of him. His eyes widened and he tapped the brake pedal. Sucking in air, he watched the car put its blinker on and turn left into a black void in the woods.

"Fuck," Mariani said, slowing down. *If I turn now, they'll see my lights behind them,* he thought and drove past the dark secluded path. "Sorry, Frankie. Just hang in there." His mind kept cranking. *I'll follow their tracks in the snow.*

Mariani continued driving up the highway for a half a mile. There were no other cars on the road. Pumping the brakes, he pulled on the shoulder and brought the SUV to a rolling stop. He whipped a U-turn and slammed on the gas.

"I'm coming, Frankie."

The wall of black forest was endless. Glimmering in the distance was a white road sign with black letters. "White Face Road," Mariani said softly, turning down the unpaved road that was blanketed with snow.

Tire tracks guided his path. It was narrow, curvy, and heavily wooded. His foot feathered the gas, headlights cutting a sliver in the darkness. *Follow those tracks*, Mariani thought, his hands tightening on the wheel, his breaths short and steady.

After listening to his tires hum for about two miles, Mariani tapped the brakes twice. There was a fork in the road before a slight elevation in the landscape. Tire tracks lead to the left, down a dark path that was on flat land. The second path lead up the medium sized hill and the snow was pristine.

Slowing down to a crawl, he turned his lights off. Rolling slowly through darkness, his head snapped to a small light twinkling down the first path. "Is that an address sign?" he asked himself softly, "That's gotta be it. Tracks lead right to it."

Mariani jammed the shifter in park, his jeep now blocking the path. He turned the key back. Climbing in the rear seat, he geared up in camouflage hunting pants and matching boots. Pulling his thin black gloves on, he reached over the back seat and opened a large half-circle case. "Time to put my training to use," he said, grabbing his compound bow and quiver that was loaded with five razor tipped arrows.

*****

Inside the log cabin, Frankie was warm on a couch with his hands duct taped together. The orange glow from the fireplace flickered in the corner of the room. His legs were extended; right one too sore to bend. Laid back, his bound hands were resting on his lap. His puffy eyes locked on the amputated hand on the coffee table. Shifting his head to the bruised sheriff, he saw a familiar lawman who only had one hand.

This is a fucking nightmare, Frankie thought and turned back to the table, eyes falling upon the cordless saw with high velocity blood spatter on the plastic guard.

"Give him what he wants, Frank," the sheriff mumbled. "This guy plays for keeps." He lifted his duct taped stub of an arm for proof. The silver tape was wet with blood and dripping on the arm of the sofa.

"Don't talk to me," Frankie said softly, sweat rolling down his side. "I'm here because of you." He twisted his body and craned his neck to glance at the three ominous men in the kitchen. Straightening himself, he looked at the saw again. *He's right though,* he thought, his body secretly quaking from head to toe. *These guys are fucking animals.*

The floor creaked from Enrique's slow steps to the family room. Blocking the glow of the fire, he stood in front of Frankie. "Two options," he said. "Give me the money or get the saw."

The air that Frankie sucked in was sharp. He couldn't speak. His eyes bounced from the sheriff's severed hand to the battery-powered cutting machine. *You can have the money,* he thought but no words came out. He froze.

Enrique nodded. "Que bien," he said and stooped down to the table, right hand reaching for the saw. Gripping the handle with his fingers, his body rose tall, the heavy saw swaying at his side. He squeezed the trigger and the saw screamed for five long seconds as the circular blade spun. "Last chance." He paused and took a step forward. "Tell me where you hid the money, or your leg will look just like the sheriff's arm. If that doesn't work, I'm gonna do the same thing to your friends. And I'll make *you* watch. Comprende?"

Oh fuck, Frankie thought in his head as his trembling body shrunk. *It ain't worth it. It's only money.* "I-I don't wanna die," he said, his voice reduced to the sound of a severely punished child. "I'll…I'll bring you to the money. Just let me live."

Enrique took a determined step forward and bent down, just inches from Frankie's face. "It doesn't work like that, mestizo," he growled. "You saw my face. You saw their faces." He paused, lifting a hand toward the goons hovering behind the couch. "I *can't* let you live. But, *if* you bring me to my money, I'll give you my word that I won't torture you *or* your friends." He paused to let out a breath. "Don't look surprised; the sheriff told me everything. I hold all the cards."

Frankie's eyes were blinking repetitively. His breaths were rapid. His forearms were shaking uncontrollably, and his left shoulder was pressed against his ear as if he were trying to hide. With his teeth clattering, his eyes rivetted to the saw. "Take the money. It's yours. Please…Ju-just l-let me live." With quivering lips, Frankie's shaking head met Enrique's eyes. "I-I won't say shit. You…you have my word."

The corner of Enrique's mouth lifted. "Once I see the mu —" "A single thud noise from behind him broke his thought. Whipping his head over his shoulder, Enrique spun his body to face the front wall. Dropping the saw on the floor, Enrique darted to the kitchen.

*****

A minute prior, Giovanni Mariani was crouching in the foliage of the thick tree line. He was stalking the ancient log cabin from the high ground. He was panting from the hike up the hill and through the woods. His compound bow was in his hands. Two vehicles were in the driveway and one of them was a dark-colored Lincoln Crown Victoria. Lights were on inside the cabin and smoke was rising from the chimney. "Two cars," he whispered to himself. "Probably four guys with guns. Maybe more."

The loud whine sound of a saw jerked Mariani's body. "Fuck!" he said under his breath, the noise stopping as suddenly as it started. With widening eyes, Mariani rose, his muscles tightening. Adrenaline was flowing through his veins as he held an arrow in his throbbing fingers. He readied the missile, drew back the bow wire, and looked at his target. He steadied his shaking arm from the resistance of the bow. Taking aim at the cabin, he inhaled a slow, deep breath. Mariani let the arrow fly into the side of the log cabin. He could clearly hear the thud from his den.

Dropping his right knee in the snow, Mariani loaded another arrow, eyes locked on the front door. "Come take a look," he said, heart pounding in his chest, breathing in short spurts. Like the trees and bushes around him, Mariani felt each gust of wind move him slightly.

Mariani's body jerked at the sight of the door swinging open. "Holy shit," he whispered, eyes locked on a man in black. The thin-framed man was holding a black handgun at his side. His feet were planted, but his head was on a swivel. Suddenly, the man's gaze froze. He was facing the black bush that Mariani was lurking in.

There's no way he can see me, Mariani thought, letting out a breath as the man started walking toward the two vehicles in the driveway. *You're mine now, asshole.*

Mariani rose and drew back once more. His sight was slightly bobbing up and down. "Breathe," he whispered to himself, his chest raising and falling slowly. The bow was now steady. The sight was locked on the man's back. "You're done," Mariani whispered, his trigger finger twitching just once.

The black razor-tripped arrow darted to and through the target's neck at the speed of sound. From the bush, Mariani watched the man faceplant in the snow. "Damn, that dude's fucked up!" Mariani said and pulled out another arrow.

*****

Frankie gazed out the window. Darkness and snowfall were all he saw. At the sound of a low buzz of commotion, his head snapped to the kitchen. His two captors were huddled together. The Hispanic man's mouth was flapping, and the bald man's head was nodding. Frankie opened his ear.

"He would have been back by now," Enrique told Thumper.

"Give him a minute," Thumper said. "He's probably walking around the cabin."

"Go out the back door," Enrique told Thumper. "Creep around the side. Come right back."

Thumper nodded his head and grabbed the shotgun off the counter. Resting it on his shoulder, he turned and opened the back door. Lowering the gun, he scanned the back yard. He tucked his exposed bald head in his shoulders as a reflex from the frigid wind. Descending the icy steps, he glanced at the half-frozen lake. Swinging the barrel toward the left, he crunched through hardened snow toward the driveway.

Thumper bent his knees and slowed his pace to a creep. Scraping his jacket on the side of the cabin, he inched his way to the front corner. He peeked and then pulled his head back. Pausing for two deep breaths, Thumper exposed his head again, scanning the front yard and then the driveway. A still body was in the snow next to the Crown Victoria.

"Scott!" Thumper yelled at his cousin who was lying face down in the snow. Blitzing to his side, he dropped to his knees.

"Scott!" He grabbed his jacket and rolled him over. Black blood was flowing from Scott Draper's neck. "What the fu—" Thumper collapsed on top of his cousin. Mariani had hit his target.

*****

With Enrique holed up in the kitchen, Frankie saw a pin hole of light in the dark tunnel of his mind. *It's been at least three minutes since that dude screamed outside,* he thought, eyes shifting from the frosty window to the sheriff, and then dropping to his bound hands. *I don't think them guys are coming back.* He twisted his arms to try to break the tape around his wrists, but it was too thick to tear.

Frankie glanced at the sheriff whose head was shaking in disapproval.

"Don't do it," the sheriff warned softly.

Craning his neck to look in the kitchen, Frankie saw the back of the Hispanic kidnapper who was peering out the window. Separated from his gang, the man looked fidgety as he bounced from window to window. Vile curse words were spewing under Enrique's breath, and he was even growling at times.

Frankie's heartbeat was pulsating throughout his body. He could hear thumping in his ears. Quickly turning back to face the front door, Frankie stabilized his quaking body with three slow breaths. *He's more concerned with his men than me,* he thought and turned his head to the right. *This sheriff better keep his mouth shut when I cut this tape.*

With his eyes on the sheriff, Frankie slowly dragged his bound hands up to his fifth pocket. His fingers were shaking as he slowly slid the knife out. Flicking the blade open with his thumb, he rested the butt of the knife against his lap and punctured a hole in the tape. *Just a little more on the bottom…*

Slipping the blade between his wrists, Frankie pretended that his hands were still bound. The tape on the top was still pristine, but the bottom had been cut free.

Frankie turned his head to the side and saw Enrique tramping toward him with a pistol in his hand.

"What the fuck are you looking at?" Enrique asked with a low menacing growl.

Frankie straightened himself. A rush of adrenaline was flowing though him. His muscles grew tight with the sound of Enrique's footsteps behind him.

Enrique planted himself three feet in front of Frankie and the sheriff. Raising his gun, he shifted his aim from Frankie to Sheriff Anderson. "You have no worth to me," he said and popped his gun twice, the earsplitting thunder reverberating off the walls.

Flinching at the explosion of sound, Frankie felt a peppering of red mist hit the right side of his face. Scrunching up his cheek muscles, he saw the sheriff's body toppling over in his direction. Frankie jerked forward in his seat and the sheriff crashed behind him. Tilting his head upward, he saw smoke funneling from the barrel of the gun. Looking past the weapon, he stared into the clenched face of the man who held it.

It's now or never, Frankie thought, inhaling air through his nostrils. With a burst of pent-up passion, Frankie sprung up and batted Enrique's gun out of his hand. Charging forward, Frankie busted the tape and drove him back. His shackles were now broken. His eyes were black with rage. He could hear the collar of his shirt being ripped as they collided against the wall. Tucking his chin, he could feel incoming punches on the top of his head.

Lowering his right arm, Frankie gripped the small knife tightly and drove it into Enrique's mid-section. Before he could pull it out, Enrique socked him in the jaw. His brain shook and he suddenly felt a sharp pain on the side of his head. *Fuck,* he thought and staggered back, the knife sliding out of Enrique's stomach.

"You're fucking dead." Enrique reached inside his jacket and pressed his hand against the wound. Wincing in pain, he growled like a cornered beast.

Shuffling backwards, Frankie tasted blood in his mouth. He cocked his arm back and held it in place. Both the knife and Frankie's hand were red with dripping blood. "Take two steps forward."

"Drop the knife and I'll let your family live."

"Fuck you!" Frankie barked and then lowered his stance. Putting his left leg forward, he protected his bruised right knee with the knife.

Enrique charged Frankie and stepped into the swinging three-inch blade. The man's fists were flying. His lips were snarling.

Twisting the knife in Enrique's side, Frankie absorbed an incoming blow with his left forearm. A fraction of a second later, his chin got rattled and it felt like brick. His legs felt numb. Another overhand right came, and Frankie collapsed to the floor, the knife bouncing by Enrique's feet.

Enrique kicked the knife against wall. Squinting, he let out a low groan. With his enemy curled up on the floor, Enrique swooped down to grab his gun.

Frankie's vision was blurry with stars. He could hear cursing in Spanish. *I'm fucked,* he thought and blindly scooted against the wall.

*****

Mariani's back was pressed against the front wall of the log cabin. A loud Spanish voice was coming from the other side of the door. Mariani's handgun was close to his chest. Stepping in front of the door, he kicked it wide open. Snapping his arm fully extended, he looked down the barrel of his gun. A black-haired man in dark clothes was spinning to meet the noise. *Not Frankie,* Mariani thought and his gun cracked four times. The bullets stopped the Hispanic man's spin abruptly, but his gun erupted once on the way down.

The wild shot clipped Mariani in the hat. With a thud, he fell inside the cabin. The cold wind rushed inside the open door and over his still body.

Slowly rising in the lingering cloud of sulfuric smoke, Frankie's breathing was rushed but his hands were steady on the gun he'd picked up from the floor. Aiming it at Enrique's gurgling form, he lowered his eyebrows and fired a single shot in the back of his head. "Buenas noches," he said and squeezed off one more. The body jerked once. "Checkmate."

Breathing heavily, Frankie stood, his hand gripping the handle of the gun. He stared down at the dead man at his feet and shook his head. A low groan from behind him sent Frankie twisting around, his eyes widening when they latched on to Mariani. "Bro!" he cried, rushing to his friend's side. His hands shook now, when they'd been steady moments before.

Frankie dropped to his knees, his free hand reaching out to touch Mariani's back. Dropping the gun, he instinctively checked for wounds. "Are you okay? Fuck, talk to me…"

Laying on his side, Mariani grumbled incoherently but managed to pull his feet from the doorway. When the door closed, he propped himself up against it. The gash on his head was gushing blood down his face. His eyes were fluttering. Frankie's friend was breathing, but the wound needed immediate attention.

As Frankie put his hand on the wound to stop the bleeding, his heart sunk. *This all my fault,* he thought in his head.

It sounded like Mariani was saying something under his breath, so Frankie listened closely.

"'Merica," Mariani rambled softly. "Misty is a whore… Never be a rat."

Smiling slightly, Frankie was about to respond when a sudden movement caught his attention. Without thought, he found the gun back in his hand as he spun around. It was Sheriff Anderson, and he was crawling toward the kitchen door. Sticking out his arm, Frankie fired a warning shot through the window and the sheriff froze still.

"Don't fucking move!" Frankie held the gun in the direction of the bleeding sheriff. With one eye trained on the sheriff, he shifted to take in Mariani once more.

"Look at me!" Frankie said to Mariani. Holding him up, he gently patted his cheek several times to get his attention. A moment later, his eye lids opened. "Are you okay?"

Trembling, Frankie's hands searched out and returned to the source of blood. "G, can you hear me? Come on, bro. Talk to me. Mariani. Wake up."

Wincing in pain, Mariani managed a weak nod as he touched the wound on his head. Looking at the blood on his fingers, he brought them to his mouth. Once the blood touched his tongue, an explosion of adrenaline shot through his veins. "Where is he?" he asked with a low rumbling voice. Rising slowly, the muscles on his face were twitching as he shook off Frankie's attempt to sit him back down.

Mariani was staggering in place, head declined toward the dead man on the floor. "You should have killed me," he mumbled with slow stumbling movements. Taking a few steps forward, he held his gun at his side.

Shoving the pistol to the back of Enrique's kneecap, Mariani pulled the trigger. The sound of the gunshot was muffled and there were no screams.

"He's dead, man," Frankie said.

"I don't think so," Mariani said and fired four more shots into Enrique's back. "Fucking punk."

After a few shakes of his head, Frankie fixed his gaze on Sheriff Anderson. "You're pretty fucking stupid," he said with his nose flared. "You sold me out to save your ass."

"Hey you," Mariani said. "Sheriff Asshole. You're next."

The sheriff stuck out his stub of an arm. "He...he cut my hand off," he pleaded. "I-I need to go to the hospital. I'm bleeding to death."

"Shut the fuck up, gramps!" Mariani yelled, "One more fucking word." He pointed his gun at the sheriff who was sitting on the floor with his back against the couch. There was the finest of tremors noticeable as he aimed the barrel straight between the sheriff's eyes.

Frankie turned his head to Mariani and nodded slightly. "Look at my arm," Sheriff Anderson whimpered in desperation. "When I t-tell them you saved my life, I'll be telling the truth. You did nothing wrong here. These guys are fucking barbarians."

Growing impatient, Mariani kicked over the table and the severed hand tumbled on the floor. Three loud reports came from Mariani's gun and Sheriff Anderson fell over.

Each gunshot made Frankie flinch even though he knew it was coming. His jaw dropped.

Mariani slipped his gun inside his jacket pocket. "We couldn't trust him."

"I know," Frankie nodded. "What now?"

Mariani pointed out the window. "I killed two guys outside with my bow," he said. "We're gonna have to drag 'em inside." He then gestured to the floor. "I left a lot of DNA. We're burning this bitch to the ground, but first I need to wrap something around my head."

*****

Frankie pressed his torn undershirt to Mariani's head wound. "Hold that," he said and started wrapping duct tape around his head. After three laps, Frankie ripped the tape. "Good as new."

"Thanks," Mariani said and pulled his winter hat over his crudely bandaged head. "How do I look?"

"You look like a fucking champion," Frankie said and looked around the room. His eyes landed on Enrique. *I bet he's got my phone and money in his pocket,* he thought and squatted beside him.

"What are you doing?"

Frankie pulled out a fat wad of cash from of the dead man's pocket. "Dude searched my house and took my loot."

A slow smile of comprehension lit up Mariani's face. "What else he got on him?"

Reaching in Enrique's breast pocket, Frankie pulled out a plastic hotel card key and a cell phone. "Bingo! My phone and his hotel key. I bet he's got a shit load of money in his room."

"Nice! What hotel?"

"Great Lake Suites."

"All right, let's pile up these bodies and set this shit on fire. Then we'll go search his hotel room. I don't think he'll miss anything."

*****

Leaning against the wind, Frankie and Mariani gazed at the orange glow that was flickering through the windows of the cabin. With each passing moment, the bodies were being cremated in a crude fashion. It was the moment they'd been longing for: the peace after the storm.

"It's over," Frankie said. "You saved my life. Thank you."

"Just glad I got here when I did."

"Me, too. He was gonna cut me to pieces."

Mariani hit Frankie's arm. "I kinda like settin' shit on fire," he said. "It feels good. Doesn't it?"

"I've never felt so good," he said. "I feel like a man who just cheated death."

17

Mariani turned the windshield wipers up a notch to match the heavy snowfall. Shifting his head to the passenger seat, he saw Frankie gazing out the side window. "Ivan's house?" he asked.

"Yeah, head there," Frankie said. "We'll clean up your wound a little bit. I think you should go to the hospital though."

"Fuck that," Mariani said. "We gotta run up in that hotel and get paid."

"What about the cameras?"

"We'll wear some ball caps and sunglasses."

"It's too risky. Maybe we could bribe Ivan to do it?"

Mariani shook his head. "Hell, no," he said. "We can't involve other people. Just me and you, brother."

"He probably wouldn't wanna go anyways."

After a few moments of critical thought, Mariani blew out an audible breath. "You know what? You might be right. I don't like cameras, and what if that asshole has a whore staying there? We might need a pawn."

"If not Ivan, who?"

"How 'bout Los or Marcel?"

"They're both probably cuddled up with their girls right about now."

"I don't think they'd want to be on camera either. Hmm."

Frankie shifted his head. "Ivan's crazy and everything, but he is resourceful."

"I think he'd sell us out in a heartbeat. I don't trust him."

"I've known him more than twenty years. He's shown me nothing but loyalty."

"He's never been tested. I trust *you*, cuz you've been tested a hundred times."

*****

Mariani parked the Jeep in front of Ivan's garage, and they both got out. Slightly limping, Frankie cut through the wind and snow. As he approached the front porch, he saw the door crack open.

"You're back," Ivan said, peeking his pale face out the door. "Is everything okay?"

"Sorry, I didn't call." Frankie stopped in the middle of the porch. "We were in the neighborhood."

Ivan waved his hand. "Come on in, homie," he said. "I didn't recognize the Jeep."

"It's mine," Mariani said, looking through Ivan's thick wire-framed glasses to meet his shifty blue eyes.

"That's a nice ride," Ivan said and turned.

They followed him inside the dark house, their steps illuminated only by the glare of the television. Entering the living room, Ivan sat down in his favorite chair before lighting up two cigarettes. After a big drag, he held his breath and pressed a button on his watch that made a beep noise.

"It's fuckin' cold out there," Mariani said, breaking the ice.

Holding in the smoke, Ivan covered his mouth till his face turned red. A dry cough forced out a gray cloud of toxic smoke. "I haven't been outside all day," Ivan said and kept coughing. "It's too cold out there."

Frankie tilted his left hand. "So…Ivan, listen, we stopped here for a couple reasons," he said, his voice controlled as he continued. "We, ah, listen man. We could really use your help."

Ivan hesitated before he spoke. "What do you need?" he asked and leaned back.

"It's a job, my friend," Frankie said. "A favor. It pays good, too." He paused dramatically and met eyes with Ivan who had a blank look on his face. "We're gonna go to the basement and let you think about it. When I come up in fifteen minutes, I hope you're ready to go."

"What's the job?"

"We're gonna rob someone who did me wrong. That's all you need to know."

"I'd rather just stay warm and smoke but let me think about it. I don't like when people do you wrong."

*****

Twenty-five minutes later, Frankie opened the basement door and entered the living room. Pulling a black suitcase on wheels, Frankie looked casual in an old pair of baggy blue jeans and a black hooded sweatshirt. "You're smoking the filter again, Iv'," he said. "Put that shit out. Let's go. We need you."

Ivan's cigarette was burnt down to the butt, yet still, he took another puff, its contents sizzling and turning bright orange. "How much will I make?" He croaked out a cloud of smoke.

"Five thousand up front," Frankie said and handed him a wrinkled envelope full of cash. "And another five thousand if you find what I'm looking for."

"Okay, homie. I'll ride with you." He lifted his wide body out of the chair.

Nodding to Ivan, Frankie smiled. "'Atta boy, Ivan," he murmured, clasping him on the shoulder. "Grab a ball cap and let's bounce."

The hard thud of footsteps coming up the stairs announced Mariani's presence. His wounds were freshly cleaned and newly dressed in gauze; duct taped under a black winter hat.

"All right boys. Let's do this." Mariani zipped up a faded black work jacket Frankie had found in the closet.

*****

In the parking lot of the Great Lake Suites hotel, Frankie sat in the driver seat of Ivan's rusty minivan. Turning first to meet eyes with a skeptical Mariani in the passenger seat, Frankie then craned his neck to coach Ivan.

"Now, remember what we talked about," Frankie said slowly and clearly. "Room 713. You have the key. It's your room; just walk in like you own the place."

"Got it," Ivan said softly, but in a stronger voice than usual. "713...Find the goods and get out." He clapped his hands once and grinned.

"It's in there somewhere," Frankie said. "He probably hid it. Look under the bed, in the closet, under the sink, and in the back of the toilet." He paused momentarily. "Look everywhere—but if you find drugs, just leave that shit for the cops to find. It will keep them off our trail."

Mariani turned in his seat and gave him a pair of thin leather gloves. "Put these on," he said and then sat back down in his seat. Reaching underneath his hat, he pressed his fingers against his wound, wincing ever so slightly.

"We'll be right here waiting for ya, bro." Frankie nodded his head a few times to give him encouragement. "You're one of a kind, Iv'. Only you could pull this off. We're counting on you, brother. If you're not out here in twenty minutes, you can count on us to have your back."

"I'll set my watch for fifteen minutes, so I won't be late," Ivan said.

With adrenaline pumping through his veins, Ivan secured his plain black baseball cap low on his head. Grabbing the suitcase on wheels, he got out of the van, adjusted his glasses, and then bowed to Frankie and Mariani.

*****

Standing in front of Enrique's suite, Ivan pulled out the card key from his navy-blue jacket. Sliding the card into the slot, he watched a small light on the panel turn green and, with that, he slowly turned the handle.

The lights are on, Ivan thought and took a short step forward. *Is someone here?* Freezing still in the doorway, his eyes cautiously swept the area—posh leather couches, a small kitchen, and even a glass dining room table.

His head tilted sideways. Rushing to the sofa, he lifted up each cushion. *Nothing,* he thought and waddled to the kitchen. After opening every cupboard, he then searched the refrigerator.

"Where the fuck is it?" Ivan asked himself and slammed the door to the fridge. Scanning the executive suite, he marched to the oak bedroom door that was cracked open.

When he opened the sturdy door, he rubbed his hand on the wall to find the switch. Flicking it on, his head snapped to a heap of clothes on the bed. *That's it.*

Ivan put his hand to his chest, feeling the irregular heartbeat with his fingers. Rushing to the bed, he swiped his arm and clothes fell to the floor. A black suitcase was resting on the bed. Ivan quickly unzipped it and found that it was filled with bricks of narcotics.

Don't take the drugs, Ivan remembered Frankie's orders. Pulling out his knife, he cut open a brick, spilled it on the bed, and then buried his nose in it like a fiend. After a big sniff, he stood tall, shoved a brick into the armpit of his jacket, and then he chuckled softly.

Resting on the bed next to the pile of drugs was a flip phone and he grabbed it. "My first cell phone," he said and put it in his pocket.

Ivan ransacked everything in the bedroom then headed for the connecting bathroom. Stepping inside, he immediately reached for the little door underneath the sink. Swinging it open, his gaze caught an olive-green backpack wedged up in one corner. Eyes widening, he grabbed it and felt its weight. Unzipping it, he let out a deep breath; the backpack was filled to the brim with stacks of cash. He raised his eyebrows then zipped it back up. "That's a lot of fucking money," Ivan said, and then listened to his inner conscience. *No one will ever know if you take two stacks right now,* he thought. *You deserve it. Frankie won't give you your fair share.*

Ivan shoved two stacks into his underwear and then left the bathroom. Crossing the bedroom, he made a beeline to the front door. Placing the backpack inside of the suitcase he'd brought with him, he then zipped it shut. As he touched the door handle, Ivan's eyes scanned the room one last time and then, suddenly, they swiveled back to the kitchen. *The oven.*

Ivan hurried to the stainless-steel appliance and whipped open the door. Inside was a suitcase similar to Frankie's, so he yanked it out and set it down. His heart was pounding almost painfully in his chest. Unzipping the flap, Ivan's droopy eyes burst open. *Score!* he thought and put two more stacks in his waistline. *Frankie's gonna be proud.*

While pulling the suitcase toward the door, the phone in his pocket started ringing. Ivan stopped in front of the sliding glass window and pulled it out. Looking at the screen, he read the name: M.

"Hello," Ivan said in a childlike voice.

"Who is this?" a man with a deep Hispanic accent asked.

"Who is this?" Ivan mocked.

"Where's Enrique?"

Ivan's watch beeped and he lifted his wrist. "I'm sorry, I think I'm out of time. Good luck finding your friend. But I think he's dead. Not quite sure though."

"Tell me your name!"

"I'd rather not say. I'm kinda in a hurry."

"I'm gonna find you and melt your fucking eyeballs with a torch."

Ivan giggled. "That doesn't sound too fun. Why don't you call back when you have something nicer to say? Maybe we could be friends."

*****

Twenty minutes had passed since Ivan had entered the hotel. Frankie and Mariani were restless in the van. Mariani staring into the passenger side rearview mirror and Frankie completely turned around in his seat.

"What the fuck is he doing in there?" Mariani asked.

Frankie shook his head. "I don't know," he said. "He should've been out by now."

"He probably found Enrique's dope. I bet he's all spun out on that shit."

"I hope he's smarter than that."

"Fuckin' A," Mariani hit the door panel. "I knew it. Now we gotta—"

Frankie cut him off. "Here he comes!"

Mariani watched his mirror, the beginnings of a smile etched out across his face. "You see that?"

"What?"

A moment before Ivan opened up the sliding side door of the van, Mariani said: "Your boy has two suitcases."

Ivan got in and slid the door shut.

"You made it!" Frankie said, clunking the transmission in reverse.

"Now, do I get some seeds in my tummy?" Ivan asked, wiggling his eyebrows.

They all erupted in laughter.

"No," Frankie said, shifting the van in drive. "But can you please tell us what's in the suitcases?"

"There's one million, two hundred and eighty thousand altogether," Ivan replied.

Mariani turned in his seat. "How the fuck do you know that?"

"I told you, he's a genius," Frankie insisted. "I bet the count's accurate." He turned his attention to Ivan. "Did you talk to anyone?"

"Who would wanna talk to me?" Ivan said, smiling briefly at the thought of his secret phone call.

"Good," Frankie said. "Good job, bro. Now, we need to get back to your house as soon as possible."

"Frankie," Ivan said. "I-I was wondering…" He paused in mid thought.

With his left hand firmly gripped to the steering wheel, Frankie looked in the rearview mirror at Ivan who was sulking. "What's on your mind, bro?"

"Since I brought you one point two mill', I thought I'd ask for a raise."

Frankie chuckled and Mariani shook his head in contempt.

"Not now, Ivan." Frankie gripped both hands on the wheel. "I'm trying to concentrate on the road. Your bald ass tires suck in the snow. We'll discuss your cut when we get home."

"But," Ivan stuttered, then spat out his selfish thoughts. "I…I just think it would be fair if we split it three ways."

"Ivan!" Mariani shouted. "Shut the fuck up!"

Ivan squirmed in his seat, clearly shaken from the sound of Mariani's thunderous voice.

"Let me drive," Frankie said, dropping his fist on the center console. "You'll get your fair share, but keep in mind — Mariani took a bullet to get this money." He glanced in the rearview then added. "Don't get all greedy on me, Ivan." And the debate ended abruptly.

*****

As they reached the top of the shining little city on the hill, Mariani cracked his window.

"Fuckin' cold out, eh," Mariani said and sparked a cigarette.

Frankie wiggled his toes. "My feet are freezing," he said. "Your heat sucks, man."

"Maybe I'll get a new car," Ivan said rudely, "when I get my raise."

"Are you fucking dense?" Frankie asked, "I just fuckin' told you…I'm trying to concentrate on the fucking road. I can barely see ten feet in front of me with all this snow."

Mariani turned around. "This is your last warning," he said. "Keep your mouth shut or you ain't getting shit."

Ivan tucked his chin and bit his lip. *I don't think they wanna fuck with me,* he thought. *I make one call and they're dead.*

Exiting the city, the boys traveled down a quiet country road. There were no buildings now, no fellow cars on the road, only the whip of snow and the company of evergreen trees on each side of them. The only light visible was Ivan's dull headlights. Behind them, there was only blackness.

Until there wasn't.

"Fuck," Frankie cried, one hand violently hitting the steering wheel at the sight of flashing blue and red lights shining in the rearview mirror. "We're getting pulled over." He paused momentarily. "Iv', don't say a word, not one peep." He pulled to the side of the road and came to a complete stop.

Frankie blinked, his heart still pounding too hard, his fingers shaking as he tried to catch his breath. They weren't getting pulled over after all, the cop flew right past them.

"Fucking pig," Mariani cried, his arms gesturing emptily.

"That fucker almost gave me a heart attack," Frankie said, still parked on the side of the road.

Mariani hit Frankie in the arm. "What are you doing? Let's get the fuck out of here."

"My heart needs to slow down," Frankie said. "My nerves are wrecked." He lit up a cigarette, cracked the window, and then put the transmission in drive. They followed in the snow tracks from the squad car, but at a much slower rate of speed.

"I feel ya'," Mariani said. "I thought we were fucked."

Frankie took another drag from his cigarette. "Maybe we needed that," he said. "We've been too lucky. This is too good to be true."

With his eyes narrowed, Frankie kept his attention on the icy, unplowed highway as the van inched closer to Ivan's house.

From the back seat, Ivan mumbled something that no one understood.

"Whud' you just say, dude?" Frankie said.

Ivan spoke up. "I said, I want one third."

"Shut the fuck up!" Frankie barked. "I'll settle this right fucking now. You ain't getting one third. But I'll give you ten percent if you can keep your rotten mouth shut."

Ivan leaned forward. "If you don't give me what I want, I'm gonna make a call."

Frankie craned his neck to look at Ivan. "Fuck you. Now you ain't getting shit."

Mariani braced himself. "Heads up!" he shouted to Frankie. "Deer!"

Frankie's eyes snapped forward once more, his body stiffening on instinct as he started to pump the brakes. The bald tires slid helplessly, uselessly. The headlights put the buck in a trance—motionless and unable to escape imminent doom. Its eyes were glistening, and its rack was huge. Frankie downshifted as a desperate attempt to stop the skidding.

There wasn't enough time. Slamming on the brakes, Frankie flinched as the animal and van collided, the buck exploding on the front bumper. Tumbling on the hood, it smashed into the windshield and flew over the top. As the van continued to slide, the beast landed on the road behind them. The van then veered into the ditch, splashing snow in the air.

For a moment no one moved; disorientated and shocked, they stared blindly out the busted windshield. Frankie's eyes locked first on Mariani and then back at Ivan. The only one not wearing a seatbelt, Ivan was crumpled up on the floor, his hands pressed against his mouth.

"You guys, okay?" Frankie asked, then he unbuckled his seat belt and looked around.

Lifting his head, Ivan removed his hands from his mouth, and then licked his upper lip. "I-I like the way my blood tastes," he mumbled.

"How 'bout you?" Frankie looked at Mariani.

"Yeah." Mariani touched his head and winced in pain. "I…I'm alright. The van's stuck though. We'll never get it out. We should start walking. It's gonna get cold real quick — and we got at least five miles to walk."

"Let's call Carlos," Frankie said, then he pulled his phone out of his pocket.

"The reception out here is shitty," Mariani said solemnly, then zipped up his jacket to his chin. "You'll never get through."

"Fuck," Frankie said with his phone in hand. "You're right. We're fucked." He turned to look at Ivan and saw blood pooling around his mouth.

"What are we gonna do?" Ivan whimpered.

"I'm gonna send Carlos a text message," Frankie said. "If he gets it, he'll find us…if not, we'll be walking all night."

"Should we stash the loot?" Mariani asked.

Frankie tilted his head. "You don't think we should bring it with us?" he said, "What if we lost it?"

"That would suck," Mariani said gravely. "But it would be a lot easier of a walk."

"We could lock it in the van," Frankie said, turning to look at Ivan who was moaning in the back.

"This asshole just threatened us," Mariani said. "Do you think I'd trust him with it?"

"He's mentally unstable," Frankie said. "It's clinical. He lashes out when he doesn't get his way. Probably needs his meds."

"That's no excuse," Mariani said. "You know what? Fuck it. Ivan, give me those fucking gloves."

Ivan took off the gloves and threw them of the floor. "Take

'em."

Mariani swooped them up and gave one to Frankie. "Here, pull the suitcase with this hand. Put the other in your sleeve. It's gonna be a long walk."

"Thanks. Good idea."

"All right," Mariani said and took in a deep breath. "Let's do this. We just gotta keep moving." He turned his attention to Ivan who was wheezing. "Look at me." He pointed at Ivan. "You threatened us. I hope you freeze to death. Fucking punk."

Ivan held his head and curled up in a ball on the back seat. "You're gonna come back to get me, and you're gonna give me one third. And if you don't, I'm gonna make the call."

"Ivan!" Frankie said, "Who the fuck you gonna call?"

"You'll see."

Mariani hit Frankie's coat. "Fuck this snake. Let him freeze."

"All right, Ivan," Frankie said. "You stay here. I know you don't mean what you're saying. You're confused, but we'll figure something out. You just gotta stay calm and stop making threats." He started taking his jacket off. "I'm not your enemy. Everything's gonna be okay."

"What are you doing?" Mariani said with a scrunched-up face.

"The guy's gushing blood," Frankie said, "I'm gonna give him my shirt, just like I did for you."

Mariani compressed his lips briefly. "He threatened us twice, man. I'd let him bleed out."

*****

Twenty minutes later, Frankie stopped walking. He let go of the suitcase and his hands found the warmth of his mouth. Breathing heavily for almost a minute created temporary comfort to his frozen fingers. "This sucks!" he raised his voice above the howling wind.

"This ain't shit," Mariani muttered with tinged lips that were white and cracking.

Frankie rubbed his hands together. "My hands are fuckin' freezing."

"Here." Mariani handed him the other glove. "Get it nice and warm for me."

Mariani paused to scan the area. He saw nothing but pine trees and darkness and snowflakes shooting in his face. Turning to face Frankie, he lowered his head. "You know Ivan's gonna be a problem, right?"

"I'll fix it. He's easy to pacify."

"Make him understand, or I'll have to put him down."

"He's harmless. Trust me. I've seen him act like this before. He's just off his meds."

*****

Darkness fell like a wet, heavy blanket as they marched forward, their breaths wheezing out thickly. Fear kept them silent as the wind howled a menacing tune. Their wet pants were completely stiff, and their bodies were frozen to the bone. Instinctively, both men walked with their heads down to avoid the blistering wind and shards of icy snow.

"Dude," Frankie said loudly. "We probably only walked two miles so far."

"That seems about right," Mariani said. "It's been about an hour. You still hangin' in there, Strunz?"

"This ain't shit," Frankie said as he leaned into the wind.

"The body, it...it starts to break down after an hour of subzero temperatures—"

"We've got time yet." Frankie assured him.

"Hypothermia, severe frostbite, gangrene…"

"Stop it, man. We ain't gonna die in this shit…."

Mariani stopped and faced Frankie. "You're right, we ain't gonna die tonight. But tomorrow, those people we set on fire — their people will start wondering where they're at."

*****

They didn't see the glare until it rose directly behind them, a beam of light suddenly exploding the landscape. They both stopped in their tracks, whipping their heads around to see headlights in the distance. The low rumble of a truck wasn't heard until it was almost upon them.

"We're saved!" Frankie said and pumped his fists.

"Hopefully, they stop," Mariani said. "Start waving your arms."

As the vehicle got closer, they noticed that it was a black pick-up truck with dealer plates. The windows were dark, but they could see two people inside. When it pulled up to them, the driver-side window rolled down.

"You boys need a lift?" Carlos shouted.

Frankie and Mariani put their hands in the air and jumped up and down. They hooted and hollered, and then they hurried to the shelter of the warm truck.

"What's up, boys?" Ivan said playfully. "I need my meds."

"You'll be home soon, my friend," Frankie promised. "Are you okay? Do you need to see a doctor?"

Ivan started laughing. "I hate doctors," he whined as Carlos sent the truck heading north.

18

At a quarter after seven in the morning, Special Agent Abbott climbed a steep hillside avenue in his unmarked government car. Agent Clark was sitting in the passenger seat. The horizon had just cracked a sliver of light, but there was still no arrest in their case.

Agent Abbott briefly stopped at a stop sign. "We'll find out right away," he said and turned right at the intersection. "If he says he was at home on the morning of November 28, we'll know he's hiding something."

"Set the trap," Agent Clark said. "There's no way he knows his vehicle was caught on camera at Joe's Diner."

"Once Mr. Buccetti gets caught in the lie, I want you to inform him that he just lied to a federal agent. Tell him it's a felony — and that — with the points on his record, he'd serve at least a year in a federal prison."

"If he tries to play dumb, I'll show him Hank Lindberg's phone records from the day before the murder. He'll see his number circled in red ink."

"That should make him sweat."

Clark laughed shortly and shook his head. "It just doesn't make sense. Why would he call Hank if he was gonna take part in his murder?"

"Coincidence. He probably just called Hank because he

needed some meth. Or maybe he needed some work done on his truck. So far, there's nothing that links him to the killers, but his connection to Hank…definitely makes him a person of interest."

"He might have stopped by and found the bodies."

"That could be the case, but you'd think he'd call 911."

Clark let out a deep breath. "He's got quite the criminal record. Maybe he didn't want to talk to the cops. Might have been rolling dirty."

Abbott slowed down and turned left up a steep incline. "Hopefully, he coughs up some information. Because as of right now, we can't prove Thumper hired the killers."

"I'm confident Thumper had Hank killed. He's got the motive; he's got phone contacts with Hank *and* the hitmen."

"On that point, I'm in agreement. Unfortunately, it's just not enough to put him away."

Clark punched the palm of his hand. "We need someone to flip on him."

"That's where little Frankie comes into play. He might be willing to say anything to stay out of jail."

"If he knows Hank, I bet he knows Thumper."

"I didn't see Thumper's number on his phone records, but he probably has a burner phone, too. Dirtbags are smart these days. They all got burner phones."

Clark nodded, turning his head slightly. "You're right. I checked the call logs on the burner phones found at the crime scene. Almost every incoming and outgoing call was from an unknown number. All burner phones. Untraceable."

"Why do you think Frankie called Hank with his personal phone?"

"Maybe he's stupid."

At the next street, Abbott turned the car right and looked

for a small house on the lower side. Two or three pine trees stood tall in every yard and made it hard to see the houses in the twilight.

"I was just thinking," Abbott said. "I bet I could get a FISA warrant. Foreign numbers are on the call logs."

"Now you're thinking. Might lead us to a bigger fish than Frank Buccetti."

Shifting his head to the left, Abbott slowed down almost to a stop. "1917?"

"Yeah, that's it." Clark pointed. "Right there."

"Okay," Abbott said and parked. "Hopefully we caught Mr. Buccetti before work."

Clark grabbed his clipboard and pushed open the door.

Abbott got out and they both crossed the narrow street, taking long strides with each step.

"No footprints," Clark said.

"No lights on," Abbott said.

Clark climbed three steps and knocked on the storm door five times.

"Walk in the front porch," Abbott said. "He can't hear you."

Clark swung open the door and they both walked inside.

"I'll show ya how to knock." Abbott pounded with the side of his fist repetitively. "FBI! Open up!"

"Mr. Buccetti!" Clark shouted. "We know you're in there."

Nothing.

Abbott pounded again. "FBI! We just have a few questions for you."

"Maybe he left early for work," Clark said softly.

"Leave a card. We'll come back tomorrow."

Clark pulled out a business card and slid it in the door crack above the knob. "What next?"

"Let's go back to the office. We're gonna have to comb through those phone records again. We need someone to squeeze."

*****

Ben Crado took a sip of coffee and set it on his oak desk. "So, Frankie," he said. "You wanted to talk about a private matter?" He cocked his head to the side questioningly. "What happened to your face?"

Frankie could feel sweat dripping down his spine. *He already knows,* he thought, looking off to the left. "I got in a fight at the bar." He returned his eyes to Ben. "Got blindsided."

Ben snorted. "If you're not gonna tell me the truth about your face, can you at least tell me what's in the satchel?"

Instead of speaking, Frankie nodded downward then placed the case on the desk in front of him. Slowly spinning it around, he unzipped it and lifted the flap.

Ben let out an audible breath. Rubbing his freshly shaved chin, his bright blue eyes locked on the case full of money.

Frankie ran his fingers through his thick wavy hair that was stiff with gel. "Ben," he said and lowered his eyes briefly. "I-I'm in big trouble. Will you *please* point me down the right path?"

"This is how you show respect? Throw money at me?"

"I meant no disrespect," Frankie said, pausing to meet eyes with Ben before sinking his head. "I know this is gonna cost a lot of money."

"Oh no," Ben sighed again. "When you walked in the door, I knew something was wrong. I-I just didn't think it would be this."

Frankie tilted his hand. "W-what do you mean?"

"I'm not sure exactly." Ben zipped up the bag. "But I know

the bikers got robbed last week. This can't be a coincidence." Ben paused to lock eyes with Frankie. "Do you know who the bikers owe that money to?"

Frankie opened his mouth just a crack.

"The Flebotomia Cartel. Do you know what flebotomia means in English?"

"No."

"It means bloodletting," Ben shook his head. "And they just sent heavy hitters from Chicago to let out some blood."

Frankie touched his forehead. "They kidnapped me, Ben."

Ben leaned forward, letting out a breathy sigh. "When was this?"

"Last night."

"My God," Ben raised his eyebrows. "You're one lucky guy. Nobody ever escapes."

"I had a guardian angel," Frankie shrugged. "Mariani was supposed to meet me after work. He said he pulled up right when they left my driveway. He followed them to a cabin up north. Right when the Mexican dude was about to cut my leg off, Mariani lured them outside. He killed two bikers with his bow. I caught the Mexican off guard."

"Hold on. Wait. Back up," Ben paused. "They kidnapped you? From your house?"

Frankie nodded. "Yeah. I came home from work and they were in my house. They clubbed me down with a bat and threw me in the trunk."

"So, they know your last name?"

"Yeah."

Ben shook his head. "That's not good."

"W-what should I do?"

Ben stood up and raised his voice. "If you don't go in hiding, you're dead! Not just you. Your mom, your stepdad, and your closest friends. These people are fucking savages."

"Please help me, Ben."

Ben walked around the table and put a heavy hand on Frankie's shoulder. "I'll do everything in my power to help you, but Frankie—you killed a top guy. They're coming for you, and if they find out I'm related to you, they'll come for me, too."

"No one knows that but me, Mariani, and my mom."

Ben leaned forward. "Tell me, why did they take you?"

"Did you see the news story about the killings up north?"

Ben nodded his head.

"We got pulled over by the sheriff that day. He smelled pot and offered to let us go for four hundred bucks. Otherwise, he was gonna search the truck. See, the gangsters thought he had the money from Hank Lindberg's house, so they cut off his arm. He must have got desperate and told them I had the money."

"Looks like he was right? How much is this right here?"

"Two hundred thousand."

"From Hank Lindberg's house?"

"Yeah."

"How much you got left?"

Frankie bit his lip. "I probably shouldn't say, should I?"

"No, but I'm family. I just need to know so I can protect you."

"My share was about five hundred thousand," Frankie said, omitting most of his winnings from the night before. "But I already spent some on a plot of land."

"Don't spend any more," Ben said. "Cuz you're gonna need it. You're gonna need money for a long trip. You're gonna need money for a safe house for your mom. You're gonna have to pay some of my guys to shadow her twenty-four hours a day. You need a damn good lawyer. And God forbid, if you go to jail, we're gonna have to pay off the guards to keep you safe. And you'll have to pay them more than the cartel is willing to pay."

"Holy fuck." Frankie sunk his head, burying his chin in his chest.

"Don't worry. We're gonna fix this, but it has to start right now."

Frankie briefly closed his eyes and let out a breath. "How long is this gonna last?"

"They don't forgive, and they never forget. I mean, I'll talk to my uncle in St. Louis. He might have some advice, or maybe an exit ramp if you're still lucky. That would cost a fortune though."

"Can you get me a price?"

"I will. But for right now, I'd pack your bags and leave today." Ben paused to reach in his desk. "Here. Take this burner phone. Toss yours in the garbage."

Frankie took the phone and put it in his pocket. "Thanks, Ben. I hope I haven't become the bane of your existence."

"Never. I'm glad you came to me. If I can't protect my family in a crisis…I'm less than a man."

19

Deputy Sheriff Carlson pulled up to the scene of an accident on the highway north of White Face Lake. Swinging the door open, he squinted at the high noon sun and saw a semi on its side, two cars in the ditch. Good Samaritans were already pulling the injured from cars. A woman waving her arms caught his attention. Carlson bolted toward her car that looked like a half-crushed pop can.

The driver-side door wouldn't open so Carlson pulled out his gun. "Cover your eyes!" he yelled and then hit the window with the butt of his gun. The glass shattered. He took off his jacket, laid it over the door, and then pulled the woman out.

After everyone was safe, Deputy Carlson and a few of the first responders searched for the dog that everyone had said was the cause of the wreck. In the ditch next to the sixteen-wheeler, he found the remains. Still latched in its mouth was what looked like a charred human hand. Bending over with black leather gloves on, Carlson grabbed the hand and shook it free.

Behind his sunglasses, Deputy Sheriff Carlson's eyebrows were low. "Get me a bag," he said and then set the blackened hand on the icy ground. *You don't find one of those every day,* he thought and shook his head. *I wonder where it came from?*

Another officer came closer when he heard the command,

the shakiness of his voice. "That's the most disturbing thing I've ever seen."

"I wish I could say the same," Deputy Carlson said.

"That's right," the officer said. "You found those mangled dead bodies last week."

"Yeah. It wasn't pretty."

A female officer walked up and handed him a large Zip-lock bag. "Here ya go, sir."

"Can ya hold that open for me?" Carlson asked and slowly put the hand inside.

"I hope you find out who it is," she said.

Deputy Carlson held the stiff bag at his side. "Yeah. I'll rush it down to Duluth. Give it to the forensics lab. They'll get us a name."

"I'll get a team together," the male officer said and looked over to the woods. "That dog couldn't have roamed too far?"

"You'd be surprised," the female traffic cop said. "A stray dog can cover a lot of ground."

"Maybe our dogs can find his tracks," the officer said.

"Good idea," Carlson said and nodded. "I'll call you when I get back. I want to help find the body."

*****

Agent Derek Clark stood next to the whiteboard holding a small stack of papers. "So, because of Lieutenant Hubert's notes and audio tapes, we know—for sure—that Thumper called Hank Lindberg on November 27 at 9:37 p.m." He pointed at the question mark under Thumper's mug shot. "Then he called the hit man's phone ten minutes later, then again at nine in the morning. That's the phone found at the crime scene in the black Lincoln Navigator."

"That's almost damning," Agent Abbott said. "But that's

all we got. Who are we gonna get to flip?"

"Mr. Scott Draper?" Clark said. "Or maybe one of the other bikers. Maybe the number three guy in their crew. What do they call him…Ax?"

"Let's try Mr. Draper first. He's a drug addict."

Clark walked to the desk and set the phone records down. "What about those foreign calls? We *need* that FISA warrant."

Before Abbott could respond, a knock at the door made them both whip around.

Clark crossed the room and opened the door.

A thin man in a shirt and tie stood in the doorway with a folder in his hand. A tall state trooper was standing at his side. "Good morning, Agent Clark. I have some information for you."

"Come on in," Clark said. "Let me introduce you to Special Agent Abbott."

"I'm Lieutenant Hubert," he said. "I met with Agent Clark yesterday."

Abbott stuck out his hand. "We appreciate the info you gave us. What else did you find?"

Hubert shook his hand and then gave Abbott the folder. "Sir, this is the Acting Sheriff of Arrowhead County, Mike Carlson. He found this evidence forty-five miles north of Duluth."

Abbott opened the folder. His eyes first took in the picture of the blackened hand, and then he read the text out loud. "The two gold rings on the severed extremity have the name Richard Anderson ingrained on the back."

"Sheriff Anderson?" Clark said, twisting to face Abbott. "You just talked to him a few days ago."

Deputy Carlson's face was long. "I was with him on Thursday. We eat breakfast at Joe's Diner almost every day. He didn't show up yesterday."

"Where's the body?" Agent Abbott asked.

*****

Frankie cruised through a green light with his phone pressed against his ear. "Ivan, you're not being cooperative. I just told you I'd meet ya halfway."

"I told *you*," Ivan said softly. "I want my fair share. Four hundred large is the least I could accept."

"I'm on my way up there. We're gonna settle this right now."

"I'm not in the mood for company."

"Look, brother. I-I might be going out of town for a while, I wanna fix this before I go. Building that house means everything to me. We're gonna be neighbors when this all clears over. We can't let a little money get between us. Okay?"

"Fine. Can you pick me up some cigarettes?"

Frankie put his blinker on. "Now that you're rich and prosperous, can I get you some quality smokes?"

"Nope, get me a carton of Black Owls. Menthol."

"Anything for you, Champ. I'll be right up."

*****

Trudging through the forest, Acting Sheriff Carlson's steps grew short. The entire twenty-man search team was exhausted and confused with the chaos of the situation. Their many flashlights were leading the way in the darkness of nightfall.

"That's it for today!" Special Agent Abbott shouted, and everyone stopped and turned back toward the vehicles, despite grumblings from Carlson.

Overpowering the acting sheriff's concerns, one of the

cadaver dogs started barking and growling. Agent Abbott, Clark, Carlson, and the rest of the team snapped their heads and spun their bodies to the sound. All four of the dogs' tails were stiff, and their heads were making fast movements, sniffing the air.

"What is it, boy?" one of the handlers asked. "Who is that?" And he unleashed the agitated German Shepherd. When the other three handlers let go, all four dogs darted deep into the woods.

Carlson swung his flashlight, shining it in the direction of the sprinting dogs. "They found something!" he shouted, then started running as fast as his heavy boots would carry him.

*****

At last, the dogs drew to a halt. Following behind them, Carlson saw a break in the trees. Crunching through the hardened snow, he looked up and found the charred remains of a building nestled on the lip of a frozen White Face Lake. The dogs were right at the doorstep, barking and signaling with raised tails.

Parked in the driveway was an SUV with tinted windows and a four-door sedan. What was left of the cabin was charred and black. The snow surrounding the cabin was dusted with ash and soot.

"Run those plates," Agent Abbott said to Agent Clark, and then he continued pressing forward. Taking the lead, he climbed the steps and slowly pushed open the carbonized door.

Acting Sheriff Carlson followed behind Abbott and scanned the room with his flashlight. In the beam of light, he saw tiny particles of carbon, floating in the air. "Oh my God."

"Let's get some light in here!" Abbott ordered the men

outside.

Agent Clark and Detective Hubert entered the cabin and the four flashlights lit up the room. They immediately noticed a heaping mound of solid objects that were resting in the center of the cabin. A thin layer of snow covered the heap.

Clark covered his mouth. "That's three dead bodies."

Hubert corrected him. "No. Four. Count the legs."

"This isn't natural," Agent Abbott swore softly before thinking silently. *These bodies are piled up like logs on a campfire.*

There was a long moment where all four men stood silent with their mouths open. It was clear to each man what they were witnessing. The remains of an arson, the purpose of which was to dispose of evidence. But the arsonists had failed.

Carlson's eyes squinted. Looking closer and, without saying anything, he dropped down to his haunches, staring at one of the bodies. "It's Sheriff Anderson," he said quietly, his voice trembling slightly.

At the weight of a hand on his shoulder, Carlson looked up to see Special Agent Abbott standing beside him. The men didn't speak, but Abbott squeezed his shoulder firmly.

Letting go of Carlson's shoulder, Agent Abbott turned, raising his voice so everyone could hear. "Don't touch anything."

Acting Sheriff Carlson shot up. "He's got no hand. It's him."

"Calm down," Agent Abbott said. "I'm going to get a team up here first thing in the morning."

"In the morning?" Carlson stomped his boot in protest. "We're here right now. I got all night."

"Sheriff," Abbott said sternly. "I'm gonna have to ask you to leave. I appreciate your help on the search. You found your man and a mountain of evidence, but this is a federal investigation and we're going to collect the evidence properly. We plan on bringing your friend's killer to justice very soon."

"Yes, sir," Carlson said, nodding his head with his lips firmly pressed together.

Lieutenant Hubert waved his flashlight over the hardwood floor. "Three guns, a bunch of shells, and a knife," he said. "We should take that with us, just in case someone trespasses overnight."

Agent Abbott turned to Clark. "Collect the evidence. I'll tape off the perimeter."

20

Around six-thirty in the evening, Carlos was sitting across from his girlfriend at their kitchen table. Tilting back his cold bottle of beer, he washed down his food.

"What'd he say when you told him he was fired," Jewlz asked while pouring a massive amount of salt on her mashed potatoes.

Carlos started laughing. "Get this, the guy actually thought he'd get away with it. I mean…" At the sudden ringing of his phone, Carlos gave Jewlz an apologetic look, and then checked to see who was calling. When he saw Mariani's name, he silenced the call. "Anyway, what was I saying? Oh, yeah, but when I confronted Ricky—"

Carlos' phone started ringing again. Scowling, he glanced over at the vibrating device. "Shit," he muttered. "It's Mariani again."

Looking up at Jewlz, he smiled. "Hold on, babe. Let me see what he needs."

Carlos swiped the screen on his phone. "Hello," he said and left the room.

"Hey," Mariani said. "Who you been with?"

"My girl. Why? What's up?"

Mariani paused then said in a low almost inaudible voice. "There's been a development. The refugee wants to talk to you...tonight."

"I concur," Carlos said. "Where at?"

"His favorite place to have a drink," Mariani said softly. "Nine o'clock. Bring Marcel. He needs to hear this, too."

Carlos took in a breath. "We'll be there," he said and hung up.

Walking back into the room with a tight smile, Carlos sat down and let out a deep breath. "I love you, Mama Bear."

"Awe," Jewlz said and treated him to a coy smile. "I love you too, Papa Bear."

Carlos smirked, then took another bite of the spiced-up swine. "I gotta return some DVDs later," he mumbled with food in his mouth.

"W-what?"

*****

Frankie Buccetti swung open the door to the Great Lake Saloon and took two steps inside. Scanning the packed night club, he failed to see his friends. *They're probably smoking,* he thought and stepped out on the back deck.

Walking outside, he felt a cold chill seeping through the collar of the black Oxford shirt he was wearing underneath his thin black jacket. Knit watch cap low on his brow, Frankie bit down on the inside of his lower lip. Avoiding eye contact with the drunk college kids, he stepped past the small tables that lined the narrow deck. In the distance, he saw Mariani lifting his drink above his head. Frankie released his lip and approached the table.

"What up, Stunz?" Mariani said, greeting him with a dark drink and a hug.

Frankie offered half a smile. "I'm still alive," he said and lifted his chin. "Grateful for that."

"You're gonna stay alive, my brother," Mariani said and lit up a cigarette.

Pulling up a chair, Frankie sat down next to the gang. Everyone was watching him cautiously and then one of them spoke.

"What the hell's going on, man?" Marcel asked, a cigarette burning in his hand. "Mariani said you got kidnapped?"

"Yeah, but it ain't over yet," Frankie said, sparking up a cigarette of his own. "We're not safe."

"What do you mean?" Carlos asked.

Frankie craned his neck to see who was in earshot. Once he turned back, he looked at Carlos then Marcel. "Ben Crado said the Flebotomia Cartel is coming for me." Though he spoke softly, there was an urgency to his voice, a rushed quality that spoke to his fear.

"How does he know that?" Marcel asked, smoke seeping from his mouth.

"Ben has a source. He said the cartel has heavy hitters in town. They've lost a lot of money in the last week. A few top men as well. He thinks they're planning on sending a violent message. Ben advised me to leave town right away."

"What?" Marcel asked quietly. "When did you hear this?"

Frankie held his hand over his mouth. "This morning. He doesn't think it's safe for you guys either. I think we should all go on vacation till this blows over."

"I got three businesses to run," Marcel snipped. "And a family to raise."

"I can't just leave," Carlos said. "I'm the manager at the car dealership. People are depending on me."

Mariani lit up a cigarette. "I don't think you guys understand," he said and blew out a line of smoke. "The cartel knows we killed their men and stole their money. We have to assume the worst. Frankie almost got cut in half with a saw. I recommend you guys leave town if you don't wanna get tortured to death."

"I'm sorry I got us in this," Frankie said, nodding his head. "It's all my fault. I-I just *had* to save Hank that day. It was stupid of me." He covered his face. "Fuck."

Carlos took a sip from his bottle of beer. "What can I do to help?"

"I'm not sure," Frankie said. "As of right now, just tell your boss there's an emergency in your family and you need to take a week off."

"All right, bro," Carlos said and shook his head. "Whatever you think is best."

"I knew it was too good to be true." Marcel sunk his head.

Carlos patted Marcel's shoulder. "Look at the bright side," he said. "Think of it as a surprise vacation. I bet your girl's gonna love it."

Mariani tilted his tall drink. When he set it down, it was empty. "Tell 'em what Ben said."

"He said we might be able to pay for protection."

"How much?" Marcel asked.

Frankie shook his head. "I have no idea; probably everything. Protection against the cartel can't be cheap."

"I don't wanna give up the loot," Mariani said with a stony look on his face. "But if it gets us off the hook, I'd do it,"

"Me too," Marcel said.

Carlos laughed shortly. "Money ain't worth nothing if you're dead."

Frankie took the last sip of his drink and set it down.

"I just don't see how they know you even exist," Marcel said.

"That old sheriff sold me out."

Marcel took a pull off his mug of beer.

Carlos flicked his cigarette off the deck. "When you think we'll be able to come back?"

"I don't know," Frankie said, "but I'm gonna find out—one way or another. Until then, I'd advise to keep your eyes open, use all precautions, and get out of town tomorrow."

Carlos stood up and shoved his chair. "I'm thirsty." His voice was hard. "I need another drink."

Frankie snubbed out his cigarette. "I'll join ya."

Carlos cuffed him on the shoulder affectionately. "Yeah, you probably need one even more than me." Looking at the rest of the group he added, "Anyone else?"

*****

Walking up to the bar, Frankie and Carlos each pulled out a stool as they flagged down the bartender. She brought them three beers and one glass of whiskey on the rocks.

"Put it on my tab," Carlos said and nodded.

Frankie wrapped his fingers around the bottle of beer. "Thanks, bro."

"No prob," Carlos said. "We're gonna make it through this."

"I hope you're right," Frankie said and took a swig.

Carlos pointed at Frankie. "Enjoy your beer. Just in case I'm wrong."

"I'm enjoying every moment with you and the boys. Might not see ya for a while."

"Don't remind me," Carlos said, shaking his head tightly. "Hey, can you take the drinks to the guys? I got to take a leak."

"Yeah, I got it," he said, and then Carlos walked into the crowd.

Left, right. Right, left. Cutting around the people milling

about, Frankie proceeded toward the back deck. "What the fuck am I gonna do with my life?" he said under his breath. "I just—"

"Shit," Frankie cried when his body suddenly collided with someone else, the impact sloshing the drinks in his hands and completely upending the wine in the other person's grip.

Looking up, an apology ready on his lips, Frankie paled at the sight of familiar blue eyes.

"Conny?" Frankie said softly, his eyebrows arching.

"Frankie!" Conny said and offered a thin smile. "What are *you* doing here?"

Frankie gazed into her squinted eyes. "Not much, just having a few drinks with the guys," he said and blinked, his eyes glancing at her hair that had changed dramatically since the last time he seen her. "New hair style?"

"You like the blond?"

"It's a little short," Frankie said. "But I like it. It's super cute. Sassy."

Conny blushed. "Well, thank you. But isn't this the exact hair cut *you* wouldn't let me get."

Looking down at the spilt drink in her hand, Frankie noticed red stains on her light gray sweatshirt. "I spilled your drink. Let me get a new one for ya."

Conny showed her wine-stained teeth. "Thanks."

Frankie ordered the drinks from the bartender then turned to face Conny. Her sharp features and soft words were bittersweet. *You broke my heart,* he thought, his mind sorting through a thousand things he wanted to tell her. He bit down on his lip then let go.

"Have you ever been to Vegas?" Frankie asked, tilting his hand.

Conny looked off to the left then faced him. "No," she said, her dark eyelids batting, her cheeks flushed from anxiety. "Why?"

"Tomorrow. Will you go with me?"

"Is this a joke?"

"Who would joke about something like that?" he asked as the bartender set the drinks on the bar. Frankie whipped out his wallet and paid the woman. Grabbing the glass of red wine, he handed it to Conny who was quick to snatch it. "All I want is one opportunity to make you happy. If you don't love me by the end of the trip, I'll walk away and fade into the distance."

"Who is this guy I'm talking to?" she asked and took a sip of her wine. "The Frankie I know wouldn't leave Duluth for me or anyone else."

"I'm not the same man I used to be."

"What changed?"

Frankie took a sip of his beer. "I'm motivated now. Let me prove it. I'll pick you up in the morning. We'll have a blast."

Conny laughed shortly. "Oh no, Frankie." She shook her head. "It ain't gonna be that easy."

"Come on, Conny. I bet we'd still get along."

Conny leaned closer. "Getting along was never the problem. You just didn't make me feel important. I-I can't be in a situation like that anymore. I'm almost forty years old."

"But you *were* important. You are important."

She took a sip and smiled sadly, looking away. She sighed. Deeply. Carefully. "I-It was nice seeing you, Frankie. My friends are waiting for me."

Frankie gently grabbed her arm. "Wait. I'm not finished yet. Two more things: You look amazing." He paused to give her the smile he knew she couldn't resist. "And I miss you a ton."

Conny's cheek twitched. "I-I'm not doing this here." She

sniffled and shifted her body slightly. "Call me tomorrow and we'll talk." With tears forming in her eyes, she turned on her heels and merged with the traffic.

"Conny." Frankie brought his hand to his heart and let out a deep sigh. *Tomorrow I'll be gone.*

*****

Walking up to the table, Carlos saw Frankie's downcast expression and knocked him on the shoulder. "Hey, tell me something good. How's the house plans coming along?"

"I made a sweetheart deal with Ivan," Frankie said. "I smoothed everything over."

Mariani leaned forward. "What?"

"Yeah. About that," Frankie said. "Look, I don't want to freak you out or anything…"

Mariani lit up a cigarette. "What the fuck does that mean."

"Ivan…well he threatened us. I know you didn't want me to pay him anything."

Mariani snorted. "How much did you pay him?"

"I paid him out of my cut."

"How much?"

Frankie took a sip of beer. "I gave him a down payment of a hundred fifty large. Pays for a plot of land and the job he did for us."

"Down payment?" Mariani swore under his breath. "You shouldn't have gave him shit." He pointed with his cigarette burning in his fingertips. "And you shouldn't build a house up there either. He's about the worst neighbor you could have."

"Ivan's harmless. He's a fucking hermit."

"So, one-fifty's the down payment? How much do you owe?"

Frankie looked away for a second. "One-fifty more."

"That's fucking ridiculous." Mariani shook his head.

Frankie held his hands out in a shrug. "The guy put in work for us. He did a good job."

"Whatever. I think it's a mistake. He'd sell you out so fast. Better hope the cops never get to him."

"Ugh." Frankie touched his fingers to his forehead. "Ivan's a sick puppy. I had to give him a bone to chew on. It's hush money."

"You know what I do with sick dogs?"

"You're not the vet."

Mariani tilted back his drink. "Trust me, I'm gonna pay Ivan a little visit someday."

"Please, don't," Frankie said. "The guy's mentally impaired. Just let it slide. He's harmless."

The sudden sound of a female voice made four heads shift.

"...Is that you?" a petite girl with shoulder-length black hair said. "Giovanni?" She walked closer to the table.

"Do I know you?" the man in question squinted his left eye.

"I'm Misty." the woman snipped. "Does that ring a bell?"

"Not really," he said. He knew exactly who it was.

Misty shook her head. "Nah," she lowered her voice. "It doesn't work like that. You just don't get to *fuck* me, then pretend like you don't know who I am."

"You're making a fucking scene," Mariani said with a low tone. "Scoot." He flickered his fingers at her like she was a stray dog.

"You're a fucking asshole." She tossed the rest of her drink in his face.

Mariani shot up out of his seat. "What the fuck!"

Frankie stood up and grabbed the back of her jacket, pulling her away from the table.

"I'm gonna have Dane and his boys fuck you up," she hissed loudly with her arms in the air.

Sliding his beer in his back pocket, Frankie forcefully guided her in the opposite direction.

*****

Staggering, one hand holding the railing of the back staircase, Misty broke free from Frankie's grip.

"Misty," Frankie said and descended after her. "Hold on. I need to talk to you."

Misty stomped down the steps. "Fuck you." She lifted her middle finger in the air.

As soon as both boots were on the pavement she started sprinting. "Help!" She kept running toward a car with a small group of people standing around it.

Stopping in his tracks, Frankie watched her run into the arms of one of them.

The biggest of the group took a step forward and spread his arms high and wide. "What's up, bitch?" the large black-skinned man barked.

"You talking to me?" Frankie threw up his arms on each side of his head.

"Yeah, I'm talking to you!" the man yelled, his finger pointing at Frankie. "You're a little bitch!"

As Frankie blinked into the darkness, a familiar silhouette formed, and Frankie's lips pulled into a snarl. "That you, Twan?" he shouted. "Bring it on, mother fucker!"

Dane let go of Misty. "You better run, bitch!" he shouted at Frankie. "It's payback time!"

"Bring it!" Frankie screamed, his hands balling into fists, his muscles flexing, his heart pounding in his chest.

*****

At the sound of loud cursing, Mariani whipped his head to the parking lot below, his eyes widening when he saw Frankie outnumbered. Shooting up out of his seat, he pointed down to the parking lot. "It's Frankie! He's in trouble." Without notice, he bolted to the staircase.

Carlos got up and grabbed Marcel by the shoulder. "Let's ride."

*****

Standing on the icy pavement, Frankie held his fists in front of his face as the four belligerents were encroaching on his person.

"First one to cross this line is gonna get fucked up!" Frankie pointed five feet in front of him.

Frankie widened his stance as Twan charged directly at him. A sharp surge of blood flowed through Frankie's veins as he planted his back foot. Reaching for his back pocket, Frankie pulled the bottle out, raised it above his head, and smashed it on Twan's face. There was an explosion of beer and glass as the tall, beefy man dropped to his knees. Twan wasn't allowed time to respond before Frankie swung his right fist forward, connecting with the side of his head. With a thud, Twan fell to the icy blacktop as Frankie put his fists up again.

Stepping up to have Twan's back, Dane Fowler caught a hard blow to his nose from Frankie's right fist. Turning away, Dane shot his hands up to his face and lowered his head.

Recoiling to hammer Dane again, Frankie got tackled to the ground by two large men with dark skin. Grunting in pain, Frankie covered his head with his arms. He could feel boots stomping on him, but his arms blocked most of the kicks.

Rocking his curled-up body, he blindly kicked back.

Suddenly the assault stopped, and Frankie saw Mariani reach for one of the men. Spinning him around, Mariani threw the first punch.

Rising to his feet, Frankie spat blood on the icy snow. At the sound of grunting, he turned to witness Carlos running a man backward and into a rusty plow truck.

Gritting his teeth, Frankie saw Dane rising to his feet. "Now it's your turn to run, bitch."

*****

From the back of the parking lot, Carlos was rolling around with a man who was about the same size as him. Grabbing ahold of the man's jacket with both hands, Carlos could feel his head getting rattled. His grip grew tighter with each blow. Pulling the man's face toward his forehead, Carlos head butted him hard and the punching stopped. Climbing to his feet, he saw a limp body with blood forming around his mouth and nose.

That dude was pretty tough, Carlos thought while he straightened his shirt collar. Turning to see tangled bodies grappling twenty feet away, he swore, and then ran to the fight.

Breathing heavily, Carlos looked down and saw Frankie behind Dane, his arm wrapped around his neck. Frankie's face was scrunching up and turning beat red.

Frankie's got that dude handled, Carlos thought, shifting to his left where he saw a struggle on the ground between Marcel and a man who was twice his size.

Treading forward like a punter, Carlos booted his head as hard as he could.

The man's body went limp.

Marcel hopped up and dusted off his shoulder. "Thanks, dog," he said in marvel of Carlos' brute power.

*****

Lungs burning from the fight, Frankie's instincts were honed in as he turned to meet his next assailant, only to see that two bodies lay unconscious at his feet, and a third lie still next to a rusty truck.

"Where's Mariani?" Frankie asked Carlos and Marcel.

Carlos shifted his head. "You hear that?"

Frankie, Carlos, and Marcel rushed to the grunting in-between two cars. Mariani was straddling Twan and dropping fists on his face. He was using both of his hands, and he was growling with each downward blow. Twan's body wasn't reacting.

Frankie's eyes grew large. "G, that's enough!" He shouted, his eyes taking in the splatter of blood on the car beside Twan. Moving forward, he grabbed for Mariani's shoulder. With a jerk, Mariani moved away, his eyes glazed over as he delivered another devasting punch to the unconscious man's nose. "Bro!" Frankie yelled. "You won! Stop. Let's get the fuck out of here!"

Mariani still wouldn't stop. The more he swung his deadly weapons; the more blood flew.

"Let's go!" Carlos shouted. "Now!"

"The *cops* are coming," Frankie said.

"I hear sirens!" Marcel insisted.

Mariani's head jerked, his eyes clearing as they caught on his friends. Shaking his head, he seemed disoriented. "This dude's a piece of shit." He shrugged. "He got what he deserved."

Frankie looked down at the critically injured man,

comatose on the pavement. His head was swelled up to the size of a pumpkin, eyes sealed shut, teeth broken out and jagged. Still, the bloody air bubbles frothing out of his mouth gave Frankie hope that the man was still alive. *Too many people saw that.*

Frankie smacked Mariani's shoulder. "You hear those sirens?" he asked, eyes shifting back and forth. "We gotta go!" And they all darted in different directions.

21

Warm underneath his covers, Frankie's deep drunken sleep was abruptly interrupted by loud pounding at his front door. His body jolted upright. *Only cops knock like that,* he thought, a tremble taking hold of his body.

"POLICE!" he heard the powerful voice travel through the walls. "Open up! We have a search warrant!"

Ripping off the blanket, Frankie jumped out of bed in his underwear. Opening the bathroom door that was connected to his bedroom, he crouched up to the window. It was dark but lifting one section of the blinds revealed light. Parked squad cars lit up the block, their cherries flashing blue and red lights. Men with long guns were standing outside his front door. "Oh fuck."

*****

Curling up in the corner of his bedroom, Frankie shivered in fear. "I'm fucked," he whispered to himself just before a loud voice bellowed throughout the house.

"Breach!"

Breathing heavily, Frankie heard glass shattering. Explosions shook the ground, and he was blinded by a flash of white-light.

"Go! Go! Go!" Frankie heard men inside his house, but not yet in his bedroom. "Get down on the ground!" an officer screamed. "Get the fuck down!"

Covering his head in the fetal position, Frankie shouted, "I'm in here. Don't shoot!"

Frankie's bedroom door opened, and a flashlight lit up the room. "Don't move, mother fucker!" the man barked. "How many people are in the house?"

"Just me," Frankie said, his hands in front of his face. Looking through the gaps in his fingers, he saw a man in camouflage pants pointing a rifle at his head.

"Are there any weapons in the house?" the man asked sternly.

"Yes," Frankie said in a panic. "Under my pillow. I am not resisting."

*****

Many hours later, Frankie sat alone in a police interrogation room, his bound hands resting on his lap. Other than a metal desk and two empty chairs across from him, the room was empty. Desolate.

Don't say shit, Frankie thought while looking at the gray brick wall. *Talking can only hurt me.*

A life in prison flashed before his eyes. He envisioned orange jump suits, shitty food, and small cell blocks. Trapped in a penitentiary of seclusion, he saw adversaries in their jail cells, sharpening

toothbrushes on the floor that were meant for him.

Pressing his hands against his head, he tried to crush the images that bombarded his senses. It felt like the walls were closing in on him. There was nothing he could do, so he closed his eyes in defeat. After a few deep breaths, Frankie's eyes snapped back open and he tilted his head up toward the clock.

"9:07 a.m.," Frankie said to himself. "Where the fuck are they? I need bail."

Bouncing his knee rapidly, he thought about the barbaric state Mariani left Twan in. *If Twan's dead, I'm fucked.*

With a click and a creak, the door opened, and Frankie's head snapped to the noise. He saw a frail old man in a black suit push open the door with a small box in his hands.

"Good afternoon," the man said and set the box on the desk.

Another man in a black suit followed him in the room and softly closed the door behind him.

Good cop, bad cop, Frankie thought, eyes shifting from the older man to the young. *Which one is which?*

Straightening himself, Frankie sat upright but sunk his head. Lines formed on his brow.

Setting a voice recorder along with two envelopes down on the table, the older man spoke: "I'm Special Agent Abbott of the F.B. I. This is Agent Clark. Do you know why the F.B.I. is interested in a local bar fight?"

Still, Frankie didn't respond.

"Anyway," Abbott continued; his voice conversational. "Fun night out on the town last night?"

Frankie raised his head questioningly.

Agent Clark squinted one eye. "Cat got your tongue?"

Frankie's chest moved up and down, but his lips were sealed.

"You probably should have stayed home last night," Agent Abbott said. "That little fight would have never happened. We might not have caught you with illegal weapons. Now we have leverage." He pressed a button on the recorder. "Mr. Buccetti, I have to record this conversation for the records." He leaned forward in his seat. "This is Special Agent Brett Abbott—interviewing Frank Buccetti—Sunday December 6th, 2015. Agent Derek Clark will also participate in this criminal interview.

"Mr. Buccetti. I'm going to remind you of your rights. You have the right to remain silent. Anything you say…can and will be used against you in the court of law. Do you understand?"

Frankie cleared his throat. "Yes, sir."

"State your full name and birthdate," Agent Abbott said.

Frankie cleared his throat again. "Frank Dominick Buccetti," he said softly, fear creeping into his shaky voice. "2-28-1980."

"Okay." Agent Abbott tapped the desk. "Let's begin. I want you to speak the truth and only the truth. Lying to a Federal Agent is a felony."

"I understand," Frankie said and crossed his arms. "But I'm going to exercise my right to remain silent. Thank you."

"I respect your choice," Agent Abbot said. "However, I think I can help you. You might want to hear what I have to say. First, let me tell you a little about myself." He paused to meet eyes with Frankie. "I've worked for the F.B.I. for the last twenty-five years. I've investigated everything from terrorism to the sex slave business. I've arrested serial killers and top-level gang leaders. I've looked evil in the eye, and as I look at you—" he shook his head. "—I don't see an evil man. I don't see a killer." He casually plopped his hand on the desk, forcing Frankie's eyes to shift to the envelope underneath his hand. "I want to believe that you're not a piece of shit, but—well, just look at what you and your friends have done." Agent Abbott slid one of two large envelopes forward.

With a trembling right hand, Frankie grabbed the envelope

and reaching inside, took out a stack of items. Placing them on the desk he looked down. There were two video tapes, four pictures, and a small stack of paperwork. He picked up the pictures and saw all four of the victims from the night before. His mouth opened the slightest and he sucked in air.

Swallowing thickly, Frankie placed the pictures carefully back on the table. He then lifted his head to face what he saw as an oppressor. "What's on the tapes?"

"One is a copy of the security camera footage in the bar," Agent Clark said. "The second tape is the sworn affidavit of Misty Berneck. We just got done speaking with her. She testifies—under subject to perjury—to having witnessed the fight...and even named two of the assailants."

Agent Abbott leaned forward sharply. "And who do you think was one of the people she named?"

Frankie lowered his head and clenched his jaw, fighting the urge to defend himself. "You know *I'm* the victim, right?" he asked, lifting his chains to point at his puffy black eye. "They started it. Look what they did to me. Did the witness mention that?"

Agent Abbott leaned back in his seat. "Victim?" He smiled thinly and cocked his head. "I don't think so. One victim is dead...and the other is a vegetable."

Frankie paled at the words he heard, his hands shaking uncontrollably, sweat rolling down his side.

Abbott folded his arms across his chest. "You're no victim. This was a brawl, Mr. Buccetti. You turned a beer bottle into a weapon, then strangled a man to death—and one of your friends bludgeoned a man to within an inch of *his* life."

"I have nothing else to say."

"Look at me!" Abbott said. "This melee is the least of your problems. I just wanted to address the fact that you killed a man in a fight, and that the guns found in your house were illegal, possibly the weapons that killed Hank Lindberg and his family. The only way you're not going to prison for the rest of your life—is if you testify under oath that you and Giovanni Mariani had a role in Hank Lindberg's murder, the kidnapping and murder of Sheriff Richard Anderson, also the murder of Enrique Chaffetz, Thaddeus Boyed, and Scott Draper. I would also need you to testify that the parking lot fight was a continuation of the feud with Mr. Chaffetz' drug ring."

Frankie's heart leapt into his throat. "I-I don't know where this is going," he said with a beet-red face. "I-I think I need advice from my lawyer. I'm confused."

Agent Abbott turned off the recorder. "Lawyer huh?" he said and collected all of the evidence on the table, securing it in the envelope. "I figured you'd say that." He handed Frankie the second package. "This is what I'll be giving to your lawyer."

Frankie scooted closer and emptied the contents on the desk. The pictures of the mutilated bodies at the Lindberg residence made Frankie's eyes widen but charred remains from the cabin forced his face to scrunch up. Besides the photos, Frankie found a detailed list of his cell phone records, with a location timestamp. This made his brow wrinkle, but the picture of his pocketknife at the cabin made him swallow the last bit of saliva in his mouth.

"What does this have to do with me?" Frankie said, eyes shifting to the left.

"Frankie," Agent Clark said with a delicate voice. "I heard that you used to be a great hockey player. I also heard you're a hard worker."

Frankie's face eased.

Agent Abbott slammed his fist on the desk—making

Frankie flinch. "If you don't give up the info, you'll never play hockey again! You'll spend the next thirty years behind bars."

Frankie lowered his eyebrows. "I have no info," he said softly. "I-I don't know any of those people. I need my lawyer. Please. I'm a United States citizen, damn it."

"Frank," Agent Clark said. "We're the F.B.I. We know everything. We have a surveillance video of you and Mr. Mariani in your truck at Joe's Diner. What a coincidence: you and him in the Meadowlands, on the day your old landlord got murdered. You say you don't know Mr. Lindberg? Well, your phone records prove you talked to Mr. Lindberg the day before his murder. We also found a number that called you. It just happens to be linked to one of the bodies you failed to burn."

"Frank!" Agent Abbott stood up and walked around the desk, leaning into his ear. "That knife in the picture has your fingerprints on it. You're fucked."

Frankie felt something throbbing in his ear. *I was kidnapped, you asshole,* he thought but didn't say anything. He just bit down on his tongue and tucked his chin. Leaning forward, he rested his elbows on his knees, but kept his fingers pressed to his forehead. While staring and the concrete floor, he let everything set in; pain, fear, anger, reality.

"There's more, Mr. Bigshot," Abbott said. "Your cellphone location on the days in question cements our case. I could charge you with seven counts of murder and conspiracy right now, *but* I want to help you shrink your sentence dramatically. I don't think you're the master mind. I think you were just along for the ride. My advice to you is give up your friend."

Frankie's lip quivered ever so slightly. "I want my lawyer," he ordered with a newfound steel in his voice. "I'll take *his* advice."

Agent Abbott sighed in frustration. "As you wish."

*****

Two days later, Frankie was sitting in that same chair, but this time his lawyer was behind the desk. Husky with a full head of gray hair, the man looked confident in a dark blue suit. Keith Sundean was tugging at his red tie when Frankie noticed the determination in the set of his jaw which left him feeling slightly hopeful.

"The circumstantial evidence is strong," Keith said and adjusted his rectangle shaped glasses. "I think we can win, but it won't be easy. The feds have a ninety-seven percent conviction rate."

Frankie's upright body fell back in his seat. *I'm doomed,* he thought and started raking his left hand through his unkempt hair. "What are the charges?"

"Since the victims in the bar fight are connected to the federal murder case, the feds will be prosecuting both cases. But as of right now, you're only charged with obstruction of justice and unlawful possession of a firearm. The federal prosecutor has ten felonies hanging over your head." He paused to pick up a sheet of paper. "In connection with the bar fight, they'll charge you with manslaughter and assault with a deadly weapon. Three counts of first-degree murder for Hank Lindberg, Candace Lindberg, and Spencer Ligget. They also plan to charge you with first-degree arson *and* three counts of second-degree murder for Enrique Chaffetz, Thaddeus Boyd, and Scott Draper. The most serious charge is the first-degree murder of Sheriff Richard Anderson."

Folding his arms, Frankie bent forward and rested his elbows on his knees. *Ninety-seven percent conviction rate,* he thought and started tapping his foot on the floor. "I don't wanna go to prison."

"Don't worry, Frankie. Most of the evidence I've seen for murder is circumstantial, *and* the only witness accusing you in the bar fight is not credible. The young woman—Miss Berneck—was inebriated, pulled over for D.U.I. They offered her a deal. Trust me. I saw the tape. See, Frankie, most of the charges are pending because their case is weak. They want you to get scared and flip on Mr. Mariani. They want to squeeze you 'till you sing…or compose."

Frankie straightened his body but tilted his head an inch. "What's compose?"

Keith gave him a fleeting smirk. "In cases with little or no physical evidence—" he said and paused briefly, "—like DNA, a murder weapon, or a credible eyewitness—they can only hope you give up an accomplice. In some cases, there's nothing to give up. That's when they start accepting false testimony. They'll let you compose or lie if it convicts a bigger fish. We call that: suborning perjury."

"That's dirty," Frankie said and clamped his jaw. *I ain't gonna compose on Mariani,* he thought. *This is my fuck up. I'll take the heat.*

Keith cracked his knuckles. "The feds play for keeps."

Frankie let out a defeated sigh. "I didn't do it, Keith." He lied out of fear of the truth. "I didn't kill anyone last night. All I did is get my ass kicked." He leveled his head. "People came to my rescue. If it wasn't for them, *I* would've been the one dead or in a coma."

"Frankie. One drunk witness from the bar said that you choked the life from of Dane Fowler, but multiple sober witnesses gave conflicting statements. They said you were attacked by four or five men, and then others joined the fight. Conflicting and contradicting witnesses are good for you. It creates doubt in the eyes of the jury. The feds were just trying to scare you—with hopes that you would give up your friend. You didn't do that, so they want to punish you until you do."

"What about the murder charges?"

Keith let out a breath. "As of right now, my main concern is the knife found at the cabin." He looked Frankie in the eye. "Your prints are on it. How does that happen?"

"I don't know?" Frankie gave a lying shrugged. "Maybe they stole it from me."

"Okay…well how about the pings on the cell phone towers at Dodge Road and White Face Lake."

Frankie felt his cheeks warming to a blush. Without thinking, he lifted his hand to cover his face and hide. His exasperated sigh was audible.

"Those two things are your biggest problems. Do you have an explanation?"

"Are you sure this room isn't bugged?"

The esteemed attorney leaned forward. "If the government recorded a conversation between a citizen and his legal representation…that would be unconstitutional. It would go against every principle we believe as Americans. It's the difference between liberty and tyranny. All charges would be dropped."

"That's reassuring," Frankie said. "But I just don't feel comfortable talking here. This place creeps me out. That dude sat in the chair you're sitting in right now. I asked for a lawyer three times. He just kept on interrogating me, telling me I'm going to prison."

"Relax, Frankie," Keith said with the slightest twitch of his cheek. "We're safe to talk here. I'm going to do everything in my power to clear your name. But make no mistake—they *do* have a case, and the feds play hardball." He got up and walked around the desk with documents in his hand. "Look at this."

Keith sat on the desk close to Frankie.

Frankie took the papers and examined them silently. Halfway through the first page, he let out another deep sigh. *What are the odds of me calling Hank that day?* he thought, eyes scanning his phone records from the day before Hank Lindberg was killed. *Every call, every text, every voicemail 'till December fourth.* Frankie pointed at one of the numbers circled in red ink. "What's this mean?"

"Look at the third page," Keith said. "It's the missed calls, texts and voicemail messages that were pinpointed on the map — in the area of Hank Lindberg's property — the day him and his family got murdered. Special Agent Abbott says that Enrique Chaffetz sent a hit squad to take out Hank Lindberg. Then a week later he kidnapped Sheriff Anderson. Their assumption is that you and Giovanni Mariani had a role in all this, but at the cabin, they think something went wrong and you killed everyone, including the sheriff. Then you allegedly set the place on fire."

Frankie sunk his head, bobbing it slightly. *With exception of Mariani killing the sheriff,* he thought, eyes staring at the floor. *I could tell him the truth, but then he'll ask why I lit the match, why I didn't call the police.*

"Those phone records prove you were in contact with Hank Lindberg and Mr. Chaffetz. The cell phone pings prove you were on Hank Lindberg's property on the day of his death. The surveillance footage at Joe's Diner from that same day further proves you were in that area. Then, on top of that, dispatch has records of Sheriff Anderson calling in your driver's licenses when he pulled you over that same day. A week later that same sheriff ends up dead." He paused to let out a breath then continued. "That's a mountain of circumstantial evidence. It begs to ask a lot of questions — but in my eyes—none of it proves murder beyond a reasonable doubt. Unfortunately for you, a jury of your peers doesn't have the same experience as me. It will be my job to convince them. But in order to mount a proper defense—we *will* need answers to all those questions."

Burying his face in the palm of his hands, Frankie was speechless. His mind was spinning with thoughts. *There are no answers, only lies.* He was shaking his head slowly, plotting his next words. *Those assholes killed the sheriff. I broke free with my knife, slashed my way to freedom. Scared to death, I burnt the cabin down.*

"It doesn't look good, Frankie. They think it's you. Trust me. I'm on *your* side, but…I need your help. I need to know what happened. I know you're not telling me everything."

Frankie sat upright and leveled his head. "Look, I-I've known Hank Lindberg for a long time," he confessed. "He let us hunt on his land that day." Throwing his arms out in frustration, Frankie felt desperation bite at his insides. "I promise. Go look. Our deer stands are still there. And we…we left some of our belongings in those stands when we heard the shooting."

"That explains the cell phone pings. Did you see anything?"

"No, but we heard everything. The gunshots scared the shit out of us. We…we left everything and got out of there. We heard people screaming in pain when we were running to the truck."

"Why didn't you call the 911?"

"I was scared. Didn't want to get caught with a gun."

"What about the phone calls from the burner phone belonging to Enrique Chaffetz? How do you know him?"

"I don't know that dude," Frankie said and lowered his

head. "But I-I think it's important I…" He stopped to take a deep breath then let it out. "I-I need to come clean with you."

Keith opened his hands. "I'm listening."

Frankie took another gigantic breath. "I-I'm sorry for keeping this from you. It's complicated. The truth is…they broke into my house, beat me with a bat, and then threw me in the trunk of a car. I got the bruises to prove it. That Chaffetz dude must have called my phone. I-I try not to answer numbers I don't know."

Frankie's lawyer placed his hand on his shoulder. "You got kidnapped?"

"Yeah."

"Why didn't you call the police when you got free?"

Frankie let out a breath. "Cuz I knew this would happen."

"I should take some pictures of all your bruises. Strip down to your boxers."

*****

Standing in front of the judge, the expression on Frankie's face was hollow. It was Monday morning, and his orange garb was replaced with a black suit and white shirt with no tie. Beside him stood his lawyer to counsel him in his arraignment.

"Mr. Buccetti," the female judge said. "Now that you've heard the charges against you, do you understand your rights?"

Frankie leaned into the microphone. "Yes, Your Honor."

"How does the defendant plead?"

"N-not guilty, Your Honor," he said with a soft, shaky voice. His freshly shaved face was flushed, and his thick wavy hair was slicked back.

Standing beside him, Frankie's lawyer exuded charm and ease. "Your Honor," Keith Sundean said. "At this time, I would like to request that my client be given the privilege of posting bail."

"Based upon the facts and nature of the charges." The Judge's head shifted in Frankie's direction before she continued. "The court cannot recall, uh, in recent Arrowhead County history, such a tragic incident which involves ten victims, including a sheriff who once served in Vietnam. The court is inclined to agree with the prosecution that for the purposes of today, bond will be denied."

"Permission to approach the bench," Keith Sundean said into the mic.

Frankie's body began to tremble as his lawyer and the federal prosecutor met in front of the judge. *No bail,* he thought to himself. *You gotta be fucking kidding me.*

Frankie's flickering flame of freedom was now extinguished. Dropping his head, his stance became deflated. His heart was constricting, plummeting with the last shred of hope.

Without bail, I could sit for two years before trial starts.

*****

Hours later, Frankie followed the corrections officer to his new cell. He was now wearing blue garb and carrying a folded blanket, a sheet, and a pillow. His heartrate elevated as he walked past all the inmates dressed just like him. Clenching his jaw, his eyes stayed on the guard's back. He didn't hear any hoots or hollers, and he didn't hear any threats, but he could feel the glares of a hundred suspected criminals.

When the guard slid open the iron door to the jail cell, Frankie took two steps inside and stopped. A stalky man with a beard was laying on the bottom bunk. Frankie's mouth opened to greet him, but the sound of the door slamming shut gave him pause. *Looks like a biker,* Frankie's thoughts prejudged the Caucasian man whose tattooed arms were folded on his chest.

"You got the top bunk," the man said with a strong baritone voice.

"That's fine with me," Frankie said softly and set his belongings on his new bed.

"Welcome to Alpha Block," the man said slowly.

Frankie looked down and saw a balding middle-aged man with short sandy-brown hair. "Thanks," he said, heart pounding with anxiety, unsure if this muscle-bound man posed a threat.

The inmate swung his feet off the bed, rising at least six feet tall.

Frankie lifted his head to face the man whose shadow he now stood in. "Frank Buccetti," he said and stuck his hand out.

"Brice Rockwell," the man said and shook it firmly. "I know who you are. You're friends with Ben Crado."

"How'd you know that?"

Brice dropped his hand on Frankie's shoulder. "Ben paid me to protect you." He removed his hand and took a step back. "Well, I got money waiting for me when I get out."

Frankie's eyebrows twitched. "Damn. Ben works fast."

"He knows you got some enemies," Brice said. "Blacks, spicks, bikers. Sounds like you single- handedly united the races. What the hell did you do to them?"

Frankie shrugged. "I-I can't really say, but I think it's uh…a hangable offense."

"They'll have to get through me first. My cousin's in here serving a parole violation. He rolls with me."

"You got a few more guys on your side?"

"Nah, just me, Dennis, and you." Brice cocked his

eyebrow. "You don't think that's enough?"

"Hey, without you I got nothing."

"He paid the guards, too. They probably got a few guys watching after you. People know you're a somebody."

"Nah, I'm a nobody. Just half a crook who happened to walk down the wrong path."

Brice smacked him on the shoulder. "Cheer up, man. You're young and respected by men like Ben. With a little luck, you might beat your case, outsmart your enemies, and do great things with your life."

"Thanks. It's been a long few days. I appreciate you stepping up for a guy you don't even know."

"Let's just say…I owe Ben a couple favors."

22

Meanwhile, in Chicago, Enrique's Boss, Martos Delgado was cursing into his phone.

Ax, the Sergeant-at-Arms of Thumper's motorcycle club interrupted. "Like I said, I haven't heard nothing."

"Probably not trying that hard though, huh?" Martos laughed. "I mean, with Thumper and his cousin out of the picture, you're the top dog of your little club."

"My people been looking," Ax said, tugging on his untamed graying beard. "Jails, hospitals, the morgue. Nothing."

Martos took a deep breath. "I guess that only leaves a couple of options."

"What's that? You think the sheriff broke free and killed our guys?"

Martos cleared his throat. "That's one scenario. Another would be that your guys killed Enrique." And then he thought what he couldn't say. *There's a third scenario, but you won't need to know about that pinche mayate when you're dead.*

"There's a flip side to that coin. Enrique could have killed *my* guys?"

"If Enrique killed them, you wouldn't be talking to me right now. You'd be a corpse, cuz he'd come for you next."

"Look, my guys are missing too," Ax said sharply. "Trust

me. If Thumper killed anyone, I'd know about it."

Martos pressed the phone close to his mouth and lowered his tone. "I don't trust no one. I won't know the truth till I look in your eyes. Then we can discuss how to move forward."

"You think it was us, don't you?"

"Prove that it wasn't. Meet me in person."

"When?"

Martos paused to think his mind. *Stupid fucking gringo. Tell me where to come blow you up.*

"You there?"

"Yeah, just thinking. Tomorrow night. You pick the place."

"The Hornet's Nest Bar and Grill. It's on Tick Lake, forty miles north of Duluth."

Martos lit up a cigarette, blew out a stream of smoke, and then the corner of his upper lip curled. "I'll be there. Bring some of your men. I want you to feel comfortable."

*****

Ax marched toward the entrance of the Hornet's Nest bar. Swinging open the door, he smiled when he saw his wrecking crew by the pool table wearing black leather vests and bushy beards.

Striding forward purposefully, his very gait caught everyone's attention. Halting, they watched him advance. Placing his hand on the shoulder of the tallest man in the club, he squeezed. "Can I talk to you for a minute?"

At the words, the group quickly disbanded, leaving the men to talk in peace.

Black Bear's skin was pale but the ink that desecrated his face and arms made him look black. He nodded then led the way to the back deck and opened the door. "What's up?"

"Remember when you said you'd follow me to the gates of

hell?" Ax asked.

The muscles on Black Bear's cheeks twitched as he looked Ax in the eyes. "Your war is my war," he said. "I'm here for ya, brother. Anything."

"Thanks," Ax said. "If I only had twenty of you, I'd feel better."

"One of me is all you need."

Ax looked out into the woods. "Um, Martos said a few things, enough to let me know he's suspicious. And we both know how he handles suspicions."

"What do you need me to do?"

"Help me set a trap." Leaning closer, Ax lowered his voice. Within minutes, he'd filled Black Bear in on his conversation with Martos, as well as his plan for how he'd deal with that man's veiled threat.

Black Bear clapped the back of his right hand into the palm of his left. "Just say the word," he said and smacked his hands again. "And it's done. We have nothing to worry about, brother. These woods ain't healthy for spics this time of the year."

"Tell the men to start planning for a war," Ax ordered.

23

Frankie stood in the lunch line with a dozen other inmates. His thick curly hair was unkempt and puffy, dark bags under his eyes. Holding a beige tray in his hand, he scanned the room for Brice and Dennis. *Where the fuck are they?* he thought. *Oh...there they —*

"Cheese or pepperoni?" the guard asked.

Frankie whipped around to face him. "Pepperoni, please," he said and the man wearing a tan and brown uniform winked, placing two slices on his plate. "Thank you." Frankie nodded.

Grabbing an apple and a small carton of milk, Frankie then veered off the line. Head down, he walked to a table against the back wall where his new friends were eating. Plopping down, Frankie looked at Brice and then Dennis. "What's up, guys?"

"A pizza party, eh," Brice said and took a bite. "Just in time for the six o'clock news."

Dennis smiled at Frankie. "Let me get your milk."

"Not today," Frankie said and opened it. "I'm thirsty."

"Just testing ya," Dennis said and tugged at his bushy orange beard. "Never give up your food. It's a sign of weakness."

"That's good to know," Frankie said and brought a piece of pizza to his mouth.

Brice squinted one eye. "You got two pieces of pizza?"

"Yeah," Frankie mumbled as he chewed his food. "Why? You only got one?"

"I've never seen anyone get two," Brice said.

Dennis laughed shortly. "How 'bout I give you some wiener for your second piece?"

"Dennis, give the guy a break. He's trying to eat."

"Hey, the guy's looking at fed time," Dennis said. "He needs to get ready. They be talkin' dirty up in there. He's gotta be able to defend himself."

Brice pointed at the TV on the wall. "Frankie." He lowered his voice. "Look at that shit. The bar's on fire."

Frankie didn't recognize the small country bar, but he started reading the subtitles. "The Hornet's Nest Bar was a known biker hang out," he read just loud enough for his friends to hear. "A survivor said three Hispanic males came in, drank a beer, and then started tossing grenades by the pool tables. A shootout pursued. Eight dead, ten injured."

"Ben was right," Brice said. "The Flebotomia Cartel wants blood."

Frankie set down the slice of pizza in his hand, choking down the food already in his mouth. "I-I just lost my appetite." *The Cartel's gonna fucking kill me,* he thought and sunk his head.

"Look at the bright side, bro," Dennis said. "There's no grenades in jail."

Stiffening suddenly, Frankie shifted to face two large black men who were walking straight up to their table, trays in both of their hands.

Without preamble, one of the men suddenly set his tray down on the table.

"You mind if we eat here, brotha?" the rotund man said with a southern accent.

"It's a free country," Frankie said, tilting his hand.

Brice set his piece of pizza on his tray.

Both men sat down, the heavier one close to Frankie. "What you in here fo', nigga?"

"Capitol murder," Frankie said. "You?"

"Drugs," the man said. "What's yo' name?"

Brice kicked Frankie under the Table.

"Uh…Frank. Frank Buccetti," he said and took a sip of his milk.

The thinner man lowered his eyebrows. "Dis the little nigga who killed Twan and Lil Dane."

Setting his milk down slowly, Frankie's heart sped up. "That's a lie."

Dennis rose from the plastic bench, spreading apart his inked-up arms. "Do we got a problem?"

The overweight inmate looked at Frankie. "Nigga, you know youz a dead man, right? These white boys can't save you foreva."

Frankie stood up and stiffened his body. "Get the fuck out of my sight."

Both men stood up, smiling menacingly down at Frankie.

With great haste, Frankie grabbed the big man's jump suit, placed his foot behind his leg and tripped him to the ground. Never letting go, Frankie found himself on top of his massive chest.

Jumping the table, Brice started stomping the man Frankie was on the ground with. Dropping to one knee, he then hammered the man's face with his fist.

The guard's whistles shrilled in the background, but Dennis continued boxing Frankie's foe.

At the sight of fists swinging, the African American congregation got up and rushed to protect their men. Guards were running and screaming. Many white men stood up. The Natives. The loners. Within a minute, a full-fledged prison brawl had started — with Frankie in the center of it all.

*****

After breakfast, Frankie was lying on the top bunk with a letter in his hands. His bruised and puffy eyes were reading a note from a name and return address he didn't recognize.

…heard your first few days on the playground didn't go so well. At least now they know you have friends. Frankie picked his head up. "Ben," he said softly then continued reading silently. *Sleep well, my friend. You're going to beat your case. You should look forward to peace when you get out. You might be broke, but you'll be safe to live a normal life.*

Frankie took a deep breath. *Sounds like his people made a deal,* he thought. *But I'd have to pay to play. Quid pro quo. Fuck it. I'd pay anything to —*

Snapping his head to the sound of the door sliding open, Frankie saw a guard standing tall.

"Buccetti," the corrections officer said with a deep voice. "You have a visitor."

Sitting up quickly, Frankie tucked the letter under his pillow. Eyes widening hopefully, he climbed down from the bed and hopped into his jail shoes. Besides his lawyer, Frankie hadn't spoken to anyone since he'd been arrested. Most of his friends — well, he consoled himself with the hope that they either didn't know or were too involved in the crimes to take a chance.

Following the guard to the visiting room, Frankie felt a sliver of hope creep up his chest. Maybe, just maybe, his mom had come to see him.

With the guard pointing to room 101, Frankie entered but

stumbled to a halt. There, directly across from him on the other side of the glass partition was none other than…

"Mom." Frankie pressed the phone tightly to his ear. "You finally came."

"Yes. I—"

"Where have you been?" The low growl of his voice didn't quite disguise the hurt buried within the question.

Diana's dark eyelids widened, her free hand coming to rest up against the glass. "I'm sorry… Frankie—W-wait. What the fuck happened to your face?"

"A fucking riot, Mom," he spat, his swelled eyes narrowing. "I got my ass kicked. I needed you. No one has come to visit me. No one."

"I-I just, I couldn't face what you'd done."

"What I've been *accused* of doing."

Nodding her head, she brushed a lock of white hair from her eyes. "Yes. Yes. That. And I was, oh Frankie, I was so angry with you. Angry with myself."

"You weren't here for me."

"I'm here now," she said and dried her eyes with a tissue, leaning forward in her seat. "What can I do to help?"

"Nothing. Just stay in hiding till your relative says it's safe. Cuz it's not safe for you right now."

"No shit, Sherlock." Diana crossed her arms. "Don't worry about me. You better watch your back in there. I can't even sleep, thinking about losing you."

"I can tell. Your eyes look almost as dark as mine."

Diana balled her hands into fists. "I've never seen your face so bruised. Does it hurt?"

"I'll live. I just need to get the fuck out of here."

"Have you ever thought about praying? Maybe God will set you free."

Frankie shook his head. "Mom, you know I don't believe in that stuff."

"What do you have to lose?" She clasped her hands. "I pray for you every night."

Burying his face in his hands, Frankie took a few deep breaths, considering her words. Dropping his hands on the counter, he just looked at her for a long moment. "I love you, Mom." He let out a heavy breath. "I appreciate the prayers. Keep 'em coming. But it would mean more to me if you could promise that you'll be at my trial."

"I'll be there," she said and coughed into her elbow. "Me and Russel will be right behind you,"

"Thank you. I'll be stronger with you by my side."

Diana folded her arms. "Does your big shot lawyer think you're gonna win?"

"He does." Frankie glanced up to the video camera. "Keith said that everything's under control."

"The news said—"

"Mom." Frankie cut her off. "Time is short. I don't care what the news said. You asked me what you can do to help. I just got an idea."

"What's that?"

He tilted his head. "I need you to sell my house. Give the money to—"

"Don't say no more." She flicked her hand. "He wanted me to ask you to start thinking about the bail fund." She paused and raised one finger. *"One million,"* she worded then set her finger down.

Frankie leaned back in his seat. *Bail fund,* he thought. *A perfect code word for Italian intervention.*

"Talk to my husky friend," Frankie said, thinking in-between words. *I need money and no one knows where mine is buried.* "Tell him I'm in trouble. Tell him I need to borrow one-fifty from him and the other deer hunter. He'll know what I'm talking about. Put that to the bail fund with the house. Should be a good enough down payment."

*****

Sitting upright in his seat, Frankie watched while his lawyer took the seat opposite him. Nonplussed, Frankie couldn't gauge if his lawyer looked pleased or frustrated.

"So, I brought the prosecutors to your hunting stand on Hank's property." Keith opened up his hands. "As you said, your belongings were still there, exactly where you said it would be. The location matched up to where the cell phone pings were on the map."

"That's good news, right?" Frankie asked, his body hopping forward in his seat. "That should exonerate me, shouldn't it?"

Keith's head slightly tilted to the left. "When you first told me about the hunting stands, I remember telling you about the risks. Your alibi gives you a logical reason to be there, but it also places you very close to the actual crime." Keith paused, leaning forward in his seat, "The prosecutors are confident this will reinforce their case."

"I remember you saying that, but don't ya think it offers reasonable doubt?"

Keith shrugged. "It does," he said. "But now it makes it even more possible that you could have done it. A juror might see reasonable doubt, but this isn't the type of exculpatory evidence that would force the prosecution to drop the charges. Don't worry. Trust me. When this goes to trial, I'll have more reasonable doubt than that. I just found out that all the spent cartridges recovered at the scene matched up with the weapons found there. Which *means*…that no other guns were used during that crime. *That* is great news for us. Your AK-47 and Glock 9mm are not the murder weapons."

"Do you believe me yet?"

"It's not what I believe, Frankie. It's what they can prove. We just need to build up the doubt for the jurors."

"How can I help more?"

Keith folded his arms. "Um. I-I'm usually against defendants taking the stand, but if you really *are* the survivor of a violent abduction—if you really witnessed Sheriff Anderson being killed—I bet the jury might feel your terror and sympathize with your actions."

"I don't know if I can do that."

"Why not? The killers were found at that cabin. You're the only eyewitness."

"My voice. I'm horrible at speaking publicly."

"Frankie. Your voice is perfect. The softer and shakier the better. You just need me to help you prepare for the gotcha questions from the prosecution."

Frankie pursed his lips. "That's what I'm worried about."

"We got time to prepare. A jury trial could take a year or two. Unfortunately, bail is still not an option. It's their leverage against you. They're betting you won't be able to handle much longer."

Frankie's head moved forward. "Two years?" he said. "That's unamerican. What the fuck? How can they make me sit with no bail? What happened to innocent until proven guilty? What happened to a speedy trial?"

"I know, I'm sorry. It's not fair. The system works in most situations, but for high-profile violent cases like this, they rule on the side of caution…for the safety of society."

"You think we can beat it?" Frankie asked, his hands

gripping his thighs, sweat rolling down his side.

"I…I can't make any promises. I'm still building your case."

"But what's your opinion?"

"As far as the murder charges, I'm pretty sure they won't be able to prove guilt beyond reasonable doubt. Now, that Mr. Twan Davis is dead, the manslaughter charge for him and Mr. Dane Fowler is fifty/fifty. They're going to destroy your character. They'll make you look so shady that the manslaughter and weapons charges might stick. But *you* were the one who was assaulted by four people. The star witness: Misty Burneck—she has zero credibility. She has a history of drugs and alcohol and theft. Not the best citizen. And her story about the bar fight—it seems convenient with her third DUI hanging over her head. It also conflicts with other witnesses."

As Frankie's body began to tremble, he bit down on his tongue momentarily. "I-I can't go to prison. I'm innocent."

"You're innocent of murder and the manslaughter, Frankie. But having guns in your possession was a crime, no matter what the circumstances. It's also a crime to give false information to federal investigators. Never talk to authorities without legal representation."

"How much time do you think I'm looking at?"

"With the points on your record, anywhere from one to ten years." Keith paused, looking at Frankie with a sly smile. "This is why it's an advantage to have an established attorney compared to a public defender. With me on your team, there's no way the judge will sentence you to more than twenty-four months."

Frankie's voice cracked. "I can't live like this for two years," he said, dropping his chin into his chest, plopping his left hand on his forehead. "These people are savages. The black gang wants me dead. The bikers want me dead. And I can tell the Hispanics are plotting on me. Sometimes, I just wanna go to sleep and not wake up till this shit's over."

"Frankie," Keith said. "Let me ask you a question: Do you have a God?"

"Not really." he shrugged. "I mean…I believe in something, but I'm not sure what. God, Universe. I don't know. There's so much evil in this world. So much suffering. If there *is* a God, why would He let so many people suffer?" Frankie paused, slouching in his seat. "Why would He make me suffer? Unless of course…I'm being punished."

Keith opened up his hands. "Frankie, His Kingdom is not of this earth. Jesus paid the ransom for all of our sins in full. He doesn't punish people on earth. He's a merciful, forgiving…loving God. You just have to believe in him. Then at some point, fall down to your knees and beg forgiveness for your sins."

"My mom's been saying the same thing for years. I just didn't want to hear it."

Keith got up and walked around the desk. Placing his hand on Frankie's shoulder, he softened his voice. "God will never lead you down the wrong path." He patted his shoulder gently. "Once you read the Bible, you'll look at the whole world differently. There's probably a Bible in your cell. Read it. It will soak up the time until trial. It will give you the strength to get through this purgatory you're living in."

24

In the wee small hours of a dark and cold morning, Martos Delgado crept up the driveway of a two-story house on the hillside of Duluth. Turning to face the two men trailing behind him, he pointed at the windows of the house in question. "When you hear the signal," he said softly, "toss the grenades through the windows and meet me at the car."

Both men nodded and Martos started marching to the back side of the house. A large picture window was facing him. *Perfect,* he thought and plunged his hand into the side pocket of his coat. *I wish this punta was in there.*

Curling his fingers around the cold steel of the pineapple grenade, Martos gripped the dense iron mass. Pulling it out, he removed the pin and then chucked it at the window. The glass cracked loudly; a small hole left in the center.

Darting down the driveway, Martos heard the distinct sound of windows shattering on the other side of the house. He turned back and saw his minions running toward him.

A massive explosion shook the ground violently and all three men ducked.

The blinding flash of light spun Martos around, and the blast wave from the second explosions rippled through the sub-zero air.

"Andale! Andale!" Martos said, yanking open the

passenger side door of an idling BMW M3.

The driver hopped in the car.

"Go! Go! Go!" Martos barked.

The driver threw the shifter in drive and slammed on the gas.

"That's what she gets," said Diego from the back seat.

Gazing at the fireball in the rearview, Martos smiled thinly. "Frankie's mom might be in hiding, but Frankie will get the message."

"Who's next?" Pedro asked, his foot tapping the brake as the car slid around the icy corner.

"With Frankie in jail," Martos said, "we'll take out his friends first. I want this pinche mayate to suffer before we rip him to pieces."

Diego briefly touched Martos' shoulder. "Let me do it, Papi. I'll get tossed in jail, then I'll stick my toothbrush in his ear."

"Do you think I'd give up my best man for this little muck?"

"How we gonna get him?" Pedro asked, now cruising at fifty miles per hour.

"I thought about paying a guard to slip some poison in his food." Martos shook his head in debate with himself. "Nah. This punta killed Enrique, a man I loved like a son. I need to send a louder message. We need to make sure no one in this shit hole town ever crosses us again."

"Look up the jail roster," Pedro said. "There must be an ese up in there."

"Nah." A short laugh left Martos' lips. "I'll find a guard with money problems. He'll tell us when the black bastard's next court date is. Then we'll ambush the paddy wagon. Take what belongs to us."

*****

Ben Crado zipped up a duffle bag and lifted his head to meet Mariani's eyes. "We're too late to save Frankie's mom's house," he said, shaking his head. "But I hope it's not too late to save his life."

"I'm ready to go right now," Mariani said. "Straight shot to St. Louis. Then I'll call your uncle Dean when I get there."

"He'll tell ya where to go. Once the money is in his boss' hands, an emissary will deliver the message to the cartel. After that…we should be safe."

"You think they'll back down?"

"They'll have no choice. The two outfits have avoided conflict for years. The truce made in the nineties was nationwide. Business is more important than revenge. They won't break the peace over Enrique Chaffetz and a little bit of money."

"Why do we gotta pay so much if there's already a truce?"

"Frankie's not a made guy," Ben sighed. "I've never asked the outfit for a favor, even though I've done a thousand favors for them. The thing is, they don't like intervening in quarrels with the cartel unless they have to. For a million bucks, they *will* move mountains."

Mariani pursed his lips. "I hope it works."

Ben nodded. "Yeah. It will. Remember, Dean and his people are my family. I vouched for you. You're one hundred percent safe. I even put in a good word for you if you want a job. They need a guy with military experience."

"I'll consider that. Thanks."

"Thank you. Without you pitching in four hundred large, we wouldn't be in this position. Every second is valuable."

"I better bounce then." Mariani shook his hand. "Catch ya

on the flip side."

*****

Pedro jerked his head at the sound of Martos' phone smashing on the wall of the motel room. His dark hard lined face leveled and turned to face Pedro.

"Fuck!" Martos barked.

Pedro and Diego flinched.

"What's wrong?" Diego asked.

"Our boss is going fucking soft," Martos said, pulling a grenade out of his jacket pocket, shaking it in his hand for emphasis. "He said my tactics are hurting business."

Diego slowly spread apart his hands. "What does that mean?"

"It means, if we don't show up in Texas in one day, our families are as good as dead."

"We can't let the mestizo slide," Diego said.

Pedro put his hand to his chest. "I don't have any family. Let me get myself arrested. I'll finish the mayate. I'll stick him."

Martos put the grenade back in his pocket, his body shifting to face Pedro. "Bien."

*****

Ivan Mortenson snubbed out two burning cigarette filters in the ashtray. "You're two months late," he said to himself and pulled out the smart phone he'd stolen from Enrique's hotel suit. "I'm running out of patience, Frankie."

Dialing Frankie's number, he pressed the phone to his ear. Ringing only once, the voice mail told Ivan to leave a message at the tone. "Frankie," he said and lit up two more cigarettes. "You gave me your word of honor." He coughed out a cloud of smoke. "You promised me payments every month. Other than the down payment, I haven't seen shit. You won't answer my calls. You don't respond to texts. I'm starting to wonder if you think I'm a chump." Ivan hit the double barrel cigarette then continued with the voice of a man who was holding his breath. "You've left me no choice. You were once my brother, but now you're my enemy." He hung up the phone and smoke erupted from his mouth.

*****

After the torching of his mother's house, Frankie had been placed in protective custody, segregated from the general population for his physical safety.

Pushing a dull pencil from a small desk like platform that stuck out from the wall, Frankie was writing his mother a heartfelt letter.

...the news of your house getting blown up broke my heart. I'm sorry a million times over. I'll be working the rest of my life trying to make it up to you. It's all my fault. I know your house was insured, but money won't replace all of your pictures, antiques, and memories.

I'm just glad you weren't in there. The nightmares I've had since then are so painful, I wake up sweating almost every night. I bet you've had nightmares about me, too. Please stay calm. I'm safe in here and you're safe out there. It would kill me if you had a heart attack from worrying about me.

My depression, inner pain, and fear has hit rock bottom. I'm afraid of being locked up like an animal for the rest of my life, and afraid of being murdered in cold blood as well. I've been told that the people who were hunting us have been convinced to halt their plans. That sounds like great news, but I still have no peace in my mind, only a passion to live.

Because no one has wrote me or visited me, sometimes it feels like

I have no friends. The only thing that brings me peace is the Bible you sent me, but that's in my heart.

Spending most of my time alone in my cell, I do pushups, I plan for the future, and I read. Thank you for never giving up on me accepting God. I was blinded by my drunken, violent, and selfish lifestyle, but now my eyes have been opened by the first part of the Bible. The forces of darkness were seeking to kill baby Jesus, and the hand of God kept Him safe and guided their path toward the light.

Anyway, I love you so much. Thank you for the prayers and support and love. It will help me win this trial and survive the threats from the forces of darkness.

God bless,

Your loving son, Frank

*****

The BMW M3 rocketed down the highway toward Texas. The engine hummed at eighty miles per hour. Both occupants were quiet. The sky was gray. Diego had his hands gripped to the wheel and Martos was gazing out the window at the wall of evergreen trees that was always there.

"Fuck Minnesota," Martos said, breaking the silence. "Nothing but trees and gringos."

"Where do you think they'll stick us next?"

"If they don't stick us in a bucket with acid, they'll put us to work in the tunnels under the border."

Diego turned his head briefly. "I thought the acid bath was for betrayal?"

"Don't think. It will only cloud your judgment. Our crew failed in a white boy town. Enrique and his crew got swallowed up by weak people." He hit the door panel hard enough to make Diego flinch. "I taught Enrique everything I know. And he still got outsmarted. I'm responsible for

Enrique, and *you* are an extension of me."

"So, we're dead men? Why herd ourselves to the slaughter?"

"I told you. Our families would pay the pri—" The buzzing in his jacket cut him off.

Reaching in his pocket, Martos pulled out his phone and looked at the screen. "It's Enrique's number," he said and swiped his thumb, bringing the device to his ear. "Who is this?"

"You can call me, Haldol," the voice said with a soft, almost feminine tone.

"Okay, Haldol," Martos said, swallowing down frustration. "I'm busy. What do you want?"

"It's not what *I* want. It's what *you* need."

Martos lowered his eyebrows. "What do you think I need?"

"I have information that would lead you to the man who killed your friend. And stole your loot."

Martos snort laughed. "Let's hear your information, gringo."

"Oh, trust me. I can't wait to tell you, but I can't do it for nothing. I don't need much. See, the man you're looking for owes me a hundred and fifty thousand. All I want is what he owes me."

"Nah, gringo. The only man I'm looking for in that shit hole town is in jail."

"Jail? Frankie? No. I know where he lives. I'll give you the address."

"Have you called the jail?" Martos smiled, thinking about Pedro. *Maybe my torpedo got him already?*

"No."

"If he's not dead, that's where he's at. Call me if he ever

makes it out alive. Maybe then we can do some business."
Martos pressed the red button on his phone.

25

One long year later, Frankie was alone in his cell, laying in his bed, reading the last page of the Bible. When he finished, he closed the book and took a deep breath. Rolling out of bed, he immediately fell to his knees, closed his eyes, and placed his hands together. Breathing in and out, he felt a slight tremble inside his body.

"Father," Frankie said with tenderness, the mantra he'd adapted in prayer. "Please forgive me for my sins. Thank you for my many blessings. Please cleanse my wicked soul of my countless sins. I-I've used violence to hurt my enemies." He paused, his face crumbling a little as it hit home...all the horrible things he did, all the excuses he made, but now he saw clearly what a monster he'd become. The crimes against humanity were flashing before his eyes. The moment he squeezed the trigger and killed the mysterious man in the black SUV. The gurgling thrash of Dane Fowler, his hands forcing his head under the bowl of urine.

Swallowing his guilt, Frankie replayed the moment he stabbed Enrique in the gut. The choice to finish the injured man by shooting him three times in the back of the head. The slow nod that gave Mariani the green light to execute Sheriff Anderson, even though he had pleaded for his life. And lastly, the swelled head of Twan and the purple face of Dane—after the strangulation—were seared in his memory for all time.

When Frankie continued praying, he did so with a meek voice. "I have lived an evil life, Father. But, can't you see I've changed? It took me a year, but I read the Bible. I've been praying almost every day, and I've even attempted to spread your good word.

"I have no right to ask this of you and I know that but…but please, set me free." He paused, sucking in a deep breath, thinking about what to say next. "I've learned my lesson. Give me another chance and I'll never hurt anyone again. I'll put that life behind me. I know, I know that doesn't make up for what I've done, but if you give me this chance, I'll dedicate my new life to helping kids avoid the path of affliction I chose to walk down—"

And Frankie's prayer was interrupted by an authoritarian voice.

"Buccetti!" the guard barked. "It's time for court."

Frankie shot up.

*****

Frankie sat alone in the far corner of a holding cell in the courthouse. His knees were bouncing uncontrollably, and his arms were folded across his chest. To calm the quaking of his body, he took deep breaths in and out. The wall in front of him had been neglected for years. Names were carved in the paint. Hundreds of them.

"Darrel was here," he said softly. "Chucky was here. Twan is a snitch." Frankie smiled and then whipped his head to the opening door, his heart sinking like it would on the freefall of a roller coaster.

"It's game time, Frankie." Keith Sundean set his briefcase down.

Frankie crossed the room and stuck out his hand. "Thank you," he said. "I know you worked hard on my case."

"Thank me when it's done," Keith said, shaking his hand firmly. "We got a battle to win."

"I'm scared," Frankie said, his voice a low rasp. "I can't stop shaking."

"Here," Keith said and handed him a stick of gum. "Try this. Might help."

"Thanks."

"I like the haircut, by the way."

Frankie nodded, his hands going up to touch the newly shaved head. "You sure about my attire though?" he asked, dropping his hands to look down at his white oxford shirt and brown slacks. "You don't think I should wear the suit jacket and tie?"

"Positive." Keith smiled. "Trust me. The plain shirt with no tie, cries out for sympathy. The jurors will be looking at you. Remember what we talked about. Don't laugh or smile. Show your grief but stand proud. Never slouch. Okay?"

"I can handle that."

"Today will be simple for you. You'll just have to watch the prosecution make Misty Burneck look like a saint. And then I'll assassinate her character. Make sure you study hard tonight. I want you to be prepared when I call *you* as a witness. If you remember everything we practiced, you'll be just fine. But Wednesday…" He paused to drop a hand on his shoulder then continued. "Wednesday will be the most difficult day of your life. You'll literally be fighting for your freedom."

The muscles on Frankie's cheek flexed, but it wasn't quite a smile.

"Let's go get 'em then!" Keith said and shook his hand once more. "You're an innocent man. Look like it."

Frankie took in air like *Indiana Jones* before his leap of faith.

*****

Keith Sundean had been cross-examining the prosecution's first witness from behind a mahogany podium. He had been chipping away at her credibility. Her blushing face told him to grab his notepad, approach the witness box, and keep chipping. "Miss Burneck, are you an alcoholic?"

"No," Misty said and brushed back her shoulder-length black hair.

"How many DUIs do you have?"

Misty squirmed in her seat. "Three."

"Would it be fair to say you have a drinking problem?"

"I'm on probation." She batted her dark eyelids. "I don't drink at all."

"Would you be willing to take a breathalyzer today?"

"Yep," She snipped. "I'll take any test you got."

Keith turned to the silver-haired Judge Stolcis who sat at a higher elevation than Misty, the flags of the nation, state, and county hanging on poles behind her. After a familiar look of contempt from the aging judge, he turned back to Misty, shaking his head tightly. "That won't be necessary, Miss Burneck." Keith flipped the page on his notebook. "On December 5, 2015—the night of the parking lot fight at the Great Lake Saloon—you were drinking, right?"

"Yep."

"Yes or no?"

"Uh, yes."

"Would it be accurate to say you were inebriated that night?"

Misty shook her head. "No."

"Okay, after the fight, you drove your vehicle under the

influence, right?"

"Yes."

"Did you get pulled over by the police?"

She nodded slowly. "Uh, yes."

"The breathalyzer you took at 2:21 a.m. read .20, correct?"

"I-I don't remember."

"Okay, the fight happened about a half hour before you failed that test. A .20 blood alcohol level means you were inebriated. Question: How can you be certain that Mr. Buccetti killed Dane Fowler if you were that drunk?"

Hearing loud grumbles, Keith twisted his head to the packed audience of the court.

"Order!" Judge Stolcis said, dropping the wood gavel.

Keith turned back to Misty.

Misty looked up to the Judge who gave her a curt nod. "Frankie has brown skin," she said. "Everyone else was either black or white. He stuck out like a sore thumb. I saw Frankie and Giovanni kicking Dane on the ground, then I watched Frankie get behind him and put him in a choke hold."

"How many people were fighting all together?" Keith flipped the page on his yellow notebook.

"Um. I know Dane was with three friends. And, uh…Frankie had at least six guys on his side. So, like ten or more."

"Miss Burneck, your original statement was ten on Mr. Buccetti's side. Which one is it? Six or ten?"

"Uh, I don't know. Seven, counting Frankie. Maybe more."

"Okay, two other witnesses say *three* men ran to the fight. They both say they counted a total of eight people involved in the fight. Four on four. You saw eleven people fighting, right?"

She gave a servile nod. "Yes."

"Seven on four. Is that your story?"

"That right."

"Okay, uh, did the fight start off with eleven people?"

"Uh, no."

"Was Mr. Buccetti all alone when Mr. Fowler and three of his friends attacked him?"

Misty slowly nodded her head. "Yes."

"Four men attacked Mr. Buccetti?"

The prosecutor shot up. "Objection. Asked and answered."

Judge Stolcis leaned forward in her tall black chair. "Sustained."

Keith shook his head and let out an exasperated sigh. "Okay. Was Mr. Buccetti on the ground, getting kicked by more than one man?"

"Uh, yes."

"Miss Burneck, was Mr. Fowler and his friends in a gang?"

"Uh. I'm not sure."

"Yes or no?"

"Uh, um." Her dark eyes shifted to the now silent audience, and then back to Keith. "Yes."

"Okay, four gang members attacked Mr. Buccetti and six other men joined the fight. Correct?"

Misty let out a breath. "Yes."

"That sounds chaotic. I understand why your numbers are off. What were *you* doing when this was happening?"

"Dane always told me to stay back if he got in a fight. I was screaming for them to get off him. Then Dane stopped moving. And then I called 911."

"You were inebriated, right?"

"No. I was fine."

"Okay, you had a good buzz going?"

"Yes."

"And you're confident that Mr. Buccetti killed Dane Fowler?"

"Dane was my boyfriend. I loved him. I'll never forget that moment as long as I live."

Keith turned to the jury and took a few steps forward. "Ladies and gentlemen of the jury, I'm going to play a surveillance tape from the night in question. From inside the Great Lake Saloon. You decide for yourself if she had a good buzz or if she was inebriated."

Keith returned to his podium, grabbed the remote control, and hit play.

Stepping closer to the jury box, Keith gestured toward the TV hanging on the wall.

"Here's Miss Burneck getting her first drink," Keith said and cleared his throat. "She seems calm and self-aware as she sips a cocktail. Now, watch the character arch as she starts taking shots. Try to count how many shots she takes." The video showed short clips of Misty as the night went on.

The clips showed Misty pounding drinks, bouncing from guy to guy, and staggering about. Aimlessly.

Keith paused the tape. "This is the final clip," he said and pressed play. "Here's Misty on the back deck, flailing her arms and stomping her feet like a child." Suddenly, the Misty on the tape jerks back her hand and violently tosses her drink in Giovanni Mariani's face.

Keith pressed pause, freezing the screen in the middle of her rage. "I think you've seen enough."

*****

Mid-morning on Tuesday, Keith Sundean took a sip of coffee, and then continued picking the brain of his first witness. "Detective Hubert," he said. "After going over all the information that Mr. Hank Lindberg disclosed to you as a confidential informant, after listening to the three recorded phone calls between Mr. Lindberg and Thaddeus "Thumper" Boyd, I'm convinced Mr. Boyd and the motorcycle gang had clear motives to murder Mr. Lindberg. Do you agree?"

"Yes, sir," Hubert said and adjusted his glasses.

"Would you say that Mr. Boyd and the hierarchy of the biker gang would be the prime suspects?"

Detective Hubert sat upright. "I'd take it a step further," he said. "I am confident that Mr. Boyd is directly responsible for Mr. Lindberg's death, *and* the other victims including Sheriff Anderson."

"Do you think Mr. Boyd hired cartel hitmen to kill Hank Lindberg? *Or* do you think he hired the defendant?"

"Could be both. The hard evidence points to the international drug syndicate. I didn't know this at the time, but they were connected at the hip with the motorcycle club. Drugs, guns, and now murder. But I *do* find Mr. Buccetti's actions troubling. I don't believe his story." Hubert rolled his head toward Frankie. "I think he's hiding something. Too many coincidences. Too many people killed in his presence."

"Troubling or guilty beyond reasonable doubt?"

"Uh, just troubling."

"I appreciate your opinion, but we deal in facts here." Keith flipped the page with authority. "Let's shift to Sheriff Anderson. Question: Is it true that Sheriff Anderson busted Mr. Lindberg with drugs in the past?"

"That's correct."

"Did that arrest lead to Mr. Lindberg becoming an informant?"

"Yes, sir."

"So, Sheriff Anderson knew Mr. Lindberg was an

informant?"

"Yes. But he didn't know what Mr. Lindberg told us."

Keith returned to his podium for another sip of coffee. "Is it possible that Sheriff Anderson told the biker gang about the informant in their crew?"

"It's possible." Hubert paused, shaking his head. "But not probable. Sheriff Anderson was one of the most respected lawmen I've ever met. He was a prisoner of war in Vietnam. I'm pretty sure he wouldn't—"

"Mr. Hubert," Keith cut him off. "*I'm* pretty sure you never took the time to check Sheriff Anderson's phone records." Keith handed him a sheet of paper. "I did. Tell me what you see."

Hubert pursed his lips while he read the phone records. "I see several calls between Sheriff Anderson and Scott Draper highlighted in pink."

"Who is Mr. Draper?"

"He was the number two in the motorcycle club. Vice President to Mr. Boyd."

"No further questions."

*****

On Wednesday morning, Judge Stolcis leaned forward in her black leather chair, her gaze looking down on a brown-haired federal prosecutor in a black suit. "Mr. Schweizer," she said into the microphone. "On behalf of the Federal Government, you can call your first witness of the day."

"The prosecution calls, Mr. Frank Buccetti," the lead prosecutor, Alan Schweizer said from behind a mahogany podium. Average height, average weight, Mr. Schweizer turned toward Frankie, his eyes studying the defendant's lowered head, his shoulders that were curled forward, and his blushing face as he stood next to his attorney.

Frankie stepped from behind the desk to the aisle. His body was secretly quaking with every step. *All eyes on me*, he thought, head shifting to the jury of his peers. *All white jury. Just my luck.*

Shoving his left hand in his pocket, he stiffly crossed the green and gold carpet to the small witness box. *Reminds me of the sin bin in hockey*, he thought and stepped inside.

"Please raise your right hand." Judge Stolcis paused while Frankie obeyed. "Do you swear to tell the truth, the whole truth, and nothing but the truth?"

"Yes, Your Honor," Frankie said with a voice so soft, so subtle, so meek, that no one but the judge understood what he said. His heart was banging away in his chest, fingers tapping on his thigh.

"Please have a seat and answer the questions of Mr. Schweizer."

The room was respectfully silent as the smirky prosecutor approached the witness booth. "Good morning, Mr. Buccetti," he said, stopping five feet in front of him. "Please state your full name, your occupation, and the city you live in."

"Frank Dominick Buccetti," he said just above a whisper. "I-I was a laborer for Superior Plumbing. I-I live in Duluth, Minnesota."

"You talk softly."

"Yes sir." Underneath his shirt, Frankie could feel sweat was rolling down his side and back.

"You're going to have to talk louder."

"I-I'm sorry, sir," Frankie said, straining out every word. "T-this is as loud as it gets."

Mr. Schweizer took a step closer. "Mr. Buccetti, I talk loudly, so try to match *my* voice."

Frankie cleared his throat and bent the microphone so it was almost touching his lips. "I'll try my best," he said a tad louder, his clammy hands interlocking on his lap.

"Mr. Buccetti. Have you ever been convicted of a felony?"

"Uh, yes, sir."

"What were your convicted of?"

Swallowing parched saliva, Frankie's eyes dropped to the bottle of water in front of him. "First degree assault." He grabbed the bottle, twisted the cap, and took a sip.

"That's right," Mr. Schweizer said and turned to the jury box, smiling. "Mr. Buccetti is a violent convicted felon. He got caught with two illegal firearms in his bedroom after he choked Mr. Dane Fowler to death. The guns, mind you, had the serial numbers scratched off.

"I started my questioning with his criminal record to show his lack of credibility and disdain for the law." Schweizer turned back to Frankie and slowly walked in his direction. "Mr. Buccetti, how do you know Hank Lindberg?"

"H-he was my landlord about fifteen years ago." Frankie felt the pulse of his heartbeat throbbing in his left ear.

"Did you...consider him a friend?"

Frankie nodded. "Yes, sir. You could say that."

"A good friend?"

Frankie shook his head. "No. But he's fixed my truck so many times...I-I guess I've grown close to him over the years."

"Did you ever buy drugs from Mr. Lindberg?"

Frankie shook his head again. "No, sir. I don't do drugs."

"Have you *ever* done drugs?"

"No."

"Not even pot?"

Frankie nibbled on the inside of his lower lip. *He can't prove that,* he thought before he lied. "No, sir."

Turning, Schweizer stepped toward the jury. "Did you see his strained face when he lied to you? That's the look he'll have every ti—"

"Objection!" Keith Sundean blurted out. "The prosecution is speculating with no evidence."

Judge Stolcis leaned into the microphone. "Sustained, unless you have evidence to the contrary, Mr. Schweizer."

Schweizer spread apart his hands. "I'll move on, Your Honor."

"Disregard Mr. Schweizer's last question and statement," Judge Stolcis said to the jury.

Turning to Frankie, Schweizer extended an open hand. "Did you call and text Hank Lindberg the day before he was murdered in cold blood?"

"Y-yes, sir."

"Yesterday, you testified that you were hunting on Mr. Lindberg's land the day he was killed. Is that correct?"

"W-with Hank's permission, I-I was hunting on the far back sixty acres."

"Hunting?" Schweizer smiled. "Funny you say that." He shook his head with contempt. "Why did you change your story? You originally told Special Agent Abbott that you didn't know Hank Lindberg. Were you lying then or now?"

"Uh, um, when I asked for a lawyer, the agent kept asking me questions. I-I was confused. Scared. I-I knew it would look bad."

"So, you lied to a federal officer?"

Frankie paused to look at his lawyer who nodded. "I did." Lines formed on his forehead.

Schweizer pivoted to face the jury. "Take note of the admission of guilt on count two." Turning back, he approached the witness bench and asked, "So, you're telling the truth now, right?"

"Yes, sir."

"Okay, I believe you. I know you were there." Schweizer let out a breath. "And I know why you changed your story." The prosecutor raised his voice a notch. "Your cell phone pings prove you were there. It's just a question of whether you were hunting man or beast." He walked up and leaned his hand on the bench. "Mr. Buccetti! Did you kill Hank Lindberg and his family?"

Flinching at the loudness of Schweizer's voice, Frankie's body leaned back in his chair. "No, sir."

"Did you have any role in his death?"

"Uh, no."

"That's right, you were just hunting. Just a coincidence, right?"

"T-that's right, sir."

"Who where you with?"

Frankie rubbed his bald head, partially covering his face with his arm. "Uh, t-that's classified."

"That's not how things work when you're under oath, Mr. Buccetti. Who were you with?"

"Objection," Keith said. "Your Honor, I would refer you to the Motion in Limine. Mr. Buccetti agreed to testify in conjunction to his own actions."

"Sustained."

"Okay, so you won't give up your accomplices. Fine. Just you. What were you hunting?"

"Deer."

Schweizer threw his hands in the air. "Mr. Buccetti, deer hunting season ended November 15th."

"Uh, I-I didn't' know that. We never shot anything, so I guess w-we didn't break the law."

"Mr. Buccetti, Hank Lindberg was an avid hunter, right?"

"I believe so."

"He didn't raise any concern on the phone? He was just going to let you poach on his land?"

"Um, the plan was to bow hunt, but we had a gun, too." Frankie raised his hand to his ear, firmly pressing a finger on the lobe. *Stop throbbing, damn it.*

"What kind of gun did you have in your possession?"

Frankie shrugged. "Uh, I-I was using a hunting rifle with a scope."

"Was it the AK-47 authorities found in your bedroom?"

"No, no." Frankie's right heel was bouncing behind the bench.

"Mr. Buccetti, *why* did you scratch the serial numbers off the guns you were caught with?"

"I didn't. A friend borrowed them to me. I needed protection. After I got kidnapped, I-I knew the gangsters would be coming for me again."

"But why were the serial numbers scratched off?"

"I don't know. Maybe the owner didn't want to be connected to it?"

"Either that or it's stolen. Either way, it's a crime."

"If it's a crime to protect myself, then I'll have to deal with that. But I didn't murder anyone."

Schweizer smiled. "That's right. You were just hunting. Did you hear anything unusual while you were...*hunting*?"

Frankie took a small sip of water. "Yes, sir. I-I heard gunshots."

"How many gunshots?"

"Uh, I'm not sure. A lot."

"How long did the shooting last for?"

"I don't know. After the first few shots, I-I climbed down

the tree and ran to my truck. I heard shooting the whole way back."

"Did you hear any screams?"

Frankie nodded his head. "Yes, sir."

Schweizer raised his voice. "Did you call 911?"

Here we go, Frankie thought. *The gotcha questions.* He said, "N-no, sir." *I got this.*

"Instead of calling 911 to save lives, what did you do?"

"I drove home," Frankie said, his eyes blinking rapidly.

"Mr. Buccetti, you didn't drive home. You drove north and got pulled over by Sheriff Anderson, didn't you?"

Frankie spun his last statement. "Uh, I-I wanted to um, take the back roads home."

"Okay, I believe you. I bet you wanted to avoid the police. But that didn't work out so well. Sheriff Anderson slowed down your escape. Mr. Buccetti, please tell the jury why you didn't tell the sheriff about your so-called friend—Hank Lindberg—who was desperately screaming out for help."

Frankie sucked in air. "I-I was scared. Selfish. I-I had a gun in my truck. And uh, I was worried that...t-that I would be accused of...." He paused to think of the right words to say. "...w-whatever was happening at Hank's house. I-I wanted to avoid sitting where I'm at right now."

"If you *did* have a small role in this triple homicide, wouldn't you lie and say the same thing?"

Keith shot up. "Objection! Badgering the witness."

*****

At the end of the day, Mr. Schweizer set the hook and Frankie yanked the bobber under the water, trying desperately to snap the line and set himself free with half the truth about the cabin on White Face Lake.

"That's right. That *was* my knife," Frankie said.

"I know it's your knife, Mr. Buccetti," Schweizer asked. "Your fingerprints are all over it. But, if you *were* violently kidnapped, brought to a cabin, beaten, *and* tortured, if you *saw* a sheriff's severed hand on a coffee table, if *you* witnessed that sheriff getting murdered, if you really *were* lucky enough to escape using that knife — *why* in the world did you set the cabin on fire and destroy evidence that could have corroborated your story — instead of doing your civic duty to call the police?"

"Uh, sir, I-I was afraid the cops wouldn't believe me."

"So, it would be fair to say you set the fire to dispose of evidence?"

Frankie shook his head. "No."

"Then, *why* did you desecrate the remains of a sheriff who once served in Vietnam?"

"Objection," Frankie's lawyer said. "Asked and answered."

"Sustained. Disregard the statement."

"Mr. Buccetti, did you profit from any of this?"

Frankie's eyes shifted to the left. "No. No, sir." He shook his head tightly.

"How much did your lawyer cost?"

Frankie blinked rapidly. "Thirty thousand dollars."

"How does a laborer from the Superior Plumbing Company afford thirty thousand dollars?"

Wiping sweat from his forehead, Frankie took a slow breath. "Uh, m-my right to have counsel is unalienable. That is *not* a question any American citizen should have to answer."

"Did you rob Mr. Chaffetz after you slit his throat."

"Uh, no. Mr. Chaffetz was the devil. I-I didn't rob him, and I didn't slit his throat." Frankie's voice cracked. "I-I knocked the smoking gun out of his hands after he shot the sheriff. Then I-I stabbed him in the gut with my pocketknife. It was me or him. He was about to shoot me in the head next. I-I had no choice." Turning toward the jury, Frankie scrunched up his face. "W-what would you do?"

26

On Friday morning, Mr. Schweizer stepped around his podium, approached the jury bench, and planted his feet in front of them. "Ladies and gentlemen," he said, opening his hands to shoulder width, his small notebook in his left hand. "Thank you for sacrificing a week of your life for the cause of justice. This entire week, I have overwhelmingly acceded our burden to prove guilt beyond any reasonable doubt. I have laid out a trifecta of guilt and lies and excuses made by the defense. A sadistic path of affliction was carved out by the defendant — three different locations, at least nine lives snuffed out. All because the defendant had a plan, a carefully constructed strategy to imbed himself in a drug syndicate until the time was right to take out the shot callers and rob them blind."

Schweizer glanced at his notes. "Fortunately, for the people of northern Minnesota, Frank Buccetti also left a trail of evidence for investigators to find along the way." Schweizer's head rolled down the jury bench, the men and women frozen still and wide eyed. "His phone records connect him with the victims. The pings off cell-towers near each crime scene place his location and track his movements from one crime to the next. The belongings and DNA Mr. Buccetti left at each crime further prove he was there.

"Mr. Buccetti also showed us his web of lies. First, he told federal investigators that he didn't know Mr. Hank Lindberg. Then he told *you* that he was deer hunting, even though deer hunting season had ended November 15th. Then, after admitting he heard the gunfight, he didn't call the police to save his so-called friend." Schweizer paused, his face scrunching up. "Imagine if *you* had heard gunshots and screams coming from your friend's house. Wouldn't *you* call authorities? I know *I* would." He paused while tapping on his chest. "Immediately."

Schweizer took just a few steps to his right. "What did Mr. Buccetti do? He fled. During his escape on the back roads, Mr. Buccetti got pulled over by Sheriff Anderson. This is the *same* Sheriff Anderson who Mr. Buccetti is charged with murdering. When given a chance to tell the sheriff about the injured people at Mr. Hank Lindberg's house, he once again chose to avoid his duty as a citizen. Why is that? Because the defendant is guilty."

Schweizer flipped the page on his notebook with vigor. "Another example of Mr. Buccetti's strained relationship with the truth is the heinous strangulation of Mr. Dane Fowler. Mr. Buccetti says it wasn't him. But Misty Burneck says she watched him put Mr. Fowler in a headlock, not letting go until Dane stopped moving. Those were her words. 'Dane stopped moving.' Can you imagine what Miss Burneck saw?... Felt?" Schweizer shook his head and took a step forward.

"But, the biggest lie in his web was the statement about the pocketknife found at the cabin on White Face Lake. The knife with *his* fingerprints on it. He gave a wild story about getting kidnapped and carving his way to safety. Then—for the third time—instead of notifying authorities, he took intentional steps to conceal his crimes. How did he do this? He actually admits to setting the cabin on fire!"

Schweizer snorted out a short laugh. "Luckily, Mr. Buccetti

is as bad at arson as he is at lying."

Schweizer shook his head. "No, Mr. Buccetti did not get kidnapped. No, he did not fight three-armed drug traffickers with a little pocketknife. No, he wasn't hunting on Hank Lindberg's land. But yes, Mr. Buccetti did strangle Dane Fowler to death. Yes, he did give false statements to federal investigators, and *yes*, he was in possession of two illegal firearms when authorities raided his home.

"The evidence is in plain sight. His guilt is clear. Frank Buccetti did—at most—murder these people. And—at least—had a role in the murders and the cover up." Schweizer cleared his throat.

"The defendant even corroborates his location at each crime scene. He doesn't deny being there. No, he *insists* he was hunting. He *claims* to have been kidnapped. He *says* he was a victim.

"No, Mr. Buccetti is *not* a victim. He *is*—in some sense—a psychotic serial killer."

Schweizer paused to scan the jury once more. "Ladies and gentlemen of the jury—today—you will be forced to make the most difficult decision of your lives. You *will* have to decide whether the defendant is guilty or not guilty on each charge. You *will* be forced to decide whether to put a killer behind bars or set him free in the society your children live in.

"I know…you *will*…make…the right decision. Thank you. The prosecution rests."

*****

After lunch recess, Keith Sundean stepped toward the jury bench with a clip board in his hand. "Good afternoon," he said and took a moment to look each juror in the eye. "Let me begin my closing argument by saying what you've heard me say over and over again. There is *zero* evidence that Frank Buccetti committed murder. Not at the Hank Lindberg residence, not at the cabin on White Face Lake, and not in the parking lot of the Great Lake Saloon. It is *scary*…that any American citizen could be so easily charged with such crimes." He paused and observed the ticks of emotion on the faces of the men and women before him.

"I want to just dive into the substance of the facts. This all started with a 911 call that ended with the sixteen-year-old son of Hank Lindberg…*dead* at the hands of Sheriff Anderson. The remains of this same Sheriff Anderson were found at a cabin on White Face Lake. In the same cabin were the remains of two high ranking motorcycle gang members and the captain of an international drug syndicate. Sheriff Anderson's phone records indicate that he was in communication with Mr. Scott Draper, a member the motorcycle gang who just happened to be found in the same ash heap. Right there, we should pause and recognize that something bigger than Frank Buccetti is going on here.

"Let me revisit that, but first, we need to understand what happened at the Hank Lindberg residence. It was an ambush. A massacre met by a heavily armed homeowner who fought back with deadly force. Who were the assailants? We don't know their names, but we know at least three of them were of Hispanic descent and could not be found in any U.S. data base. We know they used AK-47s to murder Hank and his family. We know that because the guns were lying next to their mutilated remains.

"What do you think was lying next to those guns?" He paused again before continuing. "Dozens and dozens of spent shell casings. Guess what? With exception of Mr. Lidberg's spent shell casings, every piece of brass and every bullet found at the crime scene was scientifically matched up with those weapons. That means Mr. Buccetti's AK-47 was absolutely *not* used at the crime scene."

Keith stepped to within five feet of the bench and lowered his voice. "What other facts do you have with this murder case?" He scanned the jury booth for expressions of sympathy. "Hank Lindberg was a habitual drug addict and a confidential informant. But who did Hank betray?

"The answer is: Thaddeus "Thumper" Boyd and the biker gang he was president of. Sure, Mr. Buccetti called Hank Lindberg the day before his violent death, but so did Mr. Boyd.

"That's right, the leader of a biker gang called Hank Lindberg the same day my client did. Guess who else talked to Mr. Boyd that day? Wait for it…wait for it—the mysterious Hispanic hitman found dead at Hank's house. And how do we know that? Because the phone found at the scene had Mr. Boyd's burner phone number in the call log. How do we know it was Thumper's number? Because Detective Hubert testified that he has three tapes with Hank Lindberg—the confidential informant—talking to Mr. Boyd on that same line.

"Let me ask you something. What do these people have to do with Mr. Buccetti? Nothing. Why is Frank Buccetti charged with seven counts of murder and one count of manslaughter? Because the prosecution is desperate to get a conviction even though *all* the killers are dead. They're using the fact that Frank's cell phone pinged off a tower, proving he was on Hank's land that day. Guess what? Mr. Buccetti testified under oath that he had permission from Hank Lindberg to hunt on his land. You, the jury, read the text messages on Mr. Buccetti's phone that prove it. You also saw the pictures of the duffel bag Mr. Buccetti left in the deer stand that day. How about the pop and half-eaten sandwich he must have left when he heard the gunfight?" Mr. Sundean paused for a long moment.

"Frank Buccetti was at the wrong place at the wrong time. And because of that fateful day, Thaddeus Boyd, Scott Draper, and Enrique Chaffetz kidnapped Sheriff Anderson. They thought the sheriff stole their money. They thought he would tell authorities about their treasonous deal. So, they cut his hand off with a table saw. To prevent another limb from being cut off, Sheriff Anderson must have desperately coughed up Frank Buccetti's name. A simple scapegoat to end the torture. After they forcefully took Mr. Buccetti from his home, Frank said they threatened to cut off *his* arm next if he didn't return the money.

"Since the sheriff was no longer useful to them, Mr. Chaffetz shot him in the chest to show Frank he meant business. That's when Mr. Buccetti made his last stand. The only reason Frank sits here today, is because he's a survivor. With the pocketknife found at the scene, he carved his way to safety.

"There *is* a mountain of evidence that Mr. Chaffetz and Mr. Boyd arranged the killing of Hank Lindberg and then kidnapped and killed Sheriff Anderson, but there is *zero* evidence that Frank Buccetti murdered anyone." He paused dramatically, eyes rolling down the juror box from left to right. Each man and woman were stone faced with lines in their foreheads. Many faces were red.

"One of the things you must realize when it comes to reasonable doubt, is that it is the *highest* burden in the American justice system. The Honorable Judge Stolcis will soon advise you that you need to have an abiding conviction of guilt. The evidence in this case *begs* you to doubt the prosecution's story.

"Ladies and gentlemen, when you have a prosecution that

only uses half the story and inuendo, when they *never* address bloodthirsty killers like Mr. Chaffetz and Mr. Boyd, when they *never* mention Hank's betrayal of his biker friends, when they are *silent* on the fact that Frank Buccetti's mom's house got blown up with multiple hand grenades, when you *calculate* all these facts in your mind, you probably hear something screaming at you, telling you that Frank Buccetti is *innocent* of all charges. This man is *not* guilty of murder or manslaughter. You *cannot* in good faith send a man to prison for the rest of his life when the obvious killers with unquestionable motives were found dead at the scene with scientifically confirmed murder weapons. That would be a disgrace to the cause of justice. I'm going to close by asking you to return a verdict of not guilty on all charges.

"Thank you. The defense rests."

*****

A few hours had passed, but it felt like a year. Now, waiting in the same holding cell as when it had all begun, Frankie paced back and forth with his untouched lunch sitting on the bench. Keith had warned him this would be the worst part—awaiting the verdict. His breaths were short and quick. His paces, long and heavy. With a trembling heart he thought about what he'd say if he could go in there and make one last plea to the jury. *Everything's on the line*, he thought. *My freedom is teetering on the pendulum of justice. I'm just a patsy.* But in his mind's eye, he saw the men and women of the jury with long faces and universal nods of agreement. He could hear them going down the line. *Guilty, guilty. guilty…*

Whipping his head to the creaking door, he saw Keith stepping inside.

"Frankie, they're calling us back in." Keith looked down at

his watch. "Three-hour deliberation."

"Is that good or bad?"

Keith smiled, but there was little warmth in his cautious gaze. "Could be good. Guilty verdicts usually take a bit longer."

Breathing heavily, Frankie rubbed his head. "I hope you're right," he said softly, and they shook hands.

"Stay positive. Look positive. Think positive. They never proved guilt beyond reasonable doubt."

Frankie nodded slowly, swallowing his pain and fear and doubt. Following Keith out the door, he straightened himself and lifted his chin. *I probably deserve to be convicted. I'm a sinner.*

*****

From behind the defense table, Frankie was studying the judge, then out of his peripheral vision, he took stock of the jurors who'd just re-entered the courtroom.

Behind him, he heard the sound of the general public filling back into the mahogany-paneled room. Panic flooded his system as his eyes found his mother. "I love you," she mouthed to him.

"I love you, Mom," he returned before scanning the room for the face of a friend, but to no avail. He saw only strangers.

No one else came...

When he felt Keith nudge his foot, Frankie's head snapped back around. Quickly, he straightened and faced the judge.

*****

Judge Stolcis faced the jury. "Ladies and gentlemen," she said gracefully. "You have reached a verdict. The verdict card has been handed to the bailiff." She signaled with her fingers.

"Please come forward. The clerk will read and record the verdict."

The bailiff approached the bench and handed the verdict to the clerk.

After adjusting her glasses, the female clerk leaned into the mic with the soberest of tones.

"The State of Minnesota versus Frank Dominick Buccetti," she said. "Verdict Count 1: We, the jury, upon our oaths, do find the defendant as to count 1: felony possession of a firearm — guilty."

Frankie's mom gasped. Frankie's fingers clenched down in fists at his sides. Mr. Sundean remained still.

Frankie closed his downcast eyes as the fear shuddered down his spine. Sweat was pouring down his side and back.

The clerk gently shook the sheet of paper and cleared her throat. "The State of Minnesota versus Frank Dominick Buccetti. Verdict Count 2: We, the jury, upon our oaths, do find the defendant as to count 2: giving false statements to a federal agent — guilty."

"No! No," Diana cried, her voice falling to a muffled whisper in the quiet commotion of the room.

Frankie lowered his head and took a gigantic breath. *Calm down,* he thought. *It's just a process crime.*

With a clenched jaw, his eyes skirted toward his lawyer. Only, when their eyes met, Frankie saw a man who didn't look concerned by the first two verdicts. He glared at this old man who looked so calm, so still, so at ease. *I wonder if he even cares about what happens to me?*

Breaking eye gaze with Keith, Frankie shifted back to the clerk. His blood was pulsating, every inch of his body seemed to be quaking as he waited for her to speak again.

Frankie then lowered his head, clenched his jaw, and

closed his eyes. *Please God. Please help me.*

"The State of Minnesota versus Frank Dominick Buccetti. Verdict Count 3: We, the jury, upon our oaths, do find the defendant as to count 3: manslaughter in the second-degree—" she said to the silent room. "—Not guilty."

The court room seemed to explode, hushed voices rising with mixed emotions as one-by-one, the public turned toward one another in shock, in disgust, or in victory.

The judge pounded the gavel. "Order in the court!"

The grumbles dissipated and the clerk continued.

"The State of Minnesota versus Frank Dominick Buccetti. Verdict count 4: We the jury, upon our oaths, do find the defendant as to count 4: first-degree murder—"

Frankie trembled unconsolably with a beet red face. Three seconds felt like a lifetime.

"—Not guilty," the clerk said.

At the sound of loud protest from the people in the courtroom, Judge Stolcis pounded the gavel. "Order in the court! Order in the court!"

Order out of chaos, Frankie thought and smiled from ear to ear, finally exhaling the breath he'd been holding all week. Pumping his fists, he closed his eyes and tilted his head to the sky. *Thank you, God!*

The weight of Keith Sundean's hand dropped on Frankie's shoulder. His head turned.

"We're gonna win, Frankie!" Keith said and then enthusiastically shook his hand.

"Thank you!" Frankie said. With the loud and hostile crowd behind them, they embraced each other with the jubilance of victory. Diana and Russel made it a group hug, and Frankie's smile grew.

When the Judge regained order, the clerk read the rest of

Frankie's charges. They all read the same — not guilty. Because of the fact he'd been denied bail, and that he'd served a year and a half in the county jail, the judge sentenced him to time served.

Frankie was free at last!

27

Frankie's feet were clapping along the corridor of the county jail. The exit he was not allowed near for so long was within sight. The double iron door with two small windows got closer with each bouncing step. Narrowing his eyes, he smiled as he passed through the beams of light that slanted down from the windows. At the crack of the door, Frankie's heart jolted against his chest, a rush of emotion consuming him. "Freedom," he said and shouldered the heavy door.

Blinking furiously as one step became two, Frankie didn't dare look behind him as the warmth of summer met his face and hands, the air tasting sweeter than he'd ever remembered.

The parking lot was bare except for one lone vehicle. A black pick-up truck. At Frankie's approach, the driver's side door opened, and Ben Crado stepped out.

Ben opened his arms to greet Frankie.

Frankie embraced him.

"Congratulations," Ben said. "You beat the feds, *and* the Flebotomia Cartel."

Frankie stepped back and shook his hand powerfully. "*We* beat the feds and the cartel," he said. "Thank you so much. I owe you my life."

Ben let go. "Hop in the Truck. I got the A.C. pumping."

Frankie smiled. "Take me away from this hell hole."

Ben hopped in the driver seat and shut the door. "You don't owe me your life. Just a favor. That's it. We'll talk about that another day. Today, we celebrate. *You* are a free man."

"Words can't explain how happy I am. That place was a nightmare."

Ben threw the shifter in drive. "I've been there, but now you'll get to live the dream. Just consider this a wake-up call. Go home, take a long look in the mirror, and try to decide what you want to do with your life. You're still pretty young. Nothing can stop you."

"Thank you," Frankie said. "Trust me. I got scared straight. I just want to live a totally different life than I did before." Frankie shook his head. "But I'm still kinda worried about the cartel and the bikers. Them people are evil."

Ben pursed his lips. "Don't worry. Your friends stepped up with the money, and *my* friends stepped up and made a deal. You can count on that. You're free to live your life. My advice: *never* let your guard down. *Always* carry a gun. It's smart to be prepared for the worst." Ben glanced at Frankie. "Since I bought and sold your house, can I offer you a low-key place to stay for a while?"

"Ya know what? That would be awesome. Thanks."

"Anything for you, Frankie. You been through a lot."

Frankie smiled. "Speaking of 'lot,' I own a plot of land out in the boonies. I'm gonna build a house there after I pay off my debt. How much do I owe anyways?"

Ben took his gaze off the road for a brief moment. "I wanted to celebrate before we talked about that. It's a nosebleed, but since you asked…I'll break it down for ya." Ben let out a breath. "I took fifty thousand out of the briefcase you gave me. Thirty thousand went to Keith Sundean, ten thousand to the guards, five thousand to Brice, and five thousand to put your mom up." He paused again to sigh. "The last hundred-fifty thousand went to the million-dollar insurance plan with my friends. I bought your house for a hundred-fifty thousand and threw that in the pot, too. Carlos and Marcel pitched in a hundred-fifty thousand each. And Mariani threw in four hundred large."

Frankie perked up. "Where's Mariani at?"

"I can't say." Ben turned his head to the passenger seat. "But don't worry. He's safe. That's all that matters."

"Well, if you talk to him. Uh…tell him I said thanks. Have him call me."

"He's gone off the grid. Unwilling to go to trial. You probably won't hear from him for a long time."

"You can't relay a message?"

"Not unless it's an emergency." Ben's head shifted. "He *did* leave a message for you though. He said to tell you he's proud of you. He said he loves you like a brother. And he said to bury two hundred large for him in case he ever needs it. The rest is yours."

*****

Around dinner time the next day, Marcel Tayler took a rack of ribs out of his smoker and set it on a plate. Spinning around in his sandals, he crossed the back deck and placed it on the picnic table in front of Frankie. Carlos was sitting beside him in a white polo shirt with a bottle of beer in his hand.

"Thanks, bro," Frankie said, smiling from ear to ear. "It smells awesome." Adjusting the collar of his sky-blue guide shirt, he sat upright in his seat and licked his chops.

"Good," Marcel said. "Now you can shut up and eat. You ain't paying me back nothing for Ben's insurance plan." He gestured to his home. "Take a look around. I got a farmhouse estate that my kids will inherit someday. I'm good."

Carlos plopped a heavy hand on Frankie's shoulder, squeezing tightly. "He's right. Drop it. We're even. Just happy to see you free and alive. Okay?"

"Okay." Frankie nodded. "But if you *ever* ne—"

"Ahh," Carlos cut him off. "Let's put that behind us. The past is history."

"Dig in," Marcel said. "I bet within thirty seconds you say these are the best ribs you've ever had."

Frankie pulled a piece of saucy meat off the bone and took a bite. Chewing slowly, Frankie's eyebrows raised, and he started nodding. "Yup. These are—no doubt—the best ribs I ever had."

Carlos turned his massive head to Marcel, who was wearing black shorts, a yellow golf shirt, and a thick gold chain that hung around his neck. "Let me get a plate, my brother with a different color. Them ribs look bomb."

Marcel smiled and leaned in toward Frankie. "Let that flavor set in. I'll be right back."

When Marcel went to the smoker, Frankie looked at Carlos. "You never had these ribs before?"

"I've eaten Marcel's ribs a few times, but *this* is a brand-new smoker. And I think the pork comes from the pigs on his farm. I guess his in-laws retired and moved to Florida. Gave Marcel and May a sweetheart deal on the entire property."

"Never thought I'd see Marcel become a farmer."

"I don't think he milks many cows. He probably hires people for that shit."

"Let's call him *The Farmer* from now on. *Man*…these ribs are good."

Marcel strutted up and set a plate in front of Carlos. "Enjoy."

Carlos went to work on the ribs.

Savoring the taste, Frankie's thoughts returned to his life in jail. The rectangular trays, the cafeteria packed with cruel inmates, the sub-par food that was barely edible. *I'm never going back. Never.* Each bite reminded him of the freedom he now possessed. The freedom he longed for. The freedom he thought might never come.

"What do ya think, Los?" Marcel asked.

"Best ribs around. No comparison. And I thought *I* made good ribs."

"Frankie. Do you concur?"

Frankie nodded, chewing and swallowing. "What's your secret?"

"My secret stays a secret until *you two* partner up with *me*." He pointed at his chest. "We need to open up a smoke house as soon as possible. Ribs, brisket, cornbread. If you really think they're the best ribs ever, then you should have no problem joining me right now."

Frankie set a bone on his plate. "Why do you need partners?"

"I run four businesses as it is. I'm tied up. Got my dad's recipe, my father-in-law's pigs, and some money in the bank. I need *you* to run the thing."

"I'd throw down some cash," Carlos said. "But I don't have time to work it either."

Frankie let out a breath. "I'm about to build a house on Ivan's land. I need to see how much money I got left after that."

"You tried the hard path before, and it didn't work too good for ya. I'm giving you a legitimate opportunity to run a million-dollar business. There *is* no competition in this city. We'd clean-up for sho'."

Frankie wiped his mouth with a napkin. "How much

would I need to throw in?"

Marcel started laughing and smiling, smacking Carlos on the back. "After all these years, he's finally asking the right questions! Dis brotha done changed."

Carlos hit Frankie's arm. "Yeah. The Frankie I know would have only brought up the downfalls of the restaurant business. Then he would have shot it out of the water."

"I didn't think you'd even consider it." Marcel shrugged. "Why the change of heart?"

Frankie smiled. "I'm ready to try new things. Carve a different path than before. Plus, it's a great idea. These ribs are absolutely amazing." Frankie pursed his lips, pausing to meet eyes with both of his friends. "But before I consider a lifetime business partnership with you guys…I-I have to question your loyalty for a moment. I mean…I know you guys love me like a brother, but *why* didn't you guys come visit me, or *at least* send me a letter?"

"I couldn't risk it, man," Marcel said. "I got four kids to feed. I'm sorry. Out of sight, out of mind."

Carlos blew out a sigh. "Same here, bro," he said. "We were part of it. Especially the bar fight. Look at me. If they put me in a line up, the witnesses would pick me out real quick."

"It's all good, bro," Frankie said. "It's just…I was alone for a year and a half. I-I just needed some love. Mariani didn't even come see me. No one did. Except for my mom."

"I'm sorry," Carlos said. "I'm just glad you're free. Let's hit the restart button and move forward together…as a team."

"That's good enough for me." Frankie hugged it out with Carlos and Marcel, and then they laughed…together.

After their plates were empty, the smoke from the smoker continued to rise. The smell of the barbecue lingered. A patriotic conversation mixed through the air, voices rising in competition to be heard.

"See...Independence Day wasn't the day we *won* independence," Frankie promised with a gesturing left hand. "It was the day we *declared* independence."

Carlos engaged in the conversation. "The Founding Fathers had to give this infant nation legitimacy on the world stage. Declaring independence would allow us to gain alliances, lobby for financial aid, and unite the colonies."

"We needed to recruit more soldiers," Frankie said. "And we needed France's money to pay them. But most importantly: we needed France's navy. After the Fourth of July, 1776, America got the French help we needed to achieve victory."

"It took eight long years," Carlos said, "but under the leadership of George Washington, absolute victory was achieved. So tonight—when we watch the fireworks—think about the miracle that took place two-hundred and forty years ago, that planted the seed of freedom we enjoy today."

Frankie took a sip of water. "America is flawed but think about what life would be like—under tyranny like in Iran, North Korea, or God forbid...China."

Marcel's smile grew. "Where we watching the fireworks at?"

"At the Statue of Liberty." Frankie matched his smile.

"The Statue of Liberty?" Marcel asked. "In Duluth?"

"Yeah. It's by the Aerial Lift Bridge," Frankie said. "Overlooking the bay. You can't miss it. It's one of two hundred miniature Lady Liberty statues spread out across the nation. Four in every state."

*****

As the sun set, Frankie, his friends, and their girls gathered around the mini Statue of Liberty and gazed into the night sky.

The sound of the fireworks shook the ground and echoed throughout the city as the dark sky lit up with a dazzling array of colors and shapes—each one a symbol of freedom and celebration.

Frankie watched the fireworks with the eyes of a man who was once thirsty for freedom. He remembered being denied that right. This was a reality check for an individual who needed assurance that he was actually free.

"I thought I'd never see the fireworks again," Frankie said, eyes glued to the sky.

Carlos leaned toward him. "The system worked this time. 'Merica…"

"I must be blessed."

Toward the end of the beautiful display, tens of thousands of Duluthians looked up in unison at the humungous flash in the darkness. The ground reverberated suddenly with the conclusion of the grand finale. Couples everywhere were holding each other and kissing. Carlos and Jewlz' lips were locked in a long romantic smooch. Marcel and May held hands with their heads tilted upward.

It seemed like several minutes of nonstop bombs bursting in air. The National Anthem was playing on the intercom in the background, and Frankie felt a patriotic tingle throughout his body.

"God bless America," Frankie mouthed. "My home sweet home."

28

Frankie cut through the stuffy smoke-filled room and dropped an olive-green backpack on Ivan's lap. "That's fifty thousand."

"The deal was a hundred-fifty thousand," Ivan said from his recliner with two cigarettes dangling from his lips, ash falling on his black fleece jacket.

"The deal changed, bro," Frankie said, wiping sweat from his bald head. "I had to *pay* for a lawyer. I had to *pay* for protection. And I had to *pay* for a new house for my mom to live in. I suppose you didn't hear about the cartel blowing up my mom's house, did you?"

"What does that have to do with me?" Two streams of smoke shot down from his nose.

"I paid a million dollars to make sure the cartel wouldn't kill all of us. That's who we robbed. The Flebotomia Cartel. And they wanted blood."

"You gave me your word." Ivan tossed the bag in the corner behind him like he did with trash.

Frankie sat down on the ratty sofa, his voice softening. "I did. I'm sorry. Things didn't go as planned. *Everyone* took a loss. Not just *you*."

"You're telling me all the money's gone?"

"No. I already paid you for the land next door. I got about enough to build a house over there."

"You got money for a house, but not enough to pay *me*?" He sucked on his two cigarettes.

Frankie lifted his palms to face level. "Ivan, chill out." His hands dropped to his knees. "Look, I paid you like two hundred thousand so far. That's enough to last a lifetime. How much have you spent anyways?" Frankie looked around at the neglected room that had only gotten worse in the time he'd been in jail. The only thing different was a new TV and a stereo system. Other than that, everything looked the same — fast food bags and pizza boxes strewn about the room, and an overflowing ashtray with blackened cigarette butts resting on the coffee table.

"It's none of your fucking business how much money I've spent."

"Woah…calm down, bro. No need to get an attitude. I'm just saying…it looks like you haven't spent much. You still got that same rusty minivan out there." Frankie gestured toward the driveway. "Look at this place. It's a pigsty. And you're still wearing the same dirty rags you were wearing the last time I saw you." He shook his head. "Why don't you take a shower and go spend some money?"

"Fuck you, Frankie. You used me for a stash house and robbed me. Then you spit in my face."

"Rob you? Spit in your face? I just gave you a bag full of money."

"Get the fuck out before something bad happens."

Frankie got up. "Fine. I'm out of here. Don't be surprised when the construction crew starts building my house in a few weeks."

Ivan blew out a stream of smoke. "You can build your fucking house. I don't give a fuck. But if you don't pay me the rest of my money, I'm gonna pay someone to rip out your intestines. Then I'll move into your fancy new house. Don't forget…the land's still in *my* name until you pay in full." He pointed at himself.

"Don't threaten me, Ivan!"

"It's not a threat, it's a fact."

Frankie shook his head. "I'm the only friend you've ever had. Never forget that."

Ivan shot up. "Get out, chump!"

"I'm gone." Frankie glared into Ivan's eyes that were enlarged by his thick glasses. "Anything ever happens to *me*, there won't be nothing standing in-between *you*…and Mariani."

Ivan charged Frankie and grabbed him by the shirt, shoving him. "Get out!"

Slamming his right arm down, Frankie broke Ivan's grip and filled his fists with Ivan's jacket.

Ivan swore and began flailing his arms.

Frankie's hands relocated to a higher position for better restraint. Walking Ivan backwards, clutter tripped them up and they both fell to the floor with a loud thud.

"Ahh!" Ivan screamed, reaching for his ankle.

Frankie got up and adjusted his shirt. "Are you okay?"

"No! You broke my fucking foot. Get the fuck out!"

"It was an accident. I'm sorry. Put some ice on it. You'll be fine."

"Get the fuck out!"

Frankie let out an exasperated sigh. "I hope you're okay, Ivan."

"You're fucking dead."

"Call me when you take your meds." Frankie grabbed his duffel bag and stormed out the door.

29

Frankie was sitting in a booth at Crado's Italian Restaurant. It was a Friday night in the middle of December, and he wasn't alone. Smiling on the other side of the white draped table was Conny, an appetizer plate resting between them. He felt warm in her presence, his face somewhat flushed. "You...look absolutely amazing tonight," he said, eyebrows twitching upward.

"Aw...shucks," Conny said, blinking her eyes. "Thanks! I like your new look. You look handsome without the hat."

Frankie observed her grace and charm as she giggled with a glass of wine in her hand. Her hair was brown again and had grown back to shoulder length. The navy-blue dress she was wearing was sleeveless with a short neckline. Sparkling from her ears, were a small pair of diamond earrings that looked familiar to him. *I thought she would have thrown those in the lake by now.*

The lighting in the restaurant was dim. The music soft.

Smiling and straightening the collar of his tan button-up shirt, Frankie gazed into her deep blue eyes. "I appreciate this opportunity." His voice was low, intimate as he leaned across the table, his hands reaching for hers.

"It wasn't an easy choice," she assured him, but Frankie already knew that. After she saw him in the alley brawl, she'd backed far away.

Frankie had quailed at the fury of her reaction, but he still didn't have the strength to let go. He waited through summer and fall, then on the anniversary of their breakup, Frankie was surprised to receive an email from her.

Hi, Frankie. I hope all is well. I just want you to know that I'm happy you won your trial. Sorry for the cold shoulder. Please don't blame me for being upset with you. That bar fight was ugly. The news made you look like a serial killer. I believed them all this time. Just today I looked at a picture of you. You were smiling. It made me sit and think about you and everything I know about you. I know how big your heart is. I know you'd never hurt anyone unless your life was on the line. I know you're a good man. Look, it didn't work out for us romantically, but there's no reason we can't be friends till the end. I'm sorry for doubting you.

Two years ago, today, I left you with a short text message. I ghosted you. That was wrong. I want you to give me an opportunity to regain your trust, respect, and friendship. When you were in jail, I was thinking about you. I can only imagine how bad it was. Anyways, I just want you to know that I'm here and I care.

Best regards,
Conny

Frankie took sip of water then set the glass back down softly. "Do you like the crackers and fine cheese?"

"I can't get enough," she said and lifted her shoulders to reach for the silver platter.

"I can't get enough of *you*."

"Shush…I told you. Just friends."

"You walked into that one," he said teasingly. "But in all seriousness…I-I just never thought I'd see you again. So, I'm just soaking this in."

"I never thought I'd see you either. I really thought you

were going to be found guilty. I believed the newspapers. I'm sorry."

"No need to say sorry to little ol' me," he said with his face softening, beaming at the unguarded words. "It didn't look good, but the truth was on my side. The system worked."

"I'm glad you're free."

Out of the corner of his eye, Frankie saw Ben Crado carrying a tray loaded with two porcelain bowls, steam still rising hotly off the surface. "Here he comes." They both turned their heads in his direction.

"Lobster Ravioli with Grilled Shrimp," Ben said. "What a wonderful choice." He then set the plates in front of them.

"Thank you so much," Frankie said softly with a wink and a nod. "Thanks for everything."

Ben smiled thinly. "Don't mention it," he said, noticing the empty bottle of wine. "You two sure drank that vino pretty fast. Can I get you another?" He paused, his head shifting to Frankie. "It's on the house."

Frankie shook his head. "I don't drink anymore. It's all her."

She nodded. "One more bottle, please. Thank you."

After Ben was gone, the pasta was still piping hot, but that didn't deter Conny from digging in.

"Oh, my God," she said under her breath. "This is *so* good. It brings back so many memories."

"Forget about the past," Frankie said. "We're making new memories in the present."

Feeling her face blushing, she took a sip of wine. "Maybe so."

Ben approached with a bottle of wine. He popped the cork, poured Conny a glass, then asked: "Anything else."

"No, thank you."

After Frankie had his fill, he set his fork down in the bowl. Lifting his glass of water to his lips, he looked across the table. *This is a dream come true,* he thought to himself, swallowing the ice-cold water. *Don't mess this up.* He chewed on a chunk of ice.

Frankie set his glass down. "Did you enjoy the pasta?"

"I did. It was super good."

"So…what now?"

Conny took a sip of wine. When she set it down, it was empty. "Frankie, I'm not as easy as I used to be. Your cute little smile and fancy dinner isn't going to win my heart or get in my pants."

"That's not what I meant. I mean, about me and you. I think we still get along great. It's like a day hasn't passed. When can I see you again?"

Conny smiled briefly. "Be honest with me." She pushed her hair out of her face. "What's your intentions?"

He let out a heavy sigh. "Kittenz." He smiled. "I'm not gonna lie. I want you back. But I'd take no pleasure in forcing you or persuading you back in my life. I think I've made the necessary changes to make you happy. And keep you happy. I-I know that one good night isn't going to fix everything, but maybe in time…we'll grow close again."

"This is why I blocked you out of my life two years ago." Her cheeks were just faintly flushed, her eyes glossy. "I knew if I saw you, I'd fall right back into your arms. The problem was never getting along with you. It was the fact that *you* always put your friends over me." Her voice cracked. "It felt like you didn't care."

"I'm sorry, Conny. I'm ready to listen and learn. Communication is important. Sometimes a guy needs a kick in the butt to realize the important things in life."

Frankie pulled out a hundred-dollar bill and set it on the table. He then got up and slipped into a black wool coat. After Conny put her beige jacket on, they walked arm-in-arm toward the exit.

Glancing down at the black and white checkered tile floor, Frankie was reminded of eternity, and the never-ending battle between good and evil.

Frankie waved to Ben and his wife. "See ya' next time."

The Crados waved back. "Keep in touch."

At the last moment, as Conny was walking out the door that he was holding for her, Frankie turned with his thumb up before he let go of the door.

*****

Behind the restaurant, Conny and Frankie's vehicles were parked next to each other. The two ex-lovers stood between them. They were face to face, gazing into each other's eyes underneath the glow of the streetlight.

"Are you sure you're good to drive?" Frankie asked.

Conny's hair was blowing in the wind. "I'm okay," she said. "It was just a little wine."

"It was two bottles," Frankie rebuked. "I drank water. Let me get you home safe."

She showed him the palm of her hand. "I'm fine," she said sternly. "I really had a great time tonight. I'd stay a little bit longer, but I have to work a double shift at the emergency room tomorrow. I...I want to hang out again. Sometime soon. But not tonight. Okay?"

"I understand. Can I give you a big hug at least?"

"Of course."

Frankie took a determined step forward with his arms

open. He hugged her tightly as if he might not ever see her again. His ear was next to hers. "I missed you so much."

"I missed you, too."

"I've been waiting for this moment for a very long time," he said, mimicking *Darth Sidious*. "My little brown-haired friend."

Hearing a soft groan of invitation, he turned his head at the same time as hers. Their lips touched once, then twice, and then the third time he caressed his tongue against hers.

Conny's body was melting against his, the answering thrust of her hips when he pressed her against the car. She gasped as he gripped her face with both hands as he kissed her with two years of pent-up passion.

Slowly gliding his fingers across her neck, he then followed with his lips to the spot just below her ear. *Her weak spot,* he thought just before her body fell like over ripe fruit, into his hands, just like she had predicted after dinner.

"*Not* tonight," she said softly, squirming out of his arms. She drew back but kissed him once more. Spinning around, she hurriedly fumbled the car door open, hopped in the driver seat, and then immediately started the car.

Frankie was still standing on the other side of the window with his mouth half open, shocked at the unexpected force of nature. Frozen from her abrupt halt in action.

She let out a breath and pressed a button on the inside of the door. The window rolled down. "Text me." She waved and then sped off into the coming storm.

*****

From behind the wheel of his idling SUV, Frankie sat and typed a text message into his phone: *Your beauty is unmatched.* And then he hit the send button.

Taking a deep breath only to let it out, Frankie then set the phone on his lap. Gazing out the passenger side window at the falling snow, he took time to relish every moment that she was in his arms. Picturing himself and Conny wrapped up in a whirlwind of rekindled love.

I can't believe it, he thought as he felt the cool air from the heater begin to get warm. *Ben was right about love.* He remembered Ben's words of experience. *If you love something, let it go…*

Flicking the windshield wipers on, Frankie realized that an icy build-up was immobilizing them. Opening the door, he stepped out of the truck and reached for the frozen wiper. Pounding the ice clear, he cleaned the wipers with his bare hands and then climbed back in the truck. Throwing the shifter in gear, he took his boot off the brake.

And there, snug on the snow rested his phone, which had slid off his lap when he'd exited the vehicle.

30

That same night, Ivan Mortenson was rocking in his chair with two cigarettes in his mouth and a cell phone in his hands. "Time's up, Frankie," he said to himself and tapped his thumb on the screen. "You should have paid your debt. And you shouldn't have broken my foot."

Ivan saw a capital letter *M* on the lit-up screen and the word *calling* was underneath it. He smiled and put the phone to his ear, listening to it ring as he coughed out smoke.

"Si," Martos said.

"I have new information for you, Mr. M."

31

With one hand on the wheel, Frankie pumped the brakes as he approached a now-familiar wall of trees.

"Home sweet home," he sighed as he turned down the long and winding driveway, his headlights the only spot of illumination in the otherwise densely packed woodland that crowned his property.

When he pulled up to his garage, he killed the engine. "What a night," he said softly, smiling.

With keys in his hand, he got out of the truck and shut the door. Glancing up at his new house, he grinned at the prize earned with blood and sweat and toil. The two-story home was built according to his design: cherrywood siding with ledger stones that wrapped around the bottom four feet of the house and garage. After a brief moment of bliss, Frankie hurried toward the house to hide from the ice-chilled wind.

He flew up the steps, approached the door, and whipped out his keys. As soon as he entered the house, he typed a four-digit code into the panel on the security system. After the friendly beep-beep noise, he took off his jacket and shoes. Stepping into his slippers, Frankie let out a heavy breath because he was home and free and safe. He then crossed the posh living room carpet, setting down his keychain on the oak coffee table.

Settled between the kitchen and living room was a solid oak door that led down to the basement. Reaching it, Frankie grabbed the handle. When the door swung open, he hit the light switch and proceeded down the stairs. Entering the main room, Frankie's eyes darted past the pool table off to one corner, where sports memorabilia was covering the walls. One of the small display cases glistening in the light drew him closer. His eyes caught sight of a gold medal hanging from a blue ribbon and his lips tugged upward. His high school hockey team had won the state championship his sophomore year. Back when life had been…less complicated.

Which is why…shifting, his eyes moved, taking in a newly framed picture he'd placed right next to the gold medal—the pee-wee hockey team he'd recently joined as assistant coach.

It was his first-year coaching, and he was proud to give back to the community. It was a promise he made to himself and his God. One of many promises kept.

Frankie adjusted the picture frame, so it was sitting straight. Placing a hand to his chest, he hoped that most of those kids would grow up and choose the right path—the path of sobriety, success, and peace. But he knew at least one or two of those youths were certain to drift toward the thorny path of affliction that he'd happened to walk down. *I'm not gonna let that happen,* he thought before thinking out loud. "If I can save just one kid from a life of sin—" his fingers touched the glass "—then I did my part."

*****

Bright and early the next morning, Ben Crado was loading his cash register with change when he was interrupted by the ringing of his cell phone.

Ben swiped the screen and pressed the phone to his ear.

"Hello."

"We just got a long-distance call," Ben's uncle Dean from the St. Louis organization said.

"I'm listening."

"News from our competitor in Texas. Apparently, Martos Delgado has gone rogue. Apparently, someone overheard him talking shit about his boss late last night. I guess he was making a drunken fuss about not being able to avenge the death of Enrique Chaffetz. The person heard him say something about a source in Minnesota to one of his men. Now he's nowhere to be found. I was told to warn you that your guy isn't safe."

Ben's voice lowered. "I thought we had a truce?"

Dean cleared his throat before replying. "We do. That's why they gave us the heads up."

"Well, that was nice of 'em." Ben gave an audible sigh.

"It was a smart move. Now it's on *you* to resolve it."

"Can you send my rookie on the next flight?"

"Done. Anything else I can do?"

Ben shook his head. "Do you have any idea when he left?"

"He was last seen around 1:00 last night."

"Thanks. Keep me posted."

After Ben hung up, he immediately found Frankie's number in his phone and hit the call button. It went right to voicemail. "Dammit!" He hung up and tried again. Nothing.

He put the phone in his pocket and paced back and forth. *He's probably still in bed with his girl,* he thought and tried to squish his head with his hands. *It was my stupid idea to not have his address. Plausible deniability was a mistake.*

Pulling out his phone, Ben called Frankie's mom. No answer.

He looked at the clock. It was 7:07 a.m. "Texas," he

murmured. "An eighteen-hour drive." His eyes looked up as he did the math. *If he left at 1:00 last night, he'll be here around 7:00 or 8:00.*

Time was on their side.

*****

After dinner Saturday night, Frankie sat down on the sofa in his living room and turned on the TV. Cozy in a pair of light-gray sweatpants and a pewter fleece jacket, he put his feet up on the coffee table and watched the end of the six o'clock nightly news. His eyes were on the screen, but his mind was elsewhere. He could still taste Conny's lips. He could smell her perfume. He could still hear her voice. *Not tonight.*

Frankie's long vacant gaze was interrupted by a flash of light that seeped through the blinds on the window. His head snapped to the left. The unexpected sight of headlights in the driveway stole his attention. Slowly easing his feet off the coffee table, Frankie stood up. His heart rocked against the inside of his chest. *I'm not expecting anyone.*

Silently, he approached the living room window. His eyes widened. Crouching low, he peeked out the blinds and saw a man get out of a black pick-up truck. As soon as the person slammed the door shut, the truck drove away.

Frankie's heart started to pound. "Who is that?" he worded but barely any noise came out.

The black silhouette of the man crossed the sidewalk and then climbed the stairs on the front porch. His steps were loud.

On instinct, Frankie bolted for the door. Gazing out the peephole, he saw a bald head and two blue eyes. "Holy crap," he whispered, turning quickly to deactivate the alarm. Scratching for the doorknob, he flipped the deadbolt and whipped open the door.

For a moment, the two men only stared at one another. Then Frankie smiled. "Where the hell ya been, man?" And before Mariani could even open his mouth to respond, Frankie slammed his arms around his back and tried to lift him up. After letting go, he took a step back.

"You don't wanna know," Mariani said and gripped Frankie's shoulder. "Nice haircut, by the way."

"I copied your style." Frankie waved inward. "Come in. Come in. It's freezing out here."

Mariani took two steps in the foyer and shut the door. "Holy shit," he said. "Nice fucking house, man. This must have cost a fortune."

"Thanks. Freedom motivated me." Frankie smiled. "Where you been? Who you been with? I haven't seen you for almost two years!"

"I know," Mariani said, his face contorting. "My bad. I had to stay free. I've been to prison before. And I ain't ever goin back."

Frankie turned to looked him right in the eye. "I never ratted."

"I never doubted you." Mariani slowly shook his head. "Not for one second. I thought it would be better to just...disappear."

"What made you come back?"

Mariani's body stiffened and he took in a deep breath. "Ben told me you were in trouble." Their eyes met. "I hopped on the next flight. He said he couldn't reach you, and he didn't know where you lived. I couldn't remember the street names to give Ben directions, but I knew I'd be able to find it. So, here I am."

"Trouble?" Frankie squinted one eye. "W-what kind of trouble?

Mariani pulled out his phone and hit the call button. "It would be better if he tells you." He stuck out his arm. "Here. It's ringing."

*****

Frankie pressed the phone against his ear and listened to it ring two times.

"Hello," Ben said sharply.

"It's me," Frankie said with a soft monotone voice that was easily recognizable.

"Why couldn't I get ahold of you?" Ben asked. "I thought—"

"I'm sorry." Frankie cut him off. "I-I lost my phone last night. Can't find it anywhere. Why, what's going on?"

"Listen very carefully. The guy who blew your mom's house up is on the war path again. I was told he knows how to find you."

Raising his free hand to his chest, Frankie's head snapped toward Mariani. "That's impossible. No one knows where I live."

Would it never end?

"Someone sold you out, but we can find out *who* later. This guy could be there any minute. You two need to get ready for the worst. Right now."

His nose flared and he jumped to the nearest window, pulling at the blinds. "Where should we go?" His voice was shaky, his breath heavy.

"Nowhere," Ben said. "If he *is* coming, we need to handle this tonight. Next time we won't have the heads up."

"W-what?"

"Let your boy do his thing. He ain't gonna let anything happen to you. And if it makes you feel any better—me and

Brice are parked in the woods down the road. When he passes us, I'll call that phone, and then we'll trap him in your driveway. I'm in a black truck. Don't shoot us."

"I-I can't do this. Can't we just hide in my bunker?"

"No. You *can* do it." Ben lowered his voice and spoke slower. "Just calm down. We need to end this once and for all."

Frankie let out a breath. "All right. I'll do my best."

"That's not good enough. This man won't stop until you're dead. It's *you* or *him*. Do you understand me?"

Frankie took two deep breaths and brought the phone closer to his lips. "Yeah, I get it. Thanks for the heads-up."

"Thank me later."

*****

Frankie handed the phone to Mariani. "He…he said to stay put and shoot it out."

"It's gonna be all right, bro," Mariani said. "Don't worry. We got this. We have the advantage."

"I thought it was all over." Frankie pressed his hands against his face. "I can't stop shaking."

Mariani's eyebrows dropped low, his hands shooting out and grabbing a fist full of Frankie's fleece. "It's game time, brother!" His voice was a low growl. "Pull it together. I need your help."

Closing his eyes, Frankie sucked in air and then blew it out. His eyes snapped open. "I know."

"You got any guns? I just got two pistols in my bag."

Frankie's chest and shoulders were moving up and down with each rapid breath. "I…I got guns in the bunker."

"You actually built the bunker, huh? Fuck yeah! Let's go get 'em."

"L-let me set the alarm and grab my tablet. I'll get an alert if anyone steps foot on the property. I got cameras and motion sensors everywhere."

*****

Quickly walking past the pool table in the basement, Frankie guided Mariani to the utility room. He turned on the light and they saw a furnace, a hot water heater, and a big red toolbox on wheels that was pressed up against the back wall.

"Give me a hand," Frankie said, nodding toward the toolbox. "It's super heavy."

The two former athletes heaved the bulky object to the right a few feet, revealing a circular man-hole cover on the cement floor.

Mariani gave a short laugh. "I can't believe you really built a bunker."

Frankie nodded. "Better safe than sorry."

Pulling out the bottom drawer of the toolbox, Frankie grabbed a large crowbar. He hooked the tip to the lid and, with a grunt of exertion, dragged it free.

When Frankie flipped a switch on the wall, the hole lit up. He put his toes on the first rung of a ladder welded to one side, and then slowly climbed down ten feet. From the bottom, he looked up and saw his friend descending.

With both of his feet on the floor of the subterranean bunker, Mariani smiled and scanned the dimly lit room. It was small, probably about ten square feet with a concrete floor and cinder block walls. In the right corner there was two pallets. One stacked with meals ready to eat and the other with cases of bottled water.

"Where's the guns?" Mariani asked.

"One more level down." Frankie pointed at the stockpile. "The bunker door's hidden under the rations."

Mariani smiled. "Hurry up."

Frankie grabbed a case of water and set it to the side. Mariani followed his lead, and a minute later, a storm cellar hatch was exposed.

With a grunt of effort, Frankie swung open the rectangular cast iron doors. Stooping low, he grabbed a flashlight on the ground and handed it to Mariani. "Crooks first."

Mariani took the flashlight and aimed the beam of light down the dark hole. With the steep staircase now illuminated, his boots clunked to the bottom.

Trailing right behind him, Frankie stooped down to grab an LED lantern that he'd strategically placed next to the entrance of the second sub-level. With a flick of his thumb, the entire room lit up.

"This is the common room," Frankie said, walking in the center of the room furnished with two leather couches, a coffee table, and a flat-screen television. "The kitchen and bathroom are over there, and down that hall there's two small bedrooms."

Mariani started laughing out loud. "It looks like a fucking condo!"

"I don't like it when you're on the run. Why don't you live here? You'd be off the grid."

"If we make it past our current problem, I'll consider that."

Gesturing with his hand, Frankie pointed to a large titanium door situated at the far wall. Walking past the living room and the bedrooms, he signaled Mariani to follow him. He approached the door and punched in a four-digit code. After the beep noise, he turned the knob and entered the dark room, lantern in hand.

Mariani's eyebrows shot up. "Holy shit!" he said, gazing at the gray slat board wall in front of him that displayed an array of assault rifles, shotguns, and hunting rifles with scopes. His eyes bounced from gun to gun until his cold hands finally clasped an M4A1 Assault Rifle that was black. "We're ready, brother."

"If this guy shows up," Frankie promised, "we'll be able to defend ourselves." *Forgive us, God. We have no choice.*

"If you get caught with all these guns, you'll be going to prison for life."

Frankie set the lantern on the ammo shelf against the side wall. "I'm still a felon. I'm not supposed to be around guns." He sighed. "I technically don't live here. This house and the guns are in my stepdad's name, but the land's in Ivan's name until I finish paying him off. I should have just paid him, but I-I was dragging my feet. I figured that we all took a loss with Ben's insurance plan." Frankie shrugged. "What makes him so special?"

"Speaking of the devil," Mariani said with a long pause. "I think *he's* the one who gave you up."

Nodding slowly, Frankie let out an exasperated breath. "Yeah, I mean, I don't want to believe it but..." He sunk his head. "Other than the carpenters who built the place...Ivan, Carlos, and Marcel are the only ones who know where I live. My mom hasn't even been here yet."

"Well, it *ain't* Carlos or Marcel. I'd bet my life on that."

"Oh my God." Frankie put his hand to his heart. "Ivan *did* threaten me again when I got out of jail, but...I-I didn't think he'd ever follow through with it. I just thought he was off his meds and blowing off steam like last time." He sighed heavily. "But *how* would he make contact with the cartel? And why would they want to break the truce and risk a war with the Italians."

Mariani shook his head. "I don't know, man. He must have

found some numbers in Enrique's hotel." He lifted his head to face Frankie. "It doesn't matter. Dude's coming. We better load up these guns. I'll take care of Ivan later."

32

Pulling his head out of a mound of cocaine, Ivan plopped down in his filthy green rocking chair. He sniffled twice and wiped his nose with the back of his hand.

"That sure numbed the pain," Ivan said, wide eyes bouncing from the bottle of pills on the coffee table to the 45-caliber revolver next to it. After a long look at the gun, his gaze finally landed on the plastic bottle of vodka. "What next?"

Reaching for the bottle of prescription medicine, Ivan grabbed it, popped the top, and dumped the pills down his throat, some spilling to the floor. One blink and the pint of vodka was in his hands. Bringing it to his lips, he tilted it back until it was gone. Flinging the empty bottle on the floor, he pulled out a pack of cigarettes. Instead of two, he grabbed three and put them in his mouth, lighting them with a freshly struck match.

"Why didn't Frankie just pay?" Ivan sucked in smoke and held it in, his face reddening by the second. His next words came out in a strained murmur. "I didn't want to him to die."

Frankie thinks you're a chump, a voice in Ivan's head prodded him.

Ivan coughed out a gigantic cloud. "Frankie's my only friend."

You don't have any friends, Ivan.

"Leave me alone," Ivan said and hit the cigarettes again. *I'm sick of you. Always giving me bad advice. Not today, Satan.*

You're stuck with me Ivan, his personal demon said. *You're nothing without me.*

"I'm nothing without Frankie. I just took enough pills to kill a horse."

That won't kill you. Why don't you grab the gun if you really want me out of your head?

"Thanks for the for the encouragement." Ivan grabbed the gun. "I should have never listened to you. Now Frankie's dead."

I didn't make you do anything. You did that.

"You did it!" Ivan's eyes were shifting.

Fine. I did it. So what? Frankie used you.

"He didn't have to die!"

Ivan heard the voice laughing. *If you don't like my advice, just check out. Squeeze the trigger. Or are you too weak?*

"Fuck you!" Ivan pressed the barrel against the lens of his glasses. "I put Frankie's mom in my will just to piss you off." Tears rolled down his cheeks. His hand was trembling. His heart was thumping. His trigger finger was itching the metal.

"Fuck it," Ivan said and squeezed the trigger. A loud explosion erupted, and his body crumpled to the floor.

There were no more voices in his head, only silence.

33

Still in the bunker, Mariani handed Frankie an AK-47 with a forty-shot banana clip. "Locked and loaded," he said. "Let's go up to the attic and take the high ground."

"Hold up," Frankie said and set the gun on the cement floor. "While we're down here, let me show you one last thing."

"Better make it quick. This asshole could be here any minute."

"Grab the lantern."

Mariani did as requested, a question entering his eyes when Frankie walked to the back wall of the gun room.

Looking over his shoulder, Frankie smiled. "Since we've come all this way, might as well show you the best part."

Frankie walked to the staggered stone wall in the back of the room, his hand reaching for a rectangular stone placed at waist level. "Check this out," he said, clicking the stone downward like it was a door handle. This was followed by a clunking noise and, as Frankie braced himself, both arms pressed against the stone wall. Legs splayed out and knees bent, he pushed the wall until it swung inward.

"What the fuck is that?" Mariani asked and started laughing.

Frankie nodded toward the entrance. "Step inside,

brother."

Mariani walked through the small entryway, his visible breath showed the temperature drop.

It was dark but Frankie's flashlight lit up most of the room. It was just a ten-by-ten space with cinder block walls, but one side had a manhole in it, and Frankie shined the light at the void.

"Holy shit, dude…!" Mariani shook his head with a grin. "You gotta be fucking kidding me."

"Nah man," Frankie said calmly. "No jokes here, bro. This tunnel may be the difference between life and death."

Mariani kept the beam of light on the hole. "Where does it lead?"

"About twenty yards behind the house." Frankie pointed. "Under a patch of spruce trees."

"That was a good idea. An escape tunnel might—"

The sound of Mariani's phone ringing cut him off. They both froze and looked at each other.

*****

"Hello."

"He's here!" Ben shouted. "He just passed us on the road! Black BMW. At least two in the car."

Mariani's eyebrows shot up. "What do you want me to do?"

"Just start *shooting* at them as soon as they park the car! We're about a minute behind them. We'll be in my truck. Don't shoot us!"

"We're way down in the bunker. It's gonna take a few minutes."

"They'll be there in one minute! Hurry the fuck up!"

*****

Mariani dashed to the stone wall that led to the gun room. "He's here! Let's go!" When he got to the entrance, he turned back to face Frankie. "We gotta lay down some cover fire for Ben. He needs us, right now! Let's grab the guns and run up to the attic."

"I think the tunnel would be fast—" Frankie was cut off by the alarm on his tablet. He held it up and they looked at it. The top right section of the four-way split screen showed a black sports car cruising past the garage. "He's in the driveway!"

With fast movements, Mariani breached the gunroom, picked up the rifle, and stuffed his pockets with extra magazines.

Frankie did the same and they both returned to the secret room with the escape tunnel.

"You lead the way," Mariani said. "When we get outside, follow *my* lead. Don't shoot Ben."

Crouching low, Frankie lowered his head and entered the dank tunnel, the beam of his flashlight bouncing as he scampered forward.

KABOOM! The entire complex shook violently, and the two men stumbled.

From all fours, Mariani raised his voice. "Go! Go! Go!"

*****

Frankie didn't make it another ten feet down the tunnel before another gigantic explosion rocked the foundation of the house. His crouched frame shuttered. With ringing in his ears, he pressed forward with the flashlight in one hand and an AK-47 in the other.

KABOOM!

Every few seconds there was another deafening explosion until Frankie finally reached the ladder at the end of the subterranean tunnel. He climbed the ladder, and the moment he opened the hatch, the sound of gunshots rang out. With a pounding heart, Frankie set the flashlight and gun on the snowy ground and climbed out of the hole, twenty yards behind the right corner of the house. Grabbing the rifle, he rose and turned around. The first thing he saw was his home on fire with every window glowing from within.

Mariani popped up behind him.

Bang, bang, bang! Their heads shifted to the front yard where they saw muzzle flashes further down the driveway and heard more gunshots coming from somewhere in front of the house.

Ben! Frankie thought and looked to Mariani.

Mariani crept up the tree line closer to the front of the house and Frankie followed five feet behind him. Mariani couldn't see the enemy, but he started shooting blindly. "I can't see them. Damn it."

"Me neither," Frankie answered.

In the course of forty-five seconds, Mariani emptied a clip and then reloaded. For a split second he turned back and saw Frankie dumping bullets toward the front of the house.

Mariani stopped firing and put his hand out.

Immediately, Frankie stopped firing.

Silence.

Frankie approached Mariani and they both dropped to a knee behind the cover of the tree line.

Scanning the front yard and the driveway, Mariani shook his head. "I don't like this," he said. "The silence…it's not a good sign. If Ben was alive, he'd either be shooting…or letting us know the coast is clear." He let out a heavy breath. "We gave up our position. Now we're sitting ducks. Let's fall back."

Frankie nodded his head, his eyes widening as he watched Mariani dart into the black forest. Following behind him, his adrenaline was pumping, breaths fast and heavy. *I'm sorry, Ben,* he thought as he trudged through the crunchy snow. *We should have been in the attic. Waiting.*

They rushed fifty yards deeper in the woods and took cover at the edge of a small ravine.

"We were too slow," Mariani said and let out a heavy sigh. "Now *they* got upper hand. Lucky we didn't run to the attic though. We'd be goners."

Frankie glanced at the raging light in the middle of darkness. "What are we gonna do?" his breathing was erratic and audible, visible with each frozen breath.

"They know where we were shooting from. I bet they crept around the back of the house, trying to ambush us."

Frankie's mouth cracked open, but no words came out. His eyes were shifting as he tried to reason out a survival route. "Okay. But in that case, we know where they're headed." He tried to think past the distracting beat of his heart, his words choppy, airy. "There's…only one clear exit for them. The driveway."

"Great idea. The only problem is…they could be there waiting for us. Or they could be somewhere out here. If we move, we risk giving up our location."

"We could go deeper in the woods, then cut back."

"No," Mariani said, shaking his head. "Not yet. First, we watch and listen. Rash moves make dead men."

They listened closely but didn't hear anything other than the whistling wind and the bending tree branches after each gust. They both gazed out in all directions, scanning the darkness for any movement.

Nothing.

Mariani hit Frankie's shoulder with the back of his hand. "It's now or never," he said. "Your plan is dangerous, but…we can't let him get away. We'd never be safe."

"I'm ready." Frankie held his breath while nodding.

*****

With heads on a swivel, Mariani and Frankie's eyes adjusted to the darkness. Crouching low, they used quiet, stealthy movements to carve a crooked path through the thick woods and brush and snow.

When they finally arrived at the roughage on the shoulder of the driveway, Frankie dropped to a knee. He was huffing and puffing and scrunching his face.

"Suck it up," Mariani said with a low tone, annoyed by Frankie's lack of endurance. "That car's still there. They could be anywhere. Keep your eyes and ears open."

Frankie nodded and tried to slow down his breathing.

Mariani's head was pivoting and his eyes were wide. "I hope they hop in that car and drive our way. I'll dump forty rounds in the window."

"Maybe they're dead already?" Frankie whispered. "Maybe Ben got him."

"That could be the case, but…we have to assume they're hunting us."

"W-what should we do?"

Mariani used the light of the burning house to surveil the front yard. "We either wait or go hunting."

"I could guard the driveway if you wanna hunt?"

Before Mariani could answer, the growl of a sports car starting was heard. Their heads snapped toward the front of the house. The black BMW was still parked in front of the blazing inferno, exhaust rising from the tail pipes.

Mariani's head shifted to face Frankie. "You ready?"

"Yeah." Frankie nodded, his heart dropping to his stomach.

"Let's spread out a little. We need to triangulate the kill box. I'll go twenty yards down. You stay right here. Wait for me to shoot first, then squeeze that trigger and don't stop till you're out of bullets. Then reload."

"It's him or us." Frankie closed his eyes for two seconds. *Please forgive me, Jesus.*

Mariani let out a breath, turned, and then snuck into the darkness.

*****

Sweat was dripping down Frankie's brow as he watched the idling car from the foliage. Despite the cold, he felt warm, his body shivering from abject fear. Pressing his clattering jaw against the cold stock of the rifle, his finger slightly twitched on the trigger.

What the hell are they doing in that car? Frankie's breathing sped up. *If they don't move soon, we might have to go find out.*

Crunch! A branch snapped and Frankie turned sharply.

Bang! Bang! Bang! Frankie saw a shadowy figure fall to the ground.

Dropping to the prone position, Frankie's head and eyes shifted back and forth. With a jerk, his body shuddered instinctively as another eruption of gunfire engulfed the woods behind him. And then, a different weapon reported in response.

Shuffling his body toward the crackles of gunfire, Frankie saw trees and darkness and orange flashes of light in the driveway. *Oh my God.* He popped up to a crouch, squeezing the trigger seven times as fast as he could.

The man stumbled to the ground.

Frankie let out a breath and looked around. "G!" he shouted. "Where you at?" There was no response, so he trudged down the tree line to where Mariani was before the battle. It was dark as pitch. Left, right, left. His head pivoted. "Bro!"

Nothing.

Frankie's heart rose to his throat. He paused to listen and breathe. Faintly in the distance, he heard the groans of a wounded man. He darted to the noise.

Looking down, he saw Mariani leaned up against a thick tree trunk. Blood was scattered all around him. The stained snow looked black in the darkness. Frankie felt a sharp pain in his chest as his enveloping fear and sickness of dread built up in his body.

Mariani was taking short, fast breaths and his eyes were blinking rapidly.

"Giovanni," he said. "Where are you hit?"

Instead of talking, Mariani spit blood on his chin and jacket. With his left hand, he pointed to the right side of his chest, and his right arm hung limp.

"What should I do?"

Mariani pointed to the car.

"Okay. We got two of 'em. Do you think it's safe?"

Mariani nodded slowly.

Frankie shifted then turned back to face his friend. "My keys are in the house," he said, "but I'm gonna take Ben's truck." He felt Mariani's back on the other side of the entrance wound. When he felt wetness, he looked at his hand and saw blood. "You're gonna be okay. It went in and out. I'll be right back, brother. The doctor's gonna fix you up real good." He held his hand for a long moment while staring into his eyes. "I love you, brother. Keep pressure on that wound."

After one tear rolled down Frankie's cheek, he bolted through the woods, toward the bright orange glow of the growing fire. *Please help him, Father,* he thought. *Don't let Mariani die.*

CONCLUSION

Sitting in a chair at the emergency ward waiting room, Frankie's head was buried in his hands. Slightly rocking back and forth with blood all over his clothes, he gained the squinting gazes of men, women, and children who were sitting in his proximity.

Please let them be okay, Frankie prayed silently. *Please let them —*

"Frankie," a low female voice interrupted his pleading to God.

He dropped his hands and lifted his head. Royal blue scrubs were the first thing he saw, and then he met the nurse's deep blue eyes. "Conny," he said and blinked, offering the slightest of smiles.

Dropping to a crouch, Conny grabbed his hand. "Mariani lost a lot of blood, but…the doctor said he's going to live." She sniffled and squeezed his hand tighter.

"Thank God!" Frankie bowed his head, pausing for a second with closed eyes. "What a relief." He let out a deep breath. "Mariani saved my life. I thought he was gonna die."

Conny pursed her lips. "The doctor said any longer and he'd be dead." She gently placed her hand on his shoulder. "What the hell happened, Frankie?"

He shook his head and let out a breath. "The bad guys came for me again," he said softly, letting out a painful sigh. "We stopped them." He blinked twice, his lip quivering. "W-what about Ben and Brice? Are they okay?"

"I-I'm sorry, Frankie." She shook her head slowly. "Ben didn't make it. And…Brice is in a coma. They don't think he's gonna make it either."

Frankie sunk his head and crumpled in his seat, bringing his hands up to his face. Sniffling, he tried to choke down the tears, but he couldn't stop his eyes from spilling over. "It's all my fault."

As the tears streamed down his face, Conny wrapped her arms around him and kissed the side of his head. "I'm sorry." Her voice cracked. "I-I'm just glad you're okay. I don't know what I would have done if it was you in the operating room with no vitals."

Frankie lifted his head and dried his eyes with the back of his hand. "If not for Ben, Brice, and Mariani, that *would* have been me. Dead." He softly cleared his throat. "In the last two years, I-I've gone through every possible type of pain. The heartbreak, bruises, and fear of life in prison hurt, but only now — that one of my friends is dead, another in purgatory, and my best friend is on death's doorstep — only now do I understand what the word affliction means." Frankie shook his head. "And I don't ever want to feel that again. All I want is to stay close to you."

Conny squeezed him tight. "I'm here for you, Frankie. I believe you this time." She rubbed his back in a circle then added. "Now let's go see Mariani. He was asking about you."

Frankie shot up. "You lead the way." He rested his hand on her lower back. "I'd just get us lost."

CALL TO ACTION

Thank you for reading this dream of mine. I can only hope it met or exceeded expectations. If you're anything like the old me, you'll just put *Path of Affliction* on your bookshelf to collect dust, never telling anyone about the awesome book you just read. It might seem as if no one cares about what you're reading, but they do! And I care. It would mean the world to me if you would write an honest **review** on my **Amazon author page.**

I look forward to reading every review, and plan to comment on some of them. I want to know my strengths and weaknesses, so I can make the sequel — *Order From Chaos* — even better.

Without reviews, it's impossible for a first-time author to climb the steep mountain of books. With your help, together we can bring this book to the snowy peak.

Thank you for the short time you spent in **Frank Buccetti's** boots. May the rest of your life bring health, happiness, love, peace, and success.

God bless,
Nick Campanella

ABOUT THE AUTHOR

Nick Campanella likes transforming a foggy dream into a complete story. He currently lives in Duluth, Minnesota, a shining little city on a hill, overlooking the largest freshwater lake in the world. Nick is a first-time author. He attributes his passion for writing to the only dream he ever remembered: *Path of Affliction.*

Mr. Campanella's foundation of hard work, respect, and teamwork was built on the hockey rink as a kid. His claim to glory is the fact he got a hacking penalty in the **Minnesota State High School Hockey Tournament** in 1996. After graduating high school, Nick enrolled full time at Lake Superior Community College for sociology. After two years of college—like many 21-year-old kids—Nick went down the wrong path. Alcohol and an underworld party life consumed him. His grades slipped. And then he got robbed at gunpoint by masked intruders.

Surviving the robbery with an empty wallet, Nick re-evaluated his life and what he wanted. In order to carve out a new path, he eventually dropped out of college, quit drinking, and got a full-time job. Drifting from construction to a retail business in his late twenties, Nick discovered his true passion of writing at the age of 32.

Today, **Nick Campanella** is a father who likes to take long hikes in the woods with his daughter. His old legs need the exercise. Six years ago, he had surgery on his knee. Since then, he watches more hockey than he plays, but once or twice a year, he says he likes to lace up the skates and put a lil' lumber in someone's side, just so they know he's there. (A line from Nick's favorite movie, *Slap Shot*.)